RESEARCH IN
HUMAN CAPITAL
AND DEVELOPMENT

Volume 1 • 1979

RESEARCH IN HUMAN CAPITAL AND DEVELOPMENT

A Research Annual

Editor: ISMAIL SIRAGELDIN

*Departments of Population Dynamics
and Political Economy
The Johns Hopkins University*

VOLUME 1 • 1979

 JAI PRESS INC.
Greenwich, Connecticut

ISBN NUMBER: 0-89232-019-2

Manufactured in the United States of America

CONTENTS

III. DISTRIBUTION AND EQUITY

INTRODUCTION

Ismail Sirageldin

The objective of Research in Human Capital and Development (RHCD) is to investigate a subject of fundamental importance in economics as well as in other branches of social sciences—the relationship between the development and utilization of human capital and the process of economic and social change. Our aim is to develop RHCD into a forum for important empirical and theoretical research that has in common these two basic elements of the evolution of human society. Although our scope is basically economics, we shall include relevant studies which are interdisciplinary in nature, especially those examining the structural setting of the phenomena being analyzed.

Five major areas related to human capital and development will form the scope of RHCD interest: fertility, health, education and manpower, migration, and the triangle of equity, distribution and efficiency. Most of these areas are touched on in this first volume. Our plan for future volumes is to focus on each of these topics individually. For example, Volume II will examine equity and distribution issues in the context of development and human capital; Volume III will focus on health, human capital and development; and Volume IV will examine migration within the same context. Each specialized issue will have a co-editor or co-editors — Professor Ali Khan for Volume II and Professors David Salkever and Alan Sorkin for Volume III. Most papers will be invited. Unsolicited papers, however, will be considered and all papers will be subject to external review. Papers will be judged both on their analytical merit and on the innovativeness of the ideas they present. Reports that are longer than regular journal articles are encouraged to the extent that they communicate new findings in the field.

When examining the role of human capital in the process of development, the subject of this first volume, both the supply and demand for human capital should be given equal weight and related to the nature of the market in which these forces interact. At any given stage in development, there is a corresponding structure of supply and demand for human capital of a particular quality and in particular amounts. The actual utilization of such resources will depend, among other things, on the nature of the market and the decision units' initial endowment both of human capital and other resources. This endowment is not independent of the economic and social environment.

Highlighting the important role of human capital, both as a cause and effect in the process of economic growth and development, dates back at least to Adam Smith. For Smith (11), pp. 265–266, the acquisition of talents that become a part of a person's fortune may be considered in the same light as the acquisition of a machine or instrument of trade. Smith evidently was more concerned with the development of human resources and the socio-economic setting necessary for its optimal utilization than with human capital in the modern sense. As Spengler (12), p. 36, points out, Smith's concern was mainly "to describe and seek establishment of a politico-economic environment within which man's desire and efforts to better his conditions could work optimally for himself and society."

This early concern with human capital formation and utilization was not paralleled in the history of economic analysis by a formal integration of the concept of human capital into the main body of economic theory and analytical techniques until very recently. For instance, the subject index of Schumpeter's classic, *History of Economic Analysis* (10), pp. 1231–1260, does not include a single entry on human capital or human resources. One possible reason for such slow development, according to Samuel Bowles, is the "conscious attempt [by Marx and the classical writers] to portray the class structure as they saw it, coupled with the fact that the role of education and skills in the economy was considerably less than today" [quoted in T.W. Schultz (8), p. 6]). Another possible reason is the ambiguity and multi-dimensionality of these concepts. For example, how can we estimate the returns on inputs aimed at changing a person's productivity and marketability — net of their influence on that person's preferences, attitudes and motivations which should influence the basic allocative decisions? It is this distinction between human capital as an input similar to other physical inputs as opposed to the more general concept of human resources with its multifaceted dimensions—social, economic, and psychological—that has been eluding economists and social scientists in their treatment of the subject.

In this respect, T.W. Schultz (8), p. 9 makes a fine distinction between the two concepts. In his view, the term "human resources," as opposed to human capital, serves as a

> useful descriptive term, but it is subject to ambiguities when it comes to economic analysis. Whereas natural resources and other material resources are passive economic factors in the sense that they are preference-free, *in the case of human agents it is necessary in undertaking an economic analysis to distinguish between their preferences and their abilities, including their skills and knowledge, as these abilities contribute to the possibilities of realizing their preferences.* Thus, [his] interpretation of the term "human resources" is that it encompasses all of the many attributes of a people—physical, biological, psychological, and cultural—that account for both the social values that determine preferences and the economic value of the producer and consumer services that a people render, whether they come to them as earnings or directly as personal satisfactions. The core of economic analysis rests on the assumption that preferences are given and that it is the function of economic activities to serve these preferences as best they can with the human and nonhuman capital at the disposal of the economy to obtain income streams and by transforming a part of this income by means of investment into additional forms of capital.

A systematic approach to the study of the process of human capital accumulation within an individual utility-maximizing framework had to wait for Becker's path-breaking contributions (1, 2). His theoretical framework rests on two basic propositions. The first emphasizes rational allocation of human capital over time whereby each decision maker looks forward to the future for the justification of his present action. A nucleus of this line of thought can be traced back to Irving Fisher (4). For a historical discussion see Kiker (6) and Schultz (8), pp. 6–8. The second proposition brings in the treatment of time as an essential element of cost in individual allocative decisions. An underlying premise of both is that all social phenomena should be traced back to their foundation in individual behavior [Blaug (3), p. 830]. But at the individual level, many of the difficulties arising from attempts to identify and isolate the economic dimensions of human capital from the other dimensions of human resources have not been settled to the satisfaction either of the theoretical purist or those who seek pragmatic social policy guidance.

This "methodological individualism," inherent in the modern treatment of human capital, is a natural view to take when the supply of most of those social services essential for human capital formation is in the private domain. But when many such services, e.g., health care, education, information retrieval, or labor training are either wholly or in part in the public sector (as is the case in most of the less-developed countries of the world), the theoretical developments which emphasize private calculus may not be a valid source of insights for public action. A related issue is the assumption that preferences are given. We think Griliches was right in his belief that "if we want to study the demand for children, we have to put more content into the theory and start asking why do people want to have children; what are the returns and not just the costs of this activity?" In terms of the theoretical framework, Griliches (5), p. 547, was looking for "shifters of the utility function or, alternatively, for factors that change the implicit household production function." Schumpeter (9), p. 203, was more explicit in calling for "serious research" when discussing the process of socialization of the "human element." Another important but unsettled issue in the field has to do with the dynamic nature of human capital accumulation and the role of uncertainty in such decision processes. In a developmental context, this is relevant not only to the size of the initial investment but also to its temporal allocation.

There are many other unsettled issues in the field of human capital and its relation to the process of development which need further research and discussion [see for example, T. W. Schultz (8); J. Mincer (7); Blaug (3). We do not attempt in this introduction to provide a comprehensive review but hope that RHCD as a forum for the systematic exchange of ideas will in time contribute to that body of knowledge.

The papers in this volume are grouped into three parts. Part I consists of three papers on health and fertility, with a brief discussion of the issues. Part II includes five papers concerned with education and manpower issues, followed by a discussion by Alan Sorkin. Part III includes one paper dealing with equity and social mobility.

The opening paper by Khan is an attempt to examine the relevance of human capital theory to research in fertility in Pakistan and Bangladesh— two developing countries with very low per capita incomes, relatively high mortality, and high fertility. In his rigorous review of recent development of the household production model, Khan illustrates some of the limitations on the results usually obtained in the standard theory of the consumer but which do not automatically carry over when household production is included. Khan developed two specific models: static and dynamic, and tested them empirically, using cross-sectional data. In his static model a simultaneous equation system with four endogenous variables, mainly live births, death, income, and female labor force participation, was used. This is a significant departure from the conventional single equation analysis of fertility decisions. In the dynamic model Khan's use of the probit model is also novel and provides new methodological insights in the field.

Robin Barlow's contribution offers a broad but critical review of the theoretical and empirical relationships between health and development. He presents a general model incorporating the main linkages between health and income (as an index of development) and three important social variables, namely, fertility, education, and nutrition. Barlow uses his general model as a framework for his review of the literature on health and development, indicates a number of major shortcomings in current knowledge, and suggests specific areas for future research.

Mosley's paper leads us to an analysis of a more specific situation. His analysis of health, nutrition and mortality in Bangladesh suggests that recent mortality trends in that country are largely determined by the political and social factors affecting the supply and availability of food, indicating the precarious economic condition of the majority of the population. Mosley's underlying socio-political model is tentative but illustrates the possible danger of deriving policy conclusions based on abstract models that ignore levels and changes in the basic parameters of the underlying social system. A brief discussion of the papers included in Part I is given by Sirageldin.

In part II, the paper by Morgan and Duncan is an effort to determine, for a national sample of American men and women, the effect of college quality on hourly earnings. Their findings tend to support the "Coleman notion" that the quality of the student body is more important than other school measures. But it also gives support to the notion that quality of college attended largely indicates a selection by ability, background, or motivation.

Alamgir's paper reviews some theoretical issues and models in manpower and educational planning. He examines the relevance and utility of the various models to the actual educational and manpower planning experience in Bangladesh. He emphasizes that a developmental plan that includes the educational sector should incorporate three production processes: the production of goods and services, of skills, and of the educational output.

Kelley criticizes the concept of the return on human investment as devoid of much policy relevance, especially in those developing countries characterized by large-scale unemployment and underemployment. He develops a comprehensive planning model which specifies sectoral output targets and applies it to the manufacturing sector of Venezuela. His results indicate that for the manufacturing sector as a whole, the more labor intensive techniques would generate significantly more additional jobs than the most efficient pattern.

Kristin Tornes's paper has a different perspective. She argues that the educational policies in the less-developed countries are not independent of those countries' dependency on, and exploitation by, the more-developed industrialized countries. In her analysis of the Venezuelan case, Tornes attempts to distinguish and empirically test for the difference between an explicit educational policy as usually set in the official plans and an implicit educational policy as revealed by the actual experience of administering such plans.

Carmel Chiswick seeks to explain the rapid growth in the proportion of professional workers in the United States' manufacturing sector during the period 1900–1973. Her central hypothesis is that a large part of the observed growth of professional occupations has been accompanied by factor-substituting changes in production techniques that have been mainly induced by changes in relative factor proportions. Her findings indicate no apparent shifts in the relative demand curve in favor of professional manpower and that the supply sift variable is the important exogenous variable in her model, i.e., the direct cost of higher education relative to its indirect cost can be used to predict changes in both the proportion and the relative earnings of salaried employees in manufacturing. Alan Sorkin discusses the papers presented in this part of the volume.

The last paper, by Sirageldin and Kantner, examines the concept of equity and social mobility as related to rural fertility within a socio-economic framework. They review the theoretical and empirical literature related to the social mobility-fertility hypothesis and indicate the weakness of the empirical evidence. They then present a tentative model for studying the relationships between rural fertility and what they have labelled social striving. Their discussion is tentative but raises various issues with important policy implications which have not been examined critically in the modern treatment of fertility behavior.

Much effort has gone into the production of this volume. Aside from the contributors and numerous colleagues who provided suggestions to improve the format and content of the series, we would like to thank Pam Cain for her superb editorial assistance and Ruth Skarda for an excellent job of retyping the entire manuscript.

REFERENCES

1. Becker, Gary S. (1964) *Human Capital*, 2nd ed. 1975, New York: Columbia University Press.
2. ———. (1965) "A Theory of the Allocation of Time," *Economic Journal* 75:493–517.
3. Blaug, Mark. (1976) "The Empirical Status of Human Capital Theory: A Slightly Jaundiced Survey," *Journal of Economic Literature* XIV(3):827–855.

4. Fisher, Irving. (1906). *The Nature of Capital and Income*, New York and London: Macmillan.
5. Griliches, Zvi. (1974) "Comment," in *Economics of the Family: Marriage, Children, and Human Capital*, ed. T. W. Schultz, Chicago: The University of Chicago Press.
6. Kiker, B. F. (1966) "The Historical Roots of the Concept of Human Capital," *Journal of Political Economy* 74:481–499.
7. Mincer, Jacob. (1970) "The Distribution of Labor Income: A Survey with Special Reference to the Human Capital Approach," *Journal of Economic Literature* 8:1–26.
8. Schultz, Theodore W. (1972) "Human Capital: Policy Issues and Research Opportunities," in *Human Resources*: Fiftieth Anniversary Colloquium VI, New York: Columbia University Press.
9. Schumpeter, Joseph A. (1950) *Capitalism, Socialism and Democracy*, 3rd ed., New York: Harper.
10. ———. (1954) *History of Economic Analysis*, New York: Oxford University Press.
11. Smith, Adam. (1937) *The Wealth of Nations*, New York: Modern Library.
12. Spengler, Joseph J. (1977) "Adam Smith on Human Capital," *The American Economic Review* 67(1):32–36.

PART I
HEALTH AND FERTILITY

RELEVANCE OF HUMAN CAPITAL THEORY TO FERTILITY RESEARCH: COMPARATIVE FINDINGS FOR BANGLADESH AND PAKISTAN

M. Ali Khan, THE JOHNS HOPKINS UNIVERSITY

INTRODUCTION

It is by now well accepted that even in countries exhibiting the highest rates of population growth, individual fertility, as measured by any of the conventional indices, is well within the biological maximum. Thus, child-bearing is subject to a variety of restraints. Few would contest that some of these restraints are behavioral rather than biological in nature. Alternatively put, few would contest that there are circumstances which induce individual couples to make choices as regards their family size.

Economists have investigated these circumstances. In particular they

Research in Human Capital and Development, Vol. 1, pp. 3–43.
ISBN: 0–89232–019–2

have examined whether the data could be interpreted, in the aggregate, as an outcome of a rational response to these circumstances. Can decisions concerning family size be ascribed to the same reasons that are seen to underlie decisions to obtain education, to migrate, to choose a particular job, to invest in a particular asset, to purchase health care or insurance, to buy a durable commodity and so on? More succinctly, can individual fertility decisions be interpreted as arising out of human capital theoretic considerations? Human capital theory, in the words of Blaug (11) p. 829, being concerned with the implications of the basic idea that agents "spend on themselves in diverse ways, not for the sake of present enjoyments, but for the sake of future pecuniary and non-pecuniary returns. They look forward to the future for justification of their present actions."

Whether individual couples actually make these cost-benefit calculations is really incidental to an investigator primarily concerned with measuring the importance of key variables and drawing general policy conclusions. In a different context, few economists would argue that the model of the profit-maximizing firm is useful as an analytical device only after it has been established that firms actually maximize profits, precisely defined. As Friedman taught years ago (19), what determines the worth of any model is how well it enables us to understand observed behavior. This is not to argue that there are no situations to which the model is inapplicable *a priori*. Production decisions of centrally planned economies are obvious examples of situations for which the profit-maximizing model of the firm is inappropriate. Similarly, an economic theory of fertility will have no bearing for societies for which even its basic categories make no sense, i.e., where there are no identifiable market variables or where the term "couple" has no operational significance. However, once the model is judged broadly applicable to the situation at hand, it is left for the data to deliver the final verdict as to its usefulness or to suggest how it is to be modified.

The last few years have witnessed a resurgence of active interest in applying human capital theory to fertility; see T. W. Schultz (51) for a collection of these efforts. The material has warranted surveys,[1] further expository accounts,[2] and stimulated extensions of previous viewpoints.[3] This paper is not intended as a further survey of these surveys but rather to expound some recent developments of the theory and also to illustrate them with preliminary results for Bangladesh and Pakistan based on a survey held during 1968–1969. In particular, it collects and extends the recent findings of Khan and Sirageldin (25, 26) and Sirageldin et al. (54). More generally, it presents an application of the household production model to countries where, in the words of T. W. Schultz (49), p. 20,

> illiteracy abounds, human time is cheap, and the income opportunities that women have outside the home are mainly not

jobs in the labour market. Furthermore, infant mortality is high, life expectancy at birth is low, debilitation during the adult years is substantial for reasons of inadequate nutrition and endemic diseases, and the availability of modern contraceptive techniques, including information about them is, in general, wanting.

The paper is organized in essentially two parts. Part I is devoted to the static household production model where the life cycle is reduced to one period. Part II is concerned with extensions to a dynamic or sequential setting.

1. THE STATIC ONE PERIOD MODEL

This part of the paper condenses a couple's life cycle to one period and focuses on completed family size as the relevant fertility variable. Changes occurring during the life cycle in the underlying parameters are totally ignored. Again, no attempt is made to incorporate uncertainty or sequential decision making. We defer discussion of these problems to Part II.

Section 1 presents the basic elements of the household production model in light of some recent work. Section 2 is devoted to the presentation of our specific model and Section 3 briefly discusses the findings.

1.1. The Household Production Model

The basic elements of the household production model are by now well known and well understood. For an expository account the reader should refer to Michael and Becker (38); the original statements are, of course, due to Becker (3), Lancaster (28) and Muth (41). In this section we present the model from the viewpoint of the recent work of Muellbauer (40) and Pollak and Wachter (45). It is hoped that laying out the model in this generality will emphasize both its weaknesses and strengths.

We begin with a brief exposition of the conventional theory of the consumer. This helps us to present the notation and also to have a frame of reference for the household production model. Let there be n commodities, the amount of the ith commodity being denoted by Z_i. Let Z refer to the n-tuple $(Z_1, Z_2, \ldots Z_n)$. Let the price of the ith commodity be given by p_i and p denote the n-tuple $(p_1, p_2, \ldots p_n)$. The consumer chooses that commodity bundle Z which maximizes his preferences, as embodied in a utility function U(.), and the expenditure on which is not greater than a given income I. Thus, formally, the consumer solves the following problem:

$$\text{Maximize } U(Z)$$
$$\text{subject to } p \cdot Z \leq I$$
$$Z \geq 0. \tag{1.1}$$

Let Z^* be the utility maximizing bundle chosen according to (1.1). It is certainly a function of the parameters p and I, and hence can be written as $Z^*(p,I)$ where $Z_i^*(p,I)$ is referred to as the demand function of the ith commodity. Under specific assumptions about tastes, i.e., the given utility function, the demand functions can be shown to satisfy various properties. These properties are comparative statics results, i.e., answers to questions as to what happens to the utility maximizing commodity bundles when the given parameters change.

The problem with this theory of the consumer is that it has nothing to say about the demand for commodities for which there are no market prices unless one is willing to accept that the absence of such a market price is tantamount to it being zero. In this case, the theory predicts that the demand for that commodity is infinite as long as its marginal utility is always positive. Thus, in our context, parents' limitation of their family size at n is due to the fact that their marginal utility of children beyond n is zero. Given an understandable reluctance to take such an extreme position, economists have shied away from analyzing nonmarketed commodities. Thus, economists have avoided studying "decisions about the allocation of a consumer's nonmarket time and decisions about a choice of religion, a marriage mate, a family size, a divorce, a political party, or a life style" [Michael and Becker (38), p. 381]. The household production model remedies this by focusing on "services" rather than "commodities" and by conceiving of these services as being produced by a household technology which uses as inputs both marketed and nonmarketed goods. What is important is not whether a particular commodity has a market price but whether it can be produced from inputs with market prices. As such, an implicit or shadow price can be given to a nonmarketed commodity and the consumer can use this shadow price in his decision making. All this can be formalized by assuming that the consumer solves the following problem:

$$\text{Maximize } U(Z)$$
$$\text{subject to } (Z, x, t)\varepsilon P$$
$$p.x \leq M + w(\bar{t} - t)$$
$$Z \geq 0, x \geq 0, t \geq 0. \tag{1.2}$$

Now Z refers to a n-tuple of services and x a m-tuple of inputs whose market prices are denoted by the m-tuple p. M is nonwage income, w the wage rate, $\bar{t}$ the total time available to the household, and t the amount of time it does not devote to earning the wage w. P is a characterization of the household technology by which the inputs are transformed into outputs of services. It is a collection of $(n + m + 1)$-tuples, each tuple signifying input-output pairs which are productively feasible for the household.

By redefining income I as $M + w\bar{t}$ and t as the $(m + 1)^{th}$ input whose price is w, we see that no generality is lost if we rewrite (1.2) as

$$\text{Maximize } U(Z)$$
$$\text{subject to } px \le I$$
$$(Z, x) \varepsilon P$$
$$Z \ge 0, x \ge 0. \tag{1.3}$$

In what follows we shall use (1.3) as our basic household production model and follow Pollak and Wachter (45) in referring to "services" as "commodities" and to "inputs" as "goods".

Thus the theory of the consumer as formalized by (1.3) is really a merging of the conventional theory of the consumer, i.e., (1.1), along with the theory of the producer. As such it is analytically less tractable even though it undoubtedly enables the analysis of a larger class of phenomena. It is not obvious anymore what one means by demand functions and what kind of comparative statics results can be obtained.

To begin with, let us suppose that the cost of producing a unit of commodity i is given by π_i. Certainly π_i depends on the technology and on the input prices p. Let us assume that this is all that it depends on and that marginal costs equal average costs. We can thus rewrite (1.3) as

$$\text{Maximize } U(Z)$$
$$\text{subject to } \pi(p).Z \le I$$
$$Z \ge 0. \tag{1.4}$$

Here $\pi(p)$ refers to the n-tuple of costs given by $(\pi_1(p), \pi_2(p), \dots \pi_n(p))$. Note the formal similarity of (1.4) with (1.1). Thus, under the above assumptions about the costs of producing the various commodities, the household production model reduces to the conventional theory of the consumer. Children, c, have no market prices but each child has a cost depending on the amount of inputs used for its production and the market prices of these inputs. If these "child costs," π_c, are constant per child and do not depend on other commodities the consumer acquires, the total expenditure on children is $c\pi_c(p)$. If expenditures on each of the other commodities can be similarly written, we have really constructed shadow prices for each commodity and can proceed along conventional lines. Thus the demand for commodity i will be given by $Z_i^* (\pi_1, \dots \pi_n, I)$ and will obey all the conventional comparative static properties of demand functions.

Thus the only question arises as to the conditions under which the costs can be written in this way. Rather than give these conditions directly, it may be more useful to see if we can anticipate them on intuitive grounds. Let us begin by making precise the notion of a cost function. In general terms, it tells us how much money[4] would be required to produce a given bundle of commodities $\bar{Z}$, given input prices p and assuming that this production is technologically efficient. This requirement of technological efficiency can be alternatively stated as the requirement that minimum-cost production activities are chosen from the production set. We thus have[5]

$$C(\bar{Z}, p) = \frac{\text{Minimum px}}{(\bar{Z}, x)\varepsilon P} = \{px \,|\, px \leq px' \text{ for all } (\bar{Z}, x')\varepsilon P\}. \qquad (1.5)$$

Out of all input combinations in P which produce the output $\bar{Z}$, we choose those that minimize the cost at the market prices p. It now becomes clear that, in general, the cost of producing a specified amount of commodity i depends not only on the prices p but also on how much of the other commodities are being produced. Thus, for us to be able to write the costs in a separable form as is required for (1.4), it seems intuitively obvious that we would have to restrict the technology in such a manner that the production of, say Z_i, does not depend on the production of the other commodities. We would thus have to rule out joint production. More explicitly we would have to rewrite (1.3) as

$$\begin{aligned}
&\text{Maximize U}(Z)\\
&\text{subject to } (Z_i, x^i)\varepsilon P_i \quad (i = 1, \ldots n)\\
&\qquad \sum_{i=1}^{n} x_j^i = x_j \quad (j = 1, \ldots n)\\
&\qquad p.x \leq I\\
&\qquad x \geq 0 \quad Z \geq 0. \qquad\qquad (1.6)
\end{aligned}$$

The technology P has been decomposed into n technologies P_i each consisting of a collection of input-output pairs as before but with the distinction that each produces only one output. x_j^i is the amount of the jth good used in the production of the ith commodity. We can now write the cost function π_i for the ith good as

$$\pi_i(p) = \frac{\text{Minimum px}^i}{(1, x^i)\varepsilon P_i} = \{p\bar{x}^i \,|\, p\bar{x}^i \leq px^i \text{ for all } (1, x^i)\varepsilon P_i\}. \qquad (1.7)$$

Note that this decomposition requires that one can identify the amount of a good needed to produce a specified commodity, i.e., x_j^i. This can be a stringent requirement. In the context of our original formulation of the household production model, (1.2), where nonmarketed time is explicitly treated as a good, one would have to identify its allocation to each commodity. Nerlove (42, p. S206), for example, refers to "overhead factors, say, the family house, [which] cannot in principle be allocated among the activities but must enter fully into each one.".

The remaining question about the validity of (1.4) that needs to be answered concerns the equality of marginal and average costs. Note what this requirement entails. It means that the cost of producing Z_i amount of commodity i should be Z_i times the cost of producing a unit of commodity i. This will be so if the inputs required to produce Z_i are exactly Z_i times the inputs required to produce 1 unit of commodity i, i.e., each technology P_i exhibits constant returns to scale in production.

We can now state the following important theorems without proof. We hope to have given the reader an intuitive feel for their validity. Both of these theorems are taken from Pollak and Wachter (45) who ascribe Theorem 2 to Muellbauer (40).

Theorem 1: If the household's technology exhibits constant returns to scale and no joint production, then the budget constraint in the commodity space is of the form

$$\sum_{s=1}^{n} \pi_s Z_s = I$$

where the π's depend on the good's prices and household technology but not on the commodity bundle consumed.

Theorem 2: Suppose the household's technology is continuous and zero amount of goods as inputs give a zero amount of output of commodities. Then implicit commodity prices are independent of the commodity bundle consumed only if the household's technology exhibits constant returns to scale and no joint production.

To summarize the discussion so far, we see that constant returns to scale and absence of joint production are both necessary and sufficient for the commodity demand functions to satisfy all the restrictions which conventional theory imposes and which are incorporated in empirical work. However, one could alternatively take the cost function presented in (1.5) above and rewrite (1.4) as

$$\text{Maximize } U(Z)$$
$$\text{subject to } C(Z, p) \le I$$
$$Z \ge 0. \tag{1.8}$$

This would allow us to derive demand functions, i.e., Z^* as a function of p and I, but we would have no general results on how they respond to prices and income. In particular, we would have to do without the Slutzky sign and symmetry restrictions. This is, of course, not to deny that interesting qualitative results can be obtained for specific models where the shadow prices do depend on the commodity bundle chosen. In this context we can refer to the work of Becker and Tomes (5) which generalizes the previous work of Becker and Lewis (4). They consider the following problem,

$$\text{Maximize } U(n, w, y)$$
$$\text{subject to } p_y y + n p_x x \le I$$
$$w = e + x$$
$$(n, w, y) \ge 0, \tag{1.9}$$

where n refers to the number of children each of quality w and y is a commodity with its own market price p_y. A child of quality w is produced with a good of amount x and a variable e which indicates "inherited ability, public investments in children, luck," and so on. Note that there is inherent joint production here in that n and w are jointly produced by e and x. Thus, as shown by Becker and Tomes (5), writing (1.9) in the form

$$\text{Maximize } U(n, w, y)$$
$$\text{subject to } \pi_y y + \pi_n n + \pi_w w \leq R$$
$$y, n, w \geq 0, \tag{1.10}$$

we see that $\pi_w = np_x$ and $\pi_n = xp_x$. If we substitute for x by w − e, we see that $\pi_n = (w - e)p_x$. Thus $\pi_w = \pi_w(n, p_x)$ and $\pi_n = \pi_n(w, p_x, e)$. As such they depend not only on the input prices but also on the commodity bundles chosen. Nevertheless, as shown by Becker and Tomes (5), interesting qualitative propositions can be derived. We refer the reader to their paper.

So far we have restricted ourselves to the demand functions for commodities. However, the household production model deals with both commodities and goods and we can also derive the demand functions for the goods. The derivation of these can be nicely illustrated if we reduce (1.3) to the following problem:

$$\text{Maximize } V(x)$$
$$\text{subject to } p.x \leq I$$
$$x \geq 0. \tag{1.11}$$

V(x) needs explanation. In the context of (1.3) we can determine the maximum utility that can be obtained from a given amount x of the goods without taking the budget constraint into account. In other words, given a fixed value of x,

$$\text{Maximize } U(Z)$$
$$\text{subject to } (Z, x)\varepsilon P$$
$$Z \geq 0. \tag{1.12}$$

This maximized value of the utility function[6] obviously depends on x and we denote it as V(x). Thus (1.11) again reduces the household production model to the standard theory of the consumer as presented by (1.1) but only in terms of goods. If V satisfies the standard assumptions on utility functions, we can derive demand functions for the goods which satisfy all the properties of traditional demand functions. However, the catch here is whether V satisfies the standard assumptions, particularly those relating to nonincreasing marginal rates of substitution. As Pollak and Wachter emphasize (45), p. 260, "V(x), the translation of the utility function into goods space, reflects both tastes and technology" and V does not exhibit nonincreasing marginal rates of substitution in the presence of increasing returns to scale in household production. If we now turn the matter around and look at traditional demand theory from the viewpoint of the household production model, we see that, in analyzing the demand for goods, it attributes to taste changes phenomena which may be the result of both taste and technology changes. Further, in assuming that the utility function exhibits non-increasing marginal rates of substitution, it implicitly assumes that underlying household technology exhibits nonincreasing returns to scale in addition to a similar assumption on the underlying utility function defined on commodities.

In conclusion, we can reiterate that the household production model is a significant extension of the conventional theory of the consumer but that it must be used with care and caution. As we have tried to show in this section, the results of the standard theory of the consumer, which economists take almost for granted, do not automatically carry over when household production is included. We will have occasion to reemphasize this when we turn to dynamic extensions.

1.2. A Simultaneous Equation Model

It has been generally conceded that one of the principal contributions of the theory presented in the section above is its emphasis on the simultaneity of household decisions pertaining to family size, income, labor force partici-pation, and so on. As Easterlin (17), p. 55, writes, "economics has clarified causal interrelations; for example, few economists would speak of lower fertility 'causing' higher female labour force participation, or vice versa, but would view both magnitudes as simultaneously determined by other factors." In this section, using the household production model as our frame of reference, we present a specific empirical model which attempts to take account of this simultaneity. We begin with the preliminary notation leaving a discussion of the data sources for the Appendix.

Endogenous Variables
   C : Total number of live births
   D : Number of dead children
   Y : Current monthly income in rupees
   P : Dummy variable which takes the value 1 if the wife has ever worked or is currently working at anything other than housekeeping and zero otherwise

Exogenous Variables
   H : Dummy variable which takes the value 1 if a house is owned and zero otherwise
   L : Dummy variable which takes the value 1 if land is owned and zero otherwise

AD : Dummy variable which takes the value 1 if the income during the past 12 months was adequate or more than adequate and zero otherwise

AF : Age of wife in years

AM : Age of husband in years

A : Age of wife at marriage in years

EM : Education of husband in years

EF : Dummy variable which takes the value 1 if the wife is "literate" and zero otherwise

T : The time in minutes that it takes for the wife to go to a "medical place"

F : Dummy variable which takes the value 1 if the wife is "aware of family planning" and zero otherwise

EC : Dummy variable which takes the value 1 if any of the living children have been to school and zero otherwise

N : Dummy variable which takes the value 1 if family is nuclear and zero otherwise

C_5 : Dummy variable which takes the value 1 if there is a living child less than five years of age and zero otherwise

We can now present our model. It is a simultaneous equation system that treats four variables endogenously; namely, live births, deaths, income, and female labor force participation, and includes 13 exogenous variables. I denotes the intercept.

1. *Equation for Births*

$$\beta_{11} Y + \beta_{12} D + C + \beta_{14} P = \gamma_{10} I + \gamma_{11} EF + \gamma_{12} EM + \gamma_{14} L$$
$$+ \gamma_{15} H + \gamma_{17} AF + \gamma_{18} A + \gamma_{19} N + \gamma_{110} EC + \gamma_{111} F + \gamma_{112} AD + \mu_1.$$

2. *Mortality Equation*

$$\beta_{21} Y + D + \beta_{23} C = \gamma_{20} I + \gamma_{21} EF + \gamma_{22} EM + \gamma_{23} T + \gamma_{27} AF$$
$$+ \gamma_{28} A + \gamma_{29} N + \mu_2.$$

3. *Income Equation*

$$Y + \beta_{33} C + \beta_{34} P = \gamma_{30} I + \gamma_{31} EF + \gamma_{32} EM + \gamma_{34} L + \gamma_{35} H$$
$$+ \gamma_{36} AM + \mu_3.$$

4. *Equation for Female Labor Force Participation*

$$\beta_{41} Y + \beta_{42} C + P = \gamma_{40} I + \gamma_{41} EF + \gamma_{42} EM + \gamma_{44} L + \gamma_{43} H$$
$$+ \gamma_{47} AF + \gamma_{49} N + \gamma_{412} AD + \gamma_{413} C_5 + \mu_4.$$

We begin the discussion of the specifications of our model by considering first the equation for births.

One of the primary motivations behind the above model is to isolate the determinants of completed family size. In the absence of longitudinal data for each couple, we have to devise proxies for this variable. To begin with, we restrict ourselves to those couples who by virtue of the wife's age will have a low probability of having any more children. We focused on wives between 35 to 49 years of age. There are precedents for choosing this age group as well as larger and smaller ones than this in an attempt to obtain an estimate of completed family size.[7] However, whether or not this age group is the "correct" one is an empirical matter and we go one step further. The survey questionnaire asked each couple whether they wanted any more children. We further restricted ourselves to those couples who answered in the negative. As a final means of obtaining an estimate of completed family size, we removed from our sample all those women who had no live births or no living children. The former exclusion can be justified on the ground that such women were infertile and as such they lay outside our explanatory domain. The exclusion of women aged 35–49 with no living children is less justifiable. It was done to allow the construction of the variable, Education of Children (EC). The question as to whether any of the respondent's children had ever been to school was only asked of those women who had living children. In any case the number of women in our sample who did not have any living children was small, less than two percent.

The next question concerns the construction of an adequate income variable. Unfortunately the data base at our disposal does not allow us to explore a relevant income concept. We have no knowledge about the value of a couple's savings or their assets. Apart from monthly income (and house rent if house is not owned) we have only "yes-no" information on whether a couple (i) has any savings from the past two or three years, (ii) finds its income adequate, (iii) saved any income last year, (iv) owns a house, and/or (v) owns agricultural land. We are aware of the shortcomings of our income variable, but in the absence of a better variable, we have continued to use current income Y as our basic income concept and supplemented it by using ownership of land L, and income adequacy AD, as additional explanatory variables. We expect the signs of the coefficients of both Y and L to be positive. This is in accord with Becker's observation that "an increase in income must increase the amount spent on the average good, but not necessarily that spent on each good. The major exceptions are goods that are inferior members of a broader class. Since children do not appear to be inferior members of any broader class, it is likely that a rise in long-run income would increase the amount spent on children" [Becker(2)]. Again, Keeley, listing works with a positive income effect, writes that "there is a body of empirical evidence that suggests that when a few variables such as education, urbanization are held constant, the income effect on quantity of children is positive" [Keeley (25), p. 463].

If we are justified in viewing AD as a proxy for permanent income, we expect its coefficient to be positive. This expectation also holds if we see it as a reflection of how the respondents view their economic status relative to those of their parents. We can thus argue with Easterlin (16) that those who judge themselves to be better off than their parents will have more children, everything else being constant. However, we cannot rule out the fact that AD is not really exogenous to the system but may be inversely related, in particular, to the number of surviving children. As such, the coefficient of AD may turn out to be negative.

The other relevant set of variables in terms of our theoretical schema are the price effects. The most important of these has to do with the value of the wife's time. The argument originally dates to Mincer (39) who pointed out that the higher the education, the higher the income foregone of the wife and thus the higher the shadow price of a child. Thus, everything else being constant, the higher the education of the wife, the smaller the completed family size. Given that in the countries we investigate, the literacy of the wife is low and the opportunities for her outside employment rather limited, we also supplemented EF with two other variables to capture the value of a wife's time. The first of these relates to whether the wife has ever worked outside the home and the second relates to her family structure. We expect the coefficients of both P and N to have negative signs. If the wife belongs to a nuclear family, it will be more difficult for her to find child-care help and children will be more intensive in terms of her own time. These considerations have also been recently emphasized by DeTray (14).

However, the value of a wife's time is just one of the factors that go toward the determination of the shadow price of a child. As household production theory emphasizes, the shadow price of a child is the cost at the margin of the necessary commodities that have been used on him. As such, the greater the amount of education that the child receives, the higher his shadow price, and thus the smaller the completed family size. The dummy variable EC can then be looked upon as formalizing the cost of children's education and we can expect its coefficient to be negative in keeping with these considerations.

Unfortunately, the matter is not quite as simple as this, especially given the paucity of our data. One can alternatively argue that EC is formalizing "child quality" and, as emphasized by the household production model, both the number of children and the quality of children are choice variables determined by a variety of parameters, permanent income being one. There is no presumption that either is a substitute for the other. As the value of the wife's time rises, rational parents may respond by having fewer children of "lower" quality. Alternatively, a rise in permanent income may raise expenditures on children's services manifesting itself in an increase in both completed family size and the quality of children. Thus, the relationship between C and EC becomes ambiguous. All we can say at this point is that we need better data to construct more adequate measures of the cost of children; for some ingenious preliminary attempts, see Lindert (32).

Male education as an exogenous variable is meant to reflect tastes and/or capture the effect of sociological norms. EM may also be acting as a proxy for attitudes toward family planning. Theory does not give us an unambiguous indication as to the sign of its coefficient in either of these cases; however, it seems reasonable to suppose that it would have a negative sign in the light of other work. The relationship of the coefficient of EM to EF is illuminating. Thus Keeley writes, "Leibenstein suggests that education may be measuring taste effects rather than the cost of time. One piece of evidence counter to this hypothesis is that empirically the mother's education almost always has a larger negative impact on fertility than the father's education, even in a male-dominated society such as Japan, as is documented by Masanori Hashimoto" [Keeley (25), p. 464]. In his survey Schultz is more specific:

> Because of the difficulties of measuring a permanent wage rate, particularly for women not currently in the paid labor force, education has often been assumed to be a satisfactory proxy for lifetime wage rates. When fertility is then regressed on the educational level of men and women, the women's education coefficient tends to be negative, as anticipated, and several times its standard error, while the men's education coefficient is smaller in absolute magnitude and generally less significant statistically.... (Further) the regression coefficient is more often positive for men's earnings than it is for men's education. [T. P. Schultz (46), pp. 98–99.]

The remaining consideration to be formalized is the household technology for producing child services. For one thing, this embodies in it a reflection of a couple's confidence in producing children when they want to. One variable relevant here is the family planning information available to a couple, specifically F, and also to some extent EM. Another relevant factor is some variable formalizing the *ex ante* probability of survival of a child. Finally, we have to include demographic variables such as age of the woman AF and her age at marriage A.

Consider the last two demographic variables first. If we have confidence in our assumption that women in the age group 35–49 years, wanting no more children, have in fact completed their family size, we should expect the coefficient of AF not to be significantly different from zero. However, we must recognize the posibility of birth control failures leading to excess fertility and these being positively correlated with the age of the woman. We thus expect the coefficient of AF to have a positive sign.

The effect of age at marriage is less clearcut. The lower the age at marriage, the higher the fecundity of the woman at the time of marriage and the longer the period during which the wife remains fecund. In light of these considerations we expect the coefficient of A to be negative. However, this effect may be counterbalanced in a late marriage by couples' awareness of these factors and their conscious effort to overcome them. Such couples would not have a smaller completed family size but more narrowly spaced births.

The problem with interpreting the other variables as proxies for couple's efficiency in childbearing is that the sign of coefficients cannot be predicted unless we explicitly incorporate some assumptions about couples' attitudes toward risk. Given that couples have relatively little basis to expect that they will fulfill their desires as to the number and spacing of children, do they respond to this uncertainty by overshooting and having many more children than the desired number, or do they undershoot and typically have less than the number they desire?

Recent work by T. P. Schultz (46, 48) and Ben-Porath (8, 9), building on earlier work of O'Hara (43), has clarified the relationship between fertility and mortality. With the help of simple models, these authors have, in particular, shown that "the final derived demand for births will respond positively to the incidence of child mortality only if the product of the relative change in expected cost per survivor and the price elasticity of demand for survivors is less than unity" [see T. P. Schultz (46), p. 100]. Referring to empirical work, T. P. Schultz (46, p. 101) writes, "individual and aggregate evidence from a variety of low income countries indicates that the partial relationship between fertility and child mortality is positive and statistically highly significant in such varied environments and time periods as Bangladesh (1951–1961), Puerto Rico (1950–1969), Chile (1960), and the Philippines (1968)."

Since our primary concern is with fertility, we shall be brief in discussing the remaining three equations of the model. We begin with the equation for deaths. The first consideration to be justified is the inclusion of completed family size in the mortality equation. It is easy to accept that parents respond to child deaths by adjusting their stock of children or alternatively choose a completed family size in anticipation of child deaths. However, the relationship the other way is difficult to justify on theoretical grounds. The justification we offer has to do with the fact that our variable D measures all deaths and not only infant mortality. Ideally we wanted to use the proportion of children who died under the age of three years as the relevant mortality variable but this information was only available for births after 1960. Thus C is used as an explanatory variable to take account of the fact that, *a priori*, larger families will have a larger number of deaths, everything else being constant.

The other endogenous variable in the mortality equation is current income Y. We expect well-to-do couples to have lower mortality and more specifically lower infant mortality. A similar expectation applies to more educated couples. The expected signs of T and AF need no discussion. We expect age at marriage to have, on balance, a positive effect on child mortality owing to complications arising at childbirth.

We will not discuss the equation for current income except to say that an alternative possibility is to use AD as the relevant endogenous variable. The principal difficulty is a technical one. Given that P is also a dummy, two stage least squares become even less satisfactory and the need to use simultaneous probit estimation techniques becomes more imperative.

Recent work has emphasized the simultaneity between fertility and labor force participation. Cain and Dooley (12) have fitted a model to U.S. data where the endogenous variables are children ever born per 1,000 women, proportion of married females in the labor force during the census period, and full time earnings of wives. McCabe and Rozensweig (34) have studied similar relationships in the context of developing countries. Our equation for P, however, suffers on account of a lack of a suitable earnings variable, and also on account of the definition of P. Recall that this is a dummy variable which takes the value 1 if the woman has ever worked. It is this definition of P rather than a theoretical reason that prompts us to expect the coefficient of AF to be positive. Again, the relationship between C and P is not clearcut. We refer the reader to a survey of McCabe and Rozensweig (34) who give references to rural studies where "birth rates are positively correlated with female economic activity."

The following table summarizes the discussion of our specification.

Expected Signs of the Coefficients of the Simultaneous Equation Model

	I	EF	EM	EC	P	C_s	N	L	AD	Y	D	C	AM	AF	A	T	F
C	?	−	−	?	−		−	+	+?	+	+		+	−?		?	
D	?	−	−					−				+	+	+?		−	
Y	?	+	+	?						+		?	+				
P	?	?	?				−	−	?	?	−		+		+		

Figure 1.

1.3. Results

We test the simultaneous equation model formulated in the previous section by applying it to data from Bangladesh and Pakistan. Earlier analysis for Pakistan leads us to conclude that applying the model to all of Pakistan blurs several interesting relationships [see Khan and Sirageldin (27)]. The choice is then to focus on either the urban areas or the rural areas.

Table 1.1 Multivariate Analysis for Rural Bangladeshi Women Aged 35–49 Years Who Want No More Children.

	I	EF	EM	T	L	AM	AF	A	N	EC	F	AD	C_s	Ŷ	D̂	Ĉ	P̂	R^2
LIVE BIRTHS																		
2SLS	-14.58	.42* (.10)	-.36 (.20)		.01 (.26)		-.28 (.22)	.60* (.22)	.18 (.12)	-.33 (.24)	.01 (.06)	-.45* (.19)		1.16* (.56)	1.04* (.17)		.38 (.42)	.3418
OLS	5.80	.13* (.06)	-.06 (.06)		-.17* (.06)		-.03 (.06)	-.01 (.06)	.06 (.06)	.30* (.06)	.01 (.05)	-.12* (.05)		.14* (.06)	.57* (.06)		-.004 (.06)	.4597
MORTALITY																		
2SLS	-.67	-.15* (.07)	-.01 (.03)	.01 (.07)			.21* (.07)	-.13 (.07)	.02 (.09)					-.03 (.09)		.14* (.07)		.1386
OLS	-1.50	-.17* (.06)	.01 (.06)	-.03 (.06)			.18* (.06)	-.11 (.06)	-.01 (.06)					-.08 (.06)		.56* (.06)		.4090
INCOME																		
2SLS	235.48	.03 (.07)	.16* (.07)		-.04 (.11)	-.08 (.07)										.08 (.07)	-.26* (.12)	.1125
OLS	132.71	.01 (.07)	.19* (.07)		.13* (.06)	-.09 (.06)										.16* (.07)	-.12 (.07)	.1193
LABOR FORCE PARTICIPATION																		
2SLS	1.04	-.01 (.08)	.13 (.12)		-.09 (.11)		-.33* (.18)		-.05 (.10)			.16 (.15)	-.36* (.18)	-.43* (.24)		.43* (.24)		.1163
OLS	.44	.02 (.07)	-.02 (.07)		-.23* (.07)		-.09 (.08)		.07 (.07)			-.05 (.07)	-.13 (.08)	-.11 (.07)		.16* (.07)		.1242

Figures in Parentheses = Standard Error
Number of Observations = 215
* = Significant at 10 percent level.

18

Table 1.2. Multivariate Analysis for Rural Pakistani Women Aged 35–49 Years Who Want No More Children.

Equation	I	EF	EM	T	L	AM	AF	A	N	EC	F	AD	C⁵	Y	D	C	P	R^2
BIRTHS 2SLS (C)	-68.43	-1.22* (0.38)	-0.58* (0.21)		3.06* (1.02)		0.79 (0.20)	0.24 (0.15)	-0.40* (0.20)	-0.10 (0.10)	1 27* (0 40)	2.02* (0.74)		1.80* (0.47)	1.06* (0.31)		5.61* (1.79)	0.2180
OLS	3.26	-0.06 (0.07)	0.07 (0.07)		0.003 (0.07)		0.11 (0.07)	-0.10 (0.07)	0.05 (0.07)	0.13 (0.07)	0.03 (0.07)	-0.05 (0.07)		0.01 (0.07)	0.56* (0.07)	-0.07 (0.07)		0.4153
MORTALITY 2SLS (D)	3.27	0.01 (0.08)	0.12 (0.09)	-0.27* (0.09)			0.01 (0.10)	-0.09 (0.09)	-0.12 (0.09)					-0.17* (0.09)		0.07 (0.11)		0.1250
OLS	0.50	0.06 (0.07)	0.02 (0.07)	-0.19* (0.07)			-0.01 (0.07)	-0.04 (0.07)	-0.08 (0.07)					-0.08 (0.07)		0.55* (0.07)		0.3869
INCOME 2SLS (Y)	128.5	0.07 (0.09)	0.08 (0.09)		-0.09 (0.12)	0.05 (3.09)										0.03 (0.09)	-0.39* (0.12)	0.1138
OLS	52.25	-0.03 (0.08)	0.09 (0.09)		0.14 (0.09)	0.06 (0.08)										-0.04 (0.09)	-0.09 (0.09)	0.0528
LABOR FORCE PARTICIPATION 2SLS (P)	0.75	0.08 (0.09)	0.06 (0.09)		-0.21* (0.11)		-0.01 (0.12)		0.05 (0.09)			-0.18 (0.13)	0.08 (0.11)	-0.14 (0.18)		-0.08 (0.14)		0.1818
OLS	0.601	0.08 (0.08)	0.03 (0.08)		-0.25* (0.08)		0.02 (0.08)		0.08 (0.08)			-0.25* (0.08)	0.05 (0.09)	-0.03 (0.08)		-0.18* (0.08)		0.1987

Figures in Parentheses = Standard Error
Number of Observations = 145
* = Significant at 10 percent level.

Table 1.3 Equations for Completed Family Size of Rural Women Aged 35–49 Years Who Want No More Children.

	Two Stage Least Squares		Ordinary Least Squares	
	Bangladesh	Pakistan	Bangladesh	Pakistan
I	− 15.48	− 68.43	5.80	3.26
EF	0.42**	− 1.22**	0.13**	− 0.06
	(4.20)	(3.21)	(2.17)	(0.86)
EM	− 0.36**	− 0.58**	− 0.06	− 0.07
	(1.80)	(2.76)	(1.00)	(1.00)
P	0.38	5.61**	− 0.00	− 0.07
	(0.91)	(3.13)	(0.07)	(1.00)
N	0.18	− 0.40*	0.06	0.05
	(1.50)	(2.00)	(1.00)	(0.71)
EC	− 0.33	− 0.10	0.30**	0.13*
	(1.38)	(1.00)	(5.00)	(1.86)
Y	1.16*	1.80**	0.14**	0.01
	(2.07)	(3.83)	(2.34)	(0.14)
L	0.01	3.06**	− 0.17**	0.003
	(0.04)	(3.00)	(2.83)	(0.04)
AD	− 0.45**	2.02**	− 0.12**	− 0.05
	(2.37)	(2.65)	(2.40)	(0.71)
F	0.01	1.27**	0.01	0.13*
	(0.17)	(3.19)	(0.20)	(1.86)
AF	− 0.28	0.79**	− 0.03	0.11
	(1.27)	(3.95)	(0.50)	(1.56)
A	0.60**	0.24	− 0.01	− 0.10
	(2.73)	(1.60)	(0.17)	(1.43)
D	1.04**	1.06**	0.57**	0.56**
	(6.12)	(3.42)	(9.50)	(8.00)
R^2	0.34	0.22	0.46	0.42

Figures in parentheses are t statistics.
**Significant at 2.5 percent level.
*Significant at 10 percent level.

Unfortunately, for Bangladesh only 50 observations out of a total of 265 were from urban areas and P for all of these was zero. We thus confined ourselves to rural areas. For results pertaining to urban Pakistan, see the study cited above, and for results for all of Bangladesh, see Sirageldin *et al.* (54).

The results are presented in Tables 1.1 to 1.4. There were a total of 215 observations for rural Bangladesh and a total of 145 observations for rural Pakistan. We ask the reader to compare our findings with our *a priori* expectations summarized in Figure 1 and confine ourselves to a few remarks about the surprises and about some follow-up experiments that need to be done.

The first point to be noted is that simultaneity is important. This is most transparent for the equation for completed family size fitted to Pakistani data; compare columns 2 and 4 in Table 1.3. However, the conclusion also holds for Bangladesh. Comparing columns 1 and 3 in Table 1.3, we find that ordinary least squares estimates of the coefficients of I, EC, A and L do not agree with the corresponding two-stage estimates even as regards the signs.

In the estimates of the equation for completed family size, the chief surprises are the coefficient of P for Pakistan and the coefficients of EF and AF for Bangladesh. In addition, note that even though the R^2 statistic is lower for Pakistan than for Bangladesh, a larger number of the explanatory variables are significantly different from zero in the case of Pakistan. Finally, note the difference in sign for the coefficient of AD for the two countries.

For the remaining equations, we obtain better results for Bangladesh than for Pakistan. Comparative estimates for the equations for labor force participation and the number of deaths are presented in Table 1.4. Note, in particular, the coefficient of T for Pakistan in column 4 of Table 1.4. It is significant but has the unexpected sign. T is a particularly important variable since it ensures the exact identification of the equation for completed family size. Note also that only L has a coefficient significantly different from zero in the equation for completed family size. The corresponding

Table 1.4 Determinants of Labor Force Participation and Mortality for Rural Women, Aged 35–49 Years, Who Want No More Children.

| | Labor Force Participation | | Number of Deaths | |
	Bangladesh	Pakistan	Bangladesh	Pakistan
I	1.04	0.75	− 0.67	3.27
EF	− 0.01	0.08	− 0.15**	0.01
EM	0.13	0.06	− 0.01	0.12
T			0.01	− 0.27**
L	− 0.09	− 0.21*		
AF	− 0.33*	− 0.01	0.21**	0.01
A			− 0.13*	− 0.09
N	− 0.05	0.05	0.02	− 0.12
AD	0.16	− 0.18		
C_5	− 0.36**	0.08		
Y	− 0.43**	− 0.14	− 0.03	− 0.17*
C	0.43*	− 0.08	0.14**	0.07
R^2	11.6%	18.2%	13.9%	12.5%

** t-ratio greater than 1.96.
* t-ratio greater than 1.64 but less than 1.96.

ordinary least squares estimates provide a happier picture. The reader should recall at this point that our technique of two-stage least squares is particularly inappropriate for this equation owing to P being a dummy.

The results presented above indicate directions for further experiments by revealing which relationships are important and which are not. In Figure 2, we present alternative specifications which we hope to try in the future. Figure 2 can alternatively be viewed as a qualitative summary of the results obtained thus far if we ignore most of the statistically insignificant variables. Results pertaining to the specifications of Figure 2 would also enable us to form a judgment as to the robustness of the results presented in Tables 1.1 to 1.4.

Bangladesh
$C = f(D, Y | I, EF, EM, A, AD)$
$D = f(C | I, EF, AF, A)$
$P = f(C, Y | I, C_5, AF)$
$Y = f(P | I, EM)$
f stands for a linear function.

Pakistan
$C = f(D, P, Y | I, EF, EM, AF, N, L, AD, F)$
$D = f(Y | I, T, A)$
$P = f(C | I, L, AD, EC)$
$Y = f(P | I)$

Figure 2.

A final word as regards the exact identification of the equation for completed family size. Note that in our original specification, this property is crucially dependent on the exclusion of the variables T, AM and C_5. For both Bangladesh and Pakistan one or more of these variables turned out to be insignificant for the remaining equations. As such, *ex post*, the equations for completed family size for both countries is overidentified. In the specification presented in Figure 2 above we have been sensitive to this difficulty and have overcome it for Bangladesh. The equation for Bangladesh omits the variables P, AF and C_5. AF was found to be a significant explanatory factor for total deaths and labor force participation, and C_5 to be a significant explanatory factor for labor force participation. As such, the exact identification property of the equation for C is expected, *a priori*, to be robust. The corresponding equation for Pakistan omits T, A and EC. As we emphasized earlier, T has the wrong sign in our earlier runs, and A is insignificant. Here the results would have to deliver the final verdict as to the *ex post* identification of the equation.

II. DYNAMIC EXTENSIONS

The household production model that we presented in Section 1.2 and which we used as a background to our empirical results, reduces each couple's life cycle to one period. Given the restraints and parameters pertaining to this period, utility maximizing couples make various decisions which are adhered to for the whole period. No attempt is made to incorporate uncertainty or changes in these parameters over the period. As we argued in Part I of this paper, we can still get useful insights from this model. However, it has nothing to say about the dynamic elements inherent in individual fertility decisions. In Section 1 of this part of the paper, we examine some of the issues involved and review recent attempts to incorporate these dynamic elements. Section 2 presents findings from Bangladesh and Pakistan. Section 3 furnishes other interpretations.

II.1. Toward a Dynamic Theory

Consider the household production model as formalized in the consumer's problem (1.3). We begin by examining how, under suitable reinterpretation, we can extend (1.3) to accommodate uncertainty and many time periods. The reinterpretation we have in mind has been used by Arrow-Debreu and others working in the general equilibrium theory tradition. We view identical commodities under different states of nature or in different time periods as different commodities. If the unit of time is a year, children's services during one year are regarded as a different commodity from children's services during the next year. Alternatively, children's services with a crippled wife are regarded as a different commodity than with a noncrippled wife, assuming the two states of the world involved are whether the wife meets with an accident or not. Thus, this reinterpretation really calls for the expansion of the number of commodities and goods under consideration. Assume, to begin with, that there is only one state of nature and the couple's life cycle consists of τ periods. We can now look upon x and p as $m\tau$-tuples rather than m-tuples and Z as a $n\tau$-tuples rather a n-tuple. Thus, for example, p is $[p^1, p^2, \ldots p^\tau]$ where p^i refers to the m-tuple of prices pertaining to the ith period. The reader can see that without any changes in nomenclature, (1.3) has been extended to a multiperiod framework. I now represents the total lifetime income and we can determine demand functions of any of the forms discussed in Section 1.2 for any commodity in any particular period. These would now depend, in general, on the prices of all goods in all periods. Thus, the simultaneity of decisions which (1.3) emphasized in the context of a single period can now be seen to extend to all the decisions taken over the τ periods.

If there was uncertainty and several states of nature, the vectors x, p, and z would have to be expanded still further and one could discuss the demand for the ith commodity in the jth period under the kth state of nature. This would depend, in particular, on the prices in all time periods and for all states of nature.

Thus it could be argued that presentation of the household production model as one pertaining to a single period and to an environment without uncertainty is for expository purposes only and that both underlying assumptions can be readily dropped with suitable reinterpretation. Unfortunately, this is not the whole story. Note that in our reinterpretation two crucial elements remained unchanged, i.e., the preferences and the technology of the household. In addition, all the parameters pertaining to each time period and each state of nature must be known to the decision maker at time 0. On the basis of this information, he then takes the decisions for the rest of the period. There are several problems with this schema. For one thing, the informational requirements it presupposes are so immense as to render the exercise rather futile. Even if we ignore this, there is no room for making or for correcting mistakes. More specifically, the reinterpretation does not allow for the fact that a particular decision Z_i^* can be modified in the light of decisions made before. As such, it does not incorporate sequential decision making, even for a setting with full certainty. One could argue that the sequential element is intrinsic to decisions concerning childbearing.

   Note that this difficulty cannot be solved simply by considering elements of Z as both inputs and outputs of the household technology. To see this, let there be only one commodity, children's services, and τ periods. Thus Z is a τ-tuple $(Z^1, \ldots Z^\tau)$. Let $Z(t)$ denote the restricted tuple $(Z^1, \ldots Z^t)$. We can now rewrite (1.3) as

$$\text{Maximize } U(Z)$$
$$\text{subject to } (Z^t, x^t, Z(t-1)) \varepsilon P_t \quad (t = 1, \ldots \tau)$$
$$\sum_{t=1}^{\tau} p^t x^t \leq I$$
$$Z, x^t \geq 0; Z(1) = 0. \tag{2.1}$$

It is here that the theorems presented in Section 1.2 again become relevant. If we allow children's services today to depend on marketed input and services acquired in the past, we confront joint production. Again, it is difficult to see what meaning could be given to the assumption of constant returns to scale if it is applied to all inputs going into the production of Z^t.

   The household production model written as (2.1), in emphasizing the difficulties due to joint production, also draws attention to its similarity with optimal growth theory and the dynamic theory of the firm. We can view the desired stock of children at any point in time as an analogue to the optimal stock of capital and, just as the latter can be shown to depend on the past prices, so too can the desired number of children (say C_t^*). It is this analogy that T. P. Schultz (47) exploits in his recent work. He presents a stock adjustment model of reproduction and applies it to Taiwan. We present his model below. Schultz (ibid) assumes that the desired specific number of births, C_t^*, can be written as

$$C_t^* = \alpha + \sum_{i=1}^{M} \sum_{j=1}^{n} \beta_{ij} X_{i,t-j-i} + \mu_t \qquad (2.2)$$

where $X_{i,t-j}$ is the ith exogenous variable lagged j periods. The past extends to n periods and there are M exogenous variables. μ_t is the disturbance term.

If the significant exogenous variables, for example, permanent income or the value of wife's time as proxied by her education, are constant over the life cycle, the model of Part I can be viewed as a tolerable first approximation to (2.2). The constant exogenous variables of interest would lead to a constant desired stock of capital C* which we proxy by the completed family size. However, even in this special case, we have no theory explaining how the deficit from C* is made up at any point in time. In terms of our analogy to the theory of the firm, even if we grant that we have a satisfactory theory for the determination of optimal capital stock, we have to admit that we have no theory of investment. It will be such a theory that will shed light on phenomena like child-spacing.

Note that we cannot directly apply the conventional theory of investment, and have to limit ourself to extensions to irreversible investment, say as developed by Arrow (1) and others. This is because, given costs of adjustment, a firm can invest and disinvest, whereas a couple can only add to its stock of children. If this stock is depleted, it is largely as a result of forces outside the couple's immediate control. Even if we abstract from this problem, we must face the inherent difficulties involved due to indivisibilities and the zero-one nature of the decision facing the couple. At any period of time, a couple can increase its stock by a unit after a gestation period of three-quarters of a year, or not at all. The couple is also faced with a vintage problem. Given a capital stock of a certain composition, a firm has to decide not only on how much to invest, but how to allocate that amount over machines of different vintages or types. In the context of a couple's decision, they have similar alternatives. They can either increase the quality of the children they already have or, if they decide to have another child, they have an option of wanting a boy or a girl. Of course, they cannot guarantee that they will have a child of the sex they prefer, but, if they do not, it will have consequences for future decisions. The basic point here, as Ben-Porath and Welch (10) have also emphasized, is that sex preference may result not only because of tastes, but also because of the differential costs and benefits associated with a boy or girl. This whole area though is largely unexplored territory and a general theory is lacking.

In the absence of such a theory, T. P. Schultz (1976b) proposes the following adjustment scheme:[9]

$$C_t - C_{t-1} = v(C_t^* - C_{t-1}) + f, \qquad (2.3)$$

where v is between 0 and 1 and is looked upon as the speed of reproductive adjustment. f is an excess fertility parameter signifying that couples may have children due to birth-control failures, etc., even when C_t^* equals C_{t-1}. Substituting (2.3) in (2.2), Schultz derives the following specification

$$C_t - C_{t-1} = v\alpha + f + v \sum_{i=1}^{M} \sum_{j=1}^{n} \beta_{ij} X_{i,t-j-1} \tag{2.4}$$
$$- vC_{t-1} + v\mu_t.$$

If the effect of the exogenous variables is collapsed into one lag of p periods, the above can be reduced to be simply

$$C_t = (v\alpha + f) + v \sum_{i=1}^{M} \beta_i X_{i,t-p} + (1 - v)C_{t-1} + v\mu_t. \tag{2.5}$$

Schultz discusses the econometric difficulties involved in the estimation of eq. (2.5) and applies the above specification to regional data. It is instructive, however, to see what eq. (2.5) implies in terms of our model of Part I. Abstracting from problems of simultaneity, we assume that Y, P, and D are all exogenous variables and included among the variables $X_{i,t-p}$. If the total number of live births to women aged 35–49 who want no more children is a good measure of completed family size, then $C_t = C_{t-1} \equiv \bar{C}$ and (2.5) reduces to

$$\bar{C} = (\alpha + f/v) + \sum_{i=1}^{M} \beta_i X_{i,t-p} + \mu_t. \tag{2.6}$$

As such, ordinary least squares estimation of the parameters of the birth equation would be appropriate. If, however, C_t is not completed family size, leaving out C_{t-1} biases all the estimates. Although Schultz works with regional data, his equations can be tested on cross-section data.

We now present a model due to Sirageldin and the author (53, 54), but motivate it from the viewpoint of equations (2.3) and (2.4). To begin with, note that $C_t - C_{t-1}$ is really 0 or 1. In the absence of any longitudinal data we can replace it by a dummy variable which takes the value one if the woman wants an additional child and zero if she does not. Denote such a dummy variable by AC'. We can then rewrite (2.3) as

$$AC' = g(\delta B, \delta G, Z), \tag{2.7}$$

where δB refers to the number of boys considered ideal by the woman at the time of interview minus the actual number of living boys, and δG is a similar figure for girls. Z is a vector of exogenous variables serving as proxies for excess fertility f and the speed of reproductive adjustment v. Thus, we would expect it to include the age of wife, her age at marriage, and her education. Schultz (47), p. 23, presents a table showing f by mother's education and age for Taiwan.

Alternatively, (2.4) can be written as

$$AC' = g(B, G, X), \qquad (2.8)$$

where B and G are finer measures of C_{t-1} and X is a vector of exogenous variables. Note that in (2.4) the exogenous variables $X_{i,t-j-i}$ make their appearance because of the substitution of eq. (2.2) in (2.3). As such, they represent the determinants of desired fertility at the time of interview. Thus, our exogenous variables X in eq. (2.8) include all the variables which the household production model in Part I led us to consider important. In particular, they should be sharply distinguished from the exogenous variables Z in eq. (2.7) which, as we saw, are a proxy for v and f. Thus, the motivations underlying specifications (2.7) and (2.8) are different.

II.2. Results

In this section we report results obtained by applying specific versions of equations (2.7) and (2.8) to data from Bangladesh and Pakistan. We begin with some further notation.

AC = Dummy variable which takes the value 1 if the respondent wanted any more children and zero otherwise. The precise question that was asked was, "Do you want any (more) children?"

The reader should note that the variable AC does not distinguish respondents who want only one child from those who want more than one. Further, it has nothing to say about the spacing of the desired additional children. It is therefore only an imperfect proxy for $C_t - C_{t-1}$. From this point of view, a more useful question would be, "Do you want a child next year?" Of course, whether this elicits more credible responses than the first question is a different and important consideration. We present some additional notation.

B = Number of living boys
G = Number of living girls

The next two variables can be better described if we mention the corresponding questions that were asked. The first question was "What is the appropriate number of children for a family like yours?" For those who gave a figure, the follow-up question was, "How many of these would be boys and how many girls?" The answer to this question gave us a measure of the number of boys and girls considered ideal by the respondent. We thus have

∂B : Ideal number of boys minus number of living boys
∂G : Ideal number of girls minus number of living girls

At this point, it is worth mentioning that a small proportion of the sample could not answer the first question. Such respondents were excluded. This is the reason our sample size drops from 2,658 to 2,044 in the case of Bangladesh, and from 2,461 to 2,188 in the case of Pakistan whenever we used δB and δG. Similar reductions were made when we focused on the subsample of women whose husbands were also interviewed.

$\overline{EC}$: This variable can also be better described by mentioning the corresponding questions that were asked. It was first inquired as to whether the wife thought it "necessary nowadays to educate children." Those who answered yes were further asked as to how much education was necessary for girls. Out of these answers we constructed the dummy variable as follows:
  $= 0$ if the answer to the first question was no or the answer to the second question was less than three grades
  $= 1$ otherwise

The reader should distinguish the above variable from EC defined earlier. $\overline{EC}$, in our view, measures a woman's commitment at the time of interview to the education of her children and reveals her awareness of at least part of the costs of children. EC, on the other hand, is a crude measure of the quality of the current stock of children and as such is more relevant as an explanatory factor pertaining to completed family size.

Finally, we considered the following variables:

R : Dummy variable which takes the value 1 if the respondent lives in a rural area and zero otherwise
U1 : Dummy variable which takes the value 1 if the respondent is living in an urban area of less than 100,000 people and zero otherwise
U2 : Dummy variable which takes the value 1 if the respondent is living in an urban area of equal to or more than 100,000 people and zero otherwise

Note that U1, U2, and R sum to 1 for each observation.

Before considering each table in detail, it is a good idea to get an overview. To begin with, the reader should note that we have concentrated on a subsample of women, namely, those under 40 years of age. This was done to focus, as far as possible, on the behavioral rather than biological aspects underlying a couple's decision to have children. Further, given that our dependent variable is a dummy, all the estimates are derived through the probit estimation technique. To see why ordinary least squares estimates are inappropriate, the reader should refer to, for example, Goldberger (20), p. 249, or Theil (56). For a thorough discussion of probit analysis, the reader should refer to Goldfeld and Quandt (22).

The results presented in Tables 2.1 to 2.5 alternate between the full sample of women and a subsample whose husbands were also interviewed. Tables 2.2 and 2.3 present results for the subsample in both Bangladesh and Pakistan.

Table 2.1. Demand for Additional Children in Women Aged less than 40 Years: Maximum Likelihood Estimates and Their t-statistics.

	Bangladesh			Pakistan	
	1	2	3	4	5
AD	0.320	0.292	0.311	− 0.085	− 0.084
	(5.53)	(5.03)	(4.57)	(1.46)	(1.30)
AF	− 0.040	− 0.037	− 0.071	− 0.024	− 0.022
	(7.02)	(6.07)	(11.44)	(4.25)	(3.18)
A				0.036	0.032
				(3.28)	(2.58)
B	− 0.294	− 0.293		− 0.417	
	(10.46)	(10.90)		(15.64)	
G	− 0.187	− 0.189		− 0.147	
	(7.03)	(7.31)		(5.69)	
δB			0.211		0.314
			(9.35)		(12.90)
δG			0.167		0.109
			(6.28)		(3.53)
D		− 0.021			
		(0.72)			
$\overline{EC}$		0.294			
		(5.03)			
EC	0.043		− 0.185		
	(0.60)		(2.37)		
U1	1.097	0.837	− 1.019	0.967	0.321
	(6.67)	(4.85)	(2.92)	(4.57)	(1.36)
U2	1.140	0.858	− 1.025	0.769	0.263
	(8.02)	(5.62)	(3.07)	(3.63)	(1.04)
R	1.210	0.985	− 0.909	0.940	0.337
	(9.91)	(7.64)	(2.76)	(4.66)	(1.37)
Twice log likelihood	− 735	− 761	− 841	− 710	− 850
Degree of freedom	7	8	7	7	7
Number of observations	2658	2658	2044	2461	2188
Mean of dependent variables	0.39	0.39	0.47	0.51	0.55

Table 2.2. Equations for the Demand for Additional Children in Bangladeshi Women Aged Less Than 40 Years Whose Husbands Were Also Interviewed. *Maximum likelihood estimates and their t-statistics*

	Wife's Response	Husband's Response		Wife's Response	Husband's Response
Column	1	2		3	4
AD	0.330 (2.81)	0.118 (1.00)		0.334 (2.37)	0.036 (0.26)
AF	− 0.028 (2.52)	− 0.069 (6.00)		− 0.049 (3.84)	− 0.045 (3.52)
EC	− 0.093 (0.64)	0.090 (0.66)		− 0.328 (2.09)	0.080 (0.54)
B	− 0.334 (6.12)	− 0.341 (6.75)	δB	0.279 (5.86)	0.527 (9.54)
G	− 0.172 (3.54)	− 0.170 (3.72)	δG	0.194 (3.75)	0.382 (6.99)
EM	0.023 (1.34)	− 0.033 (1.87)		0.024 (1.18)	− 0.014 (0.70)
Y	− 0.000 (1.09)	− 0.000 (0.46)		− 0.000 (0.16)	− 0.000 (0.75)
U1	0.658 (1.97)	2.961 (8.23)		− 2.452 (3.44)	− 4.227 (5.53)
U2	1.021 (3.41)	2.422 (7.52)		− 2.131 (3.11)	− 4.941 (6.41)
R	1.114 (4.52)	2.959 (10.32)		− 2.037 (3.06)	− 4.334 (5.87)
Twice log likelihood	− 225	− 300		− 261	− 395
Degrees of freedom	9	9		9	9
Number of observations	702	702		552	648
Mean of dependent variable	0.37	0.57		0.43	0.58

Critical value of Chi-Squared Statistic at 0.995 level with 9 degrees of freedom = 23.59.

The use of the subsample is obviously necessary when we compare the wife's attitude toward having more children with that of her husband. However, as emphasized in our discussion of the data, this limitation is also necessary whenever we want to include current income as an explanatory variable. If the effect of current income was significant, our results pertaining to the full sample would be seriously biased. Given that it is not significant for the subsample, the presumption is that a similar conclusion holds for the full sample. Earlier work by Khan and Sirageldin (1976) and Sirageldin *et al.* (54) attempted to substantiate the robustness of the specifications underlying the coefficients of Table 2.1.

The results show interesting differences between Bangladesh and Pakistan. Income adequacy has a uniformly positive effect on the probability of Bangladeshi women wanting additional children. The coefficient hovers around 0.3 for the full sample as well as for the subsample. The substitution of δB and δG for B and G makes little difference to its value. The t-statistics

Table 2.3. Equations for the Demand for Additional Children in Pakistani Women Aged Less Than 40 years Whose Husbands Were Also Interviewed.

| | Maximum likelihood estimates and their t-statistics | | | |
	Wife's Response	*Husband's Response*	*Wife's Response*	*Husband's Response*
Column	1	2	3	4
AD	− 0.248 (2.44)	0.292 (2.60)	− 0.287 (2.52)	0.062 (0.46)
AF	− 0.033 (3.17)	− 0.065 (5.55)	− 0.047 (4.41)	− 0.090 (7.11)
A	0.048 (2.42)	− 0.003 (0.14)	0.048 (2.28)	0.024 (1.00)
B	− 0.381 (8.52)	− 0.462 (9.90)	δB 0.383 (9.36)	0.540 (10.53)
G	− 0.141 (3.16)	− 0.179 (3.83)	δG 0.229 (4.63)	+ 0.243 (4.36)
EM	− 0.002 (1.19)	− 0.002 (1.54)	0.002 (1.11)	− 0.001 (0.38)
Y	0.000 (0.81)	− 0.000 (0.37)	0.000 (0.40)	− 0.000 (0.16)
U1	1.085 (2.85)	3.173 (6.95)	0.387 (0.85)	1.699 (3.17)
U2	0.838 (2.22)	3.433 (7.50)	0.257 (0.58)	2.180 (4.04)
R	1.127 (3.10)	3.332 (7.61)	0.392 (0.90)	2.085 (4.02)
Twice log likelihood	− 259.16	− 370.61	− 320.64	− 389.54
Degrees of freedom	9	9	9	9
Number of observations	842	842	753	670
Mean of dependent variable	0.50	0.67	0.55	0.70

Critical value of Chi-Squared Statistic at 0.995 level with 9 degrees of freedom = 23.59.

are also uniformly high. These results are consistent with the predictions of relative income hypotheses like Easterlin's which hypothesize a positive effect of income adequacy on fertility. As can be seen from columns 2 and 4 of Table 2.2, the effect of a husband considering his income adequate is not quite so strong a factor in explaining his desire to have additional children. The coefficient of AD loses both in magnitude and, more importantly, in significance with the substitution of δB and δG for B and G.

The situation of Pakistani women as regards the effects of income adequacy is totally reversed. The coefficient of AD is uniformly negative for the total sample and increases in magnitude and significance for the subsample of women whose husbands were also interviewed. However, when we consider the husbands' response (see column 2 in Table 2.3), the coefficient of adequacy remains significant but changes sign. On the substitution of δB and δG for B and G in the equation for husbands' responses, the change in coefficient of income adequacy is similar to what we obtained for Bangladesh.

The age of the wife has broadly similar effects on desired additional fertility in both Bangladesh and Pakistan. Its coefficient is negative and relatively small in magnitude, with uniformly high t-statistics.

The other coefficient worthy of notice is the one corresponding to the wife's age at marriage. For Pakistan it is uniformly positive and significant. Thus, increasing the age at marriage only increases the probability of wanting additional children. Note that wife's age at marriage has insignificant explanatory power in terms of a husband's response. Age at marriage is not included as an explanatory variable for the regressions pertaining to Bangladesh. This is in keeping with earlier findings as to its insignificant effect [Sirageldin *et al.* (54)].

Recall that the variables EC and $\overline{EC}$ are intended to measure the quality of children and the future commitment of parents to their quality. They have no effect on desired additional fertility in Pakistan [see Khan and Sirageldin, (26)] and were not included in the specifications reported here. For Bangladesh, the results greatly merit further investigation. Consider column 2 in Table 2.1. Here $\overline{EC}$ has a significant coefficient but opposite in sign to what we would expect. The higher the commitment to children's education, everything else being constant, the greater the probability of having additional children. When we use the variable EC instead, we find its coefficient nonsignificant, see column 1. Looking at columns 1 and 2 in Table 2.2, we see that this result holds also for the wives' and husbands' responses in our subsample. However, on substitution of δB and δG for B and G, we find EC is a significant negative factor in the explanation of wife's probability of wanting additional children, see column 3 in Table 2.1 and 2.2.

This lack of consistency in the Bangladeshi data as regards the effects of EC and $\overline{EC}$ is also seen in the coefficient of total child deaths. For the sample as a whole it is not significantly different from zero, but it has a negative significant impact for the subsample as reported in Sirageldin *et al.* (54). It is difficult to explain this inconsistency, especially given the fact that the subsample is distinguished only by virtue of the husbands' being interviewed rather than by some other socio-economic or demographic variable. The results in Table 2.2 are presented with D excluded. For Pakistan, D is not a significant explanatory variable.

We now come to what we consider our most interesting findings. These relate to son preference or, in terms of this paper, the effect of the composition of the stock of current children on desired additional fertility. Note that the number of living boys is the single most important explanatory factor both for Bangladesh and Pakistan. This is in terms of the magnitude of the coefficient as well as the associated t-statistic. The next most important factor is the number of living girls. Both of these variables exert, as expected, a negative influence on desired additional fertility. What is most interesting from our point of view is the differential effect of this negative inducement. Thus, for Bangladesh, the coefficient of B is around one and a half times the coefficient of G, whereas the corresponding figure for Pakistan is around three. These ratios remain constant not only when we substitute δB and δG for B and G, but also when we shift to the consideration of a husband's response as distinct from that of his wife.

The significance of the statement that the coefficient of boys β_B is α times that of the coefficient of girls β_G can be underscored by computing τ where this is given by the formula

$$\tau = \frac{\hat{\beta}_B - \alpha \hat{\beta}_G}{\sqrt{\{\mathrm{Var}(\hat{\beta}_B) + \alpha^2 \mathrm{Var}(\hat{\beta}_G) - 2\alpha \mathrm{Cov}(\hat{\beta}_B, \hat{\beta}_G)\}}}. \tag{2.9}$$

τ is distributed as a t-statistic whose critical value at the 95 percent level is 1.96. We computed τ for the coefficients of B and G given in columns 1 and 4 of Table 2.1 by letting α equal respectively 1.5 and 3. The values came out to be 0.31 and 0.73.

The implications of the statement that the effect of son preference on desired additional fertility in Bangladeshi women under 40 years of age is of the order 3 to 2, whereas for comparable Pakistani women, it is of the order 3 to 1 can be made clearer if we consider Tables 2.4 and 2.5.

Both tables emphasize the effect of a marginal change in the independent variable on the probability of wanting additional children. The reader should note that the change in probability (AC = 1) for a change in a particular exogenous variable X_i depends on the particular value of the vector of explanatory variables. This is because of the nonlinear structure of the probit model and is a departure from the conventional linear model. The probit model emphasizes that the influence of a particular variable depends on the values ascribed to the other explanatory variables. Given this nonlinearity, there are two ways to proceed. The first is illustrated in Table 2.4.

Table 2.4. Percentage Change in the Probability of Wanting Additional Children for a Change on the Independent Variables.

$$\partial P/\partial X_i$$

	Bangladesh*		Pakistan**	
	$P = 90\%$ or 10%	$P = 50\%$	$P = 90\%$ or 10%	$P = 50\%$
AF	− 0.70%	− 1.59%	− 0.44%	− 0.95%
AD	5.63%	12.76%	− 1.47%	− 3.38%
B	− 5.27%	− 11.97%	− 7.31%	− 16.56%
G	− 3.34%	− 7.58%	− 2.58%	− 5.84%
EC	0.76%	1.72%		
A			0.63%	1.43%

*The figures are based on the coefficients presented in Column 1 of Table.
**The figures are based on the coefficients presented in Column 4 of Table.

Let the values of the independent variables be such that the probability of wanting additional children is 90 percent. A marginal increase in B decreases, say, for Bangladesh, this probability by 5.27 percent. In particular, the reader should compare the row corresponding to B with the corresponding coefficients for G.

The alternative procedure is to give specific values to each of the exogenous variables and then calculate the changes in the probability of having children

Table 2.5. Dependence of the Probability of Wanting Additional Children on Sex Composition*

Number of Girls \ Number of Boys	0	1	2	3	4
0	68.4/77.8	57.5/64.1	46.0/47.7	38.2/31.8	24.5/18.7
1	61.8/73.6	50.0/58.4	38.6/42.0	31.2/26.7	18.9/15.0
2	54.4/68.6	42.5/52.6	31.6/36.3	25.1/22.1	14.0/11.8
3	46.8/63.2	35.6/46.8	25.1/30.9	19.5/18.0	10.4/ 9.1
4	39.4/57.5	28.8/41.0	19.8/26.0	14.7/14.4	7.3/ 7.0

*The first figure in each cell is based on the coefficients of Column 1 in Table 2.1. It is based on a Bangladeshi woman who finds her income adequate, whose age is 27.24 years, whose children have been educated, and who lives in a rural area. The second figure in each cell is based on the coefficients on Column 4 in Table 2.1. It is based on a Pakistani woman who finds her income adequate, whose age is 27.24 years, whose age at marriage is 16.0 years, and who lives in a rural area.

for a marginal change in a specific exogenous variable. The advantage of this method, compared to the first, is that it can also be applied to situations where the marginal or infinitesimal changes in the exogenous variables do not make sense. Thus B can really only increase in terms of single units. We have taken this aspect into account in Table 2.5. For a Bangladeshi woman of specific characteristics the change in the probability of wanting additional children is 57.5–46.0 percent = 11.5 percent when she increases her stock from one to two boys.

The figures in Table 2.5 illustrate rather nicely the implications for desired additional fertility of son preference being of the order 3 to 2 or 3 to 1. Indeed, if we go beyond Table 2.5 to more extravagant[10] values of the number of boys and girls, the implications become dramatically pronounced. The probability of a Pakistani woman with seven sons wanting additional children is only 1.6 percent; for a woman with corresponding characteristics, but with seven daughters instead of seven sons, the probability of wanting additional children is around 40 percent. The corresponding figures for a Bangladeshi woman are 10 percent and 20.3 percent.

It should be emphasized that Tables 2.4 and 2.5 are based on the estimates presented in columns 1 and 4 of Table 2.1. We could have equally well calculated corresponding tables for the other equation whose estimates are presented in Tables 2.1 to 2.3. Alternatively, Tables 2.4 and 2.5 are as reliable as the estimated equations on which they are based.

II.3. Other Approaches and Interpretations

The results presented in Section II.2 were motivated as an application of the theory of investment to fertility decisions. At any given point in time, couples adjust to their desired fertility, with the speed of adjustment depending on a variety of factors, particularly those relating to the age of the woman and the duration of her marriage. The stock of desired fertility, however, is determined principally by a variety of socio-economic variables suggested by the household production model. Putting the two together by substituting for the stock of desired fertility, we obtained a specification relating desired additional fertility to demographic and socio-economic variables. In particular, we derived the composition and magnitude of the current stock of children as an explanatory factor.

There is another interpretation which we can give to our specifications, particularly to eq. (2.8) which is in terms of B and G as opposed to δB and δG. In the model of Part I, completed family size was seen as a result of various influences, economic or otherwise, which the couple faced in the past. It were these influences that we attempted to capture in our independent variables. However, one always has a certain amount of uneasiness about this. Are the values of the variables as revealed at the time of interview really the ones relevant to decision making extending over long periods in the past? Some, undoubtedly, are relevant. This is particularly so with regard to education variables. But others are equally deficient. Even if we ignore income and income adequacy, there is always a leap of imagination involved when we use labor force participation or mortality variables. One could argue that a more satisfactory approach would be to apply the household production model to explain decisions taken at the time of interview. The same theoretical influences would operate, but we could use our explanatory variables with more confidence. The problem with this is, of course, how much credence can be given to answers about projected family size, given the couple's position at the time of interview. Do the respondents really appreciate the figures they give as to the number of additional children they would like to have?

A way around this difficulty is to use AC as the relevant proxy. One could argue that it captures projected fertility with the correct degree of precision. Under this interpretation, the question underlying the construction of AC is precisely the one that we need, and the difficulty of interpretation that we faced in the use of AC as a proxy for $C_t - C_{t-1}$ is no longer relevant.

However, here we come up with the difficulties of applying the household production model to a variable which is not continuous but can only take the values 0 and 1. This is a problem of qualitative choice behavior. At a heuristic level, one can approach this problem in the vocabulary of the probit estimation technique. Let the probability of the ith couple wanting additional children be given by

$$\Pr(AC_i = 1) = \int_I^\infty f(z)\,dz \qquad (2.10)$$

where z is a random variable with a density function $f(z)$ defined on $-\infty \leq z \leq \infty$. I is some index depending on a vector of exogenous variables X and can be written as βX. Thus the probability of wanting additional children is the probability that z exceeds I. If the n couples are all governed by eq. (2.10), the likelihood function is given by

$$L(X, \beta) = \prod_{AC_i = 0}\left(\int_{-\infty}^{\beta X} f(z)\,dz\right) \prod_{AC_i = 1}\left(\int_{\beta X}^\infty f(z)\,dz\right). \qquad (2.11)$$

If we assume that f is the normal density, choosing β to maximize L gives us the maximum likelihood probit estimates of β.

The reason why this procedure is heuristic lies in our not having specified the consumer's utility maximization problem analagous to (1.1). In particular, we do not investigate how the index I depends on the exogenous variables. Further, the likelihood function (2.11) assumes that every individual is alike. Fortunately a fairly complete and coherent theory which addresses itself to these problems has been developed by Mcfadden and his associates [Mcfadden (36); Domencich and Mcfadden (15)]. We shall not go into this development except to point out that Mcfadden (37) reports an application (due to D. Sant) of this theory to desired additional fertility. The specification he works with is identical in spirit to the one we reported in Section II.2.

We now move away from desired additional fertility as the dependent variable to mention two other developments which attempt to incorporate dynamic elements in the economic theory of fertility.

The first approach is due to Heckman and Willis (24) and extends the probit model to a multiperiod framework. The decision underlying equations (2.10) and (2.11) pertained only to one period: the future. Suppose, however, that we had information on whether a woman had a child in the jth period, j running from 1 to n. Let the probability of having a child in any period be given by eq. (2.10) and let these probabilities be independent over the n periods. Then the probability of getting a child in the jth period is given by

$$\left\{ \int_{-\infty}^{I} f(z)dz \right\}^{j-1} \left\{ \int_{I}^{\infty} f(z)dz \right\}. \tag{2.12}$$

We can thus construct a likelihood function corresponding to eq. (2.12) and estimate the coefficients embedded in I. Note that $j = 1$ reduces eq. (2.10) to (2.11).

Heckman and Willis, however, proceed beyond eq. (2.12) and relax the assumption that the probability of having a child in a particular period is independent of the outcome in other periods. They write that:

> Serial correlation may naturally arise if there are unmeasured random variables which remain at, or near, the same level over time for a given individual but which are randomly distributed among individuals. For example, unmeasured components of fecundability (e.g., semen counts of husbands, tastes for coital activity, and varia- tions in contraceptive efficiency) plausibly have a persistent compo- nent for the same individual across time periods although these components may vary widely among individuals. Similarly impor- tant economic variables may be missing in a given body of data [Heckman and Willis (24), p. 122].

For generalization of eq. (2.12) to incorporate serial correlation and for empirical results, the reader is referred to their paper.

Note that the question of unobservables such as fecundability is not really a dynamic issue. It biases the estimates in the same way as would be the case on leaving out any significant variable. The link-up with dynamic questions comes in when we make the assumption that these unobservables are more or less constant over time but vary across individuals. A dynamic framework allows us to exploit this differential variance.

This directly leads us to the second development in the incorporation of dynamic elements which complements the approach of Heckman and Willis. This is to use birth intervals as a basic observation of analysis. In such a context we could pool the birth intervals and use the unobservable, fecundability, as one of the explanatory variables. This would allow application of the recently developed "components of variance" literature by Goldberger (21), Chamberlain and Griliches (13), and others. Birth intervals as a unit of analysis to capture the dynamic effects of mortality on fertility behavior have been used by Ben-Porath (9) and Ben Porath and Welch (10). However, they do not concern themselves with the question of incorporating unobservables.

III. CONCLUDING REMARKS

In this paper we have attempted to show the relevance of human capital theory to research on fertility in Bangladesh and Pakistan, two countries whose per capita income levels are among the lowest in the world and whose birth rates are among the highest. The results reported in this paper enable us to draw some general conclusions as regards the methodology for future work.

There seems little doubt of the valuable insights that human capital theory furnishes in this area. We saw in both parts of the paper how a particular specification could be better understood when examined in the light of human capital theory. For example, in Part I, education of the female could be more pursuasively looked on as a proxy for the value of a wife's time rather than as a parameter of tastes. Similarly, the specification in Part II could be usefully viewed in the vocabulary of the stock adjustment model. All this adds to a deeper understanding of the subject material and gives rise to further hypotheses and emphasizes the need for more discriminating tests.

Indeed, in our view one of the more important benefits of the application of human capital theory to fertility research lies in the directions it pinpoints for further work. This applies both to the collection of additional data and to the development of further statistical techniques. As regards the former, the theory makes precise for the designers of survey questionnaires the type of information that is required. As we saw in both sections I.2 and II.2, we were severely hampered by a lack of a suitable income variable and data pertaining to savings. The same holds for data on education of children. It is also hoped that future data sets would allow the construction of variables indicating the differential costs of boys and girls. This would enable us to probe more deeply into the causes that underlie son preference. Finally, the empirical results presented, especially in Part II, cry out for verification on data sets on the same individuals but collected at different points in time.

Our results also provide a counterexample to the widely held view that improvements in statistical estimation techniques have a limited practical use since the data is typically rather crude and unreliable. As we saw in connection with the variable AC (signifying the demand for additional children), this may be the principal reason for the inadequacy of conventional techniques. Again, a cursory examination of Table 1.3 shows how ordinary least squares estimates can greatly diverge from their two-stage counterparts. Indeed, the specification of Part I calls for a simultaneous probit estimation and for the specification in Part II, we have yet to justify the use of probit rather than logit, Tobit, Goldberger constrained Tobit, etc. All this is, of course, not to argue that diminishing returns to improvement in technique do not eventually set in; only that a judgment must be made in the context of the model and care taken to avoid extreme positions in either direction.

In conclusion, it must also be mentioned that human capital theory itself benefits from application to fertility research. The latter, in posing its own particular problems, stimulates development of the theory along lines hitherto unexplored. Thus a study of fertility brings to the fore problems generated by dichotomous choice variables, the irreversible nature of investment in children's services, and sequential decision making in an inherently uncertain setting. Needless to say, this list will grow longer as further development will reveal how much more there is to be investigated and learned.

IV. APPENDIX

The analyses reported in this paper are based on cross-sectional data obtained from a national survey conducted in 1968–1969 in what was then an undivided Pakistan consisting of the present Bangladesh and Pakistan. For Bangladesh, 3,088 currently married women under the age of 50 were interviewed. For Pakistan, the corresponding figure was 2,910. The design of the survey followed closely the conventional designs of extended KAP-type surveys. It had, however, some important modifications such as more socio-economic information, a detailed pregnancy history and interviews with both husbands and wives in a household. Emphasis was given to measuring program inputs as conceived and utilized by the population. An independent assessment of the availability of family planning and health facilities was also made during the enumeration process. The universe of the sample consisted of all households in Bangladesh and Pakistan (except those in the tribal areas). The sample was multistage and internally self-weighted within rural and urban strata. For more details on sample selection, see Hardee and Sirageldin (23), Pakistan Family Planning Council (44), and Sirageldin (53).

I am grateful to Ismail Sirageldin for getting me interested in this area and, more specifically, for several stimulating discussions over the last two years. My indebtedness in this paper to our joint work is evident. I would also like to acknowledge the valuable research assistance of Farida Shah and Pam Cain. Errors are only mine.

FOOTNOTES

1. See Simon (52), Leibenstein (30), Easterlin (17), Ben-Porath (6), T. P. Schultz (46), among others.
2. See Michael and Becker (38), Ben Porath (6), among others.
3. See Leibenstein (29, 31), Easterlin (17), and Terleckyj (55).
4. This is only for ease of exposition; any other numeraire good would serve just as well.
5. Note that for $C(\bar{Z}, p)$ to be well defined, the set of all input bundles producing $\bar{Z}$ must be closed and bounded from below.
6. Note that V is an analogue of the indirect utility function in the space of goods.
7. See, for example, the work of Frieden, Gardner and Willis reported in columns 9 to 11 of Table 4.B in T. P. Schultz (46).
8. This refers only to the underlying parameters; parents remain uncertain as to the birth outcome.
9. The reader should note that in his paper, Schultz uses δ where we have used v and indexes f and δ by "a".
10. The use of the term "extravagant" is intentional to emphasize that we are going beyond the values of the explanatory variables in our sample.

REFERENCES

1. Arrow, K. J. (1968) "Optimal Capital Policy with Irreversible Investment," in *Value, Capital and Growth*, ed. J. N. Wolfe, Edinburgh: Edinburgh University Press.
2. Becker, G. S. (1960) "An Economic Analysis of Fertility," in *Demographic and Economic Change in Developed Countries*, Universities-National Bureau Conference Series No. 11, Princeton, N. J.: Princeton University Press.
3. ———. (September 1965) "A Theory of the Allocation of Time," *Economic Journal* 75.
4. ———, and H. G. Lewis. (1973) "On the Interaction between the Quantity and Quality of Children," *Journal of Political Economy* 81 : s288.
5. ———, and Nigel Tomes. (1976) "Child Endowments and the Quantity and Quality of Children," *Journal of Political Economy* 84 : s5143–s5162.
6. Ben-Porath, Y. (1974) "Notes on the Microeconomics of Fertility," *International Social Science Journal* XXVI : 5302–5314.
7. ———. (1975) "Fertility and Economic Growth: Some Micro-Economic Aspects," *Maurice Falk Institute Discussion Paper* No. 756. Also presented at Toronto Meetings of the Econometric Society.
8. ———. (1976a) "Fertility Response to Child Mortality: Micro Data from Israel," *Journal of Political Economy* 84 : 163–178.
9. ———. (1976b) "Child Mortality and Fertility—Issues in the Demographic Transition of a Migrant Population," paper presented at the NBER Conference on Population and Economic Change in Less Developed Countries.

10. ———, and F. Welch. (1976) "Do Sex Preferences Really Matter, *Quarterly Journal of Economics* XC:285–307.
11. Blaug, M. (1976) "Human Capital Theory: A Slightly Jaundiced Survey," *Journal of Economic Literature* XIV:827–855.
12. Cain, G. C., and M. D. Dooley. (1976) "Estimation of a Model of Labour Supply, Fertility and Wages of Married Women," *Journal of Political Economy* 84:s179–s200.
13. Chamberlain, Gary, and Zvi Griliches. (1975) "Unobservables with a Variance-Components Structure: Ability, Schooling and the Economic Success of Brothers," *International Economic Review*: 422–449.
14. DeTray, D. (1976) "On the Microeconomics of Family Behavior in Developing Societies," preliminary paper presented at the IUSSP Conference on Household Models of Economic-Demographic Decision Making held in Mexico City.
15. Domencich, T. A., and D. Mcfadden. (1975) *Urban Travel Demand: A Behavioral Analysis*, Amsterdam: North Holland Publishing Company.
16. Easterlin, R. A. (1969) "Towards a Socioeconomic Theory of Fertility: A Survey of Recent Research on Economic Factors in American Fertility," in *Fertility and Family Planning: A World View*, eds. S. J. Behrman *et al.*, Ann Arbor· University of Michigan Press.
17. ———. (1975) "An Economic Framework for Fertility Analysis," *Studies in Family Planning* 6:54–63.
18. ———. (1978) "The Economics and Sociology of Fertility: A Synthesis," in *Historical Studies of Changing Fertility*, ed. Charles Tilly, Princeton, N. J.: Princeton University Press.
19. Friedman, M. (1953) "The Methodology of Positive Economics," in *Essays in Positive Economics*, Chicago: Chicago University Press.
20. Goldberger, A. S. (1964) *Econometric Theory*, New York: John Wiley and Sons.
21. ———. (1973) "Unobservable Variables in Economics," in *Frontiers in Econometrics*, ed. Paul Zarembka, New York: Academic Press.
22. Goldfeld, S. M., and R. E. Quandt. (1972) *Nonlinear Methods in Econometrics*, Amsterdam: North Holland Publishing Company.
23. Hardee, G. and I. Sirageldin. (1970) "A Flexible Interaction Model for Analyzing Sample Survey Data for Planning and Evaluation of Fertility Control in Pakistan," *CENTO Symposium on Demographic Statistics, Karachi* (1968), published August 1970 by the Office of U.S. Economic Coordinator for CENTO Affairs.
24. Heckman, J. J., and R. J. Willis. (1975) "Estimation of a Stochastic Model of Reproduction: An Econometric Approach," in N. E. Terleckyj, ed., *Household Production and Consumption*, New York: Columbia University Press.
25. Keeley, M. S. (1975) "An Interpretation of the Economic Theory of Fertility," *Journal of Economic Literature* XIII:461–468.
26. Khan, M. Ali, and I. Sirageldin. (1975) "Education, Income and Fertility in Pakistan," preprint. Forthcoming in *Economic Development and Cultural Change*.
27. ——— and ———. (1977) "Son Preference and the Demand for Additional Children in Pakistan," *Demography* 14:481–496.
28. Lancaster, K. J. (1966) "A New Approach to Consumer Theory." *Journal of Political Economy* 74:132–157.
29. Leibenstein, H. (1973) "The Economic Theory of Fertility Decline," *Quarterly Journal of Economics* 89:1–31.
30. ———. (June 1974) "An Interpretation of the Economic Theory of Fertility," *Journal of Economic Literature* XII.

31. ———. (1975) "On the Economic Theory of Fertility: A Reply to Keeley, *Journal of Economic Literature* XIII: 469–471.
32. Lindert, P. H. (1978) *Fertility and Scarcity in America*, Princeton, N. J.: Princeton University Press.
33. ———. (1976) "Child Costs and Economic Development," preliminary paper presented at the N.B.E.R. Conference on Population and Economic Change in Less Developed Countries.
34. McCabe, J., and M. R. Rosenzweig. (1974) "Female Labour Force Participation and Fertility in Developing Countries," *Yale Economic Growth Centre Discussion Paper No. 216*.
35. ———, and ———. (1976) "Female Labour Force Participation, Occupational Choice, and Fertility in Developing Countries," *Journal of Development Economics* 3: 119–140.
36. Mcfadden, D. (1973) "Conditional Logit Analysis of Qualitative Choice Behavior," in *Frontiers of Econometrics*, ed. P. Zarembka, New York: Academic Press.
37. ———. (1975) Comments on "Estimation of a Stochastic Model of Reproduction: An Econometric Approach," in N.E. Terleckyj, ed., *Household Production and Consumption*, New York: Columbia University, Press.
38. Michael, R. T., and G. S. Becker. (1973) "On the New Theory of Consumer Behavior," *Swedish Journal of Economics* 75: 378–396.
39. Mincer, J. (1963) "Market Prices, Opportunity Costs and Income Effects," in *Measurement in Economics: Studies in Mathematical Economics and Econometrics in Memory of Yehuda Grunfield*, ed. C. Christ *et al.*, Stanford, Calif.: Stanford University Press.
40. Muellbauer, J. (1974) "Household Production Theory, Quality and the Hedonic Technique," *American Economic Review* LXIV: 977–994.
41. Muth, R. F. (1966) "Household Production and Consumer Demand Functions," *Econometrica* 34: 699–708.
42. Nerlove, M. (March-April 1974) "Household and Economy: Toward a New Theory of Population and Economic Growth," *Journal of Political Economy* 82.
43. O'Hara, D. J. (1972) *Changes in Mortality Levels and Family Decisions Regarding Children, R-914*, Santa Monica, Calif.: The Rand Corporation.
44. Pakistan Family Planning Council (1969) *Survey Design and Development: National Impact Survey*, Lahore, Pakistan: Government of Pakistan.
45. Pollak, R. A., and M. L. Wachter. (1975) "The Relevance of the Household Production Function and Its Implications for the Allocation of Time," *Journal of Political Economy* 83: 255–278.
46. Schultz, T. P. (1976a) "Determinants of Fertility: A Microeconomic Model of Choice," in *Economic Factors in Population Growth*, ed. A. J. Coale, London: Macmillan.
47. ———. (1976b) "Consequences of Development and Family Planning for Completed Fertility and Birth Rates in Taiwan, 1966–1974," preliminary paper presented at the IUSSP Seminar on Economic-Demographic Decision Making held in Mexico City.
48. ———. (1976c) "Interrelationships between Mortality and Fertility," in *Population and Development: The Search for Selective Interventions*, ed. R. G. Ridker, Baltimore: The Johns Hopkins University Press.
49. Schultz, T. W., ed. (March-April 1973) "New Economic Approaches to Fertility," *Journal of Political Economy* 81.
50. ———. (March-April 1974a) Marriage, Family, Human Capital and Fertility," *Journal of Political Economy* 82.

51. ———, ed. (1974b) *Economics of the Family: Marriage, Children and Human Capital*, Chicago: University of Chicago Press.
52. Simon, J. L. (1974) *The Effects of Income on Fertility*, Chapel Hill, N. C.: Carolina Population Center.
53. Sirageldin, I. (1975) "The Survey Method in Family Planning Research and Evaluation," in *Population and Development in Southeast Asia*, eds. J. F. Kantner and Lee McCaffrey, Lexington, Mass.: Lexington Books.
54. ———; M. Ali Khan; A. Ariturk; and F. Shah. (1976) "Fertility Decisions and Desires in Bangladesh: An Econometric Investigation," *The Bangladesh Development Studies* IV:329–350.
55. Terleckyj, N. E., ed. (1975) *Household Production and Consumption*, New York: Columbia University Press.
56. Theil, Henry. (1971) *Principles of Econometrics*, New York: John Wiley and Sons.

HEALTH AND ECONOMIC DEVELOPMENT: A THEORETICAL AND EMPIRICAL REVIEW

Robin Barlow, UNIVERSITY OF MICHIGAN

That healthy men produce more (not that they can but that they actually do) is logical but has only been proved in a small number of limited situations [Davies (15)].

INTRODUCTION

Between 1960 and 1970 real GNP per capita, commonly accepted as an index of economic development, rose by about 40 percent in the world as a whole [United Nations (61)]. Over the same period the world's crude death rate, an indicator of health conditions, fell by about 25 percent [United Nations (60)]. What was the connection, if any, between these two trends?

Research in Human Capital and Development, Vol. 1, pp. 45–75.
ISBN: 0–89232–019–2

To what extent does health promote development, and to what extent does development promote health? A substantial amount of research has been devoted to these questions by economists, demographers, public health specialists, and others during the last thirty years. The purpose of this paper is to review some of the contributions to this literature, especially those pertaining to less-developed countries.

Much of the literature uses the framework of human capital theory. To the extent that better health leads to higher income, expenditures made by an individual or a community to improve health can be viewed as resulting in the acquisition of a capital asset which generates revenues in future years and which may also be subject to depreciation. Rates of return or benefit-costs ratios may therefore be computed for health investments, entirely analogous to those computed for investments in physical capital. Educational expenditures can also be viewed as generating human capital, and indeed both the theory and the empirical research on investment in human capital are more advanced in the educational field than in health.

Once the economic payoff to particular health programs has been calculated, raw material exists for evaluating the policies pursued by ministries of public health and other agencies whose activities affect health conditions. Is the present deployment of the resources available to the ministry—for example, between curative care and preventive care—the best that could be achieved? This kind of question, which is in the realm of health planning, is not one which this paper attempts to cover. Our concern here is with measurement rather than optimization, and with positive matters rather than normative.

Therefore we do not confront in this paper the issue of the weight which the health planner ought to place on economic objectives relative to humanitarian and other noneconomic objectives. In fact, economic objectives seem to play very little part in the decisions made by ministries of public health. But even if economic objectives are deemed to be totally irrelevant for health planning, it is still of interest to investigate the various links between health and the economy. Knowledge of the causes of better health and rising income is valuable for its own sake. And as regards the practical uses of that knowledge, even if a ministry of public health chooses to ignore the economic consequences of health programs, other decision-making bodies like a ministry of economic development may prefer not to.

We start our discussion of health and development by defining these two concepts more precisely. A general model of the relationships between health and development is then outlined. The empirical studies which have been done in this field can be viewed as attempts to estimate one or more components of the general model. The model therefore serves to organize our subsequent discussion of the empirical work, and also indicates gaps which need to be filled by future research.

Two general impressions emerge from our review. The first is that the empirical studies are on the whole not very convincing. As Ruderman notes, they are "characterized … more by anecdotal evidence than by quantitative analysis" [Ruderman (56)]. Subjective and unverified opinions abound: "an intensive [hookworm] control programme in the Darjeeling district was believed by the manager of a large tea-garden to have increased labor efficiency by over 25 percent" [Winslow (69), p. 19]. Where more scientific methods are attempted, the number of sampled observations is often very inadequate.[1] Correlations between two variables are reported without careful analysis of what the direction of causation might be. Correlations between two variables are reported without adequate efforts being made to account for all the other factors which significantly affect one variable or the other. Variables are represented by proxies which scarcely approximate them at all. Explanatory variables turn out to be so highly correlated with each other that it is impossible to disentangle their separate effects.

Second, it is difficult to draw broad generalizations from the empirical conclusions. Even when these conclusions are based on sound statistical procedures, they are only persuasive within their own narrow context. Take a study of the effects of a particular disease on the level of per capita income. The effects discerned in a specific population are not likely to be reproduced at all exactly in some other population. This is because disease-causing agents (viruses, parasites, etc.) differ in potency from place to place, because levels of immunity (inherited or acquired) differ among human populations, because types of treatment for the diseases are not uniform, because income-leisure preferences vary from group to group, as do labor market conditions, and so forth. It is hardly surprising that schistosomiasis is found to be positively associated with absenteeism in one part of the world [Foster (18)], and negatively in another [Weisbrod *et al.* (67)]. The relationships between health and economic development are so complex that the definitive study in this area will never be made.

DEFINITIONS

The reason for our interest in health and economic development is that both contribute positively to human welfare or utility. But the particular definitions of health and development that have been used in empirical work have often been deficient as measures of utility. To take the economic side first, the most common variable used is real income or output—total income or output if the observations are individuals or families, and per capita income or output if the observations are district or national aggregates. Among the shortcomings of these variables as measures of utility are the following:

1. As conventionally measured, income or output excludes the value of

certain goods and services which clearly add to consumption and utility. Examples are domestic services provided by unpaid family members, the value of home-grown food and of owner-occupied shelter, and other nonmarketed commodities.

2. Changes in per capita income do not indicate how the distribution of income is changing, and social welfare may be deemed to be as much a function of the distribution of income as of its total or per capita amount. Median income may be falling while mean income is rising, and the former may well be judged to be more important than the latter from the viewpoint of social welfare.

3. Some output causes a loss of utility, as when pollution of the environment occurs as a result of manufacturing processes, but the conventional measures of income or output make no allowance for this.

Despite these shortcomings, it is probably true that the conventional measures are acceptable proxies for the broader concept of material well-being or economic development which we would like to be able to measure. Large increases in per capita real income are normally associated with significant improvements in the typical family's standard of living. It is unlikely that the use of per capita income rather than some broader measure of development has led to spurious empirical conclusions about the links between health and development.

On the health side, two kinds of variables have been used in the empirical work. First are measures of the existence or prevalence of a particular disease. When the units of observation are individuals, the variable indicates whether or not the individual has the disease in question. When the units of observation are communities, it is the fraction of the community with the disease that is measured. These variables are then correlated with economic variables like hours worked, output per hour, and so forth.

The definitional problems in this approach mostly concern the accuracy of diagnosis. Is the prevalence of malaria accurately indicated by the spleen rate (the percentage of a sampled population with enlarged spleens)? How reliable are official statistics on the number of deaths caused by tuberculosis? There is often much disagreement among medical experts on such points. By its very nature, this approach can provide only a small part of the picture describing the general state of health in a society. There is no more reason to accept the incidence of malaria as a measure of general health than there is to accept the consumption of wheat as a measure of economic development.

The second kind of health variable attempts to reflect health conditions as a whole. Most commonly selected, because of the ready availability of data, is some measure of mortality like the crude death rate or the infant mortality rate. Measures of health-care resources, like the number of hospital beds per capita, are also sometimes employed as indicators of general health conditions.

The deficiencies of resource measures as indicators of health are rather severe. A resource variable like hospital beds measures at best the *change* in health conditions brought about by hospitals rather than the *level* of health attained. The point might be made that most hospitals are concentrated in urban areas, where the level of health attained is generally better than elsewhere. But if that is the argument, it would be better to proxy health directly with an urbanization variable rather than indirectly with hospitals. And then, of course, one would be explaining urbanization rather than health.

As for death rates, they provide only a partial indicator of health. Most people would agree that a measure of health conditions ought to reflect the extent of *morbidity* in a population (defined here following Mushkin and others as the fraction of time when sickness causes absence from normal activities) and also its degree of *debility* (causing poorer performance of those activities) [Mushkin (47)]. The correlations between various measures of mortality, morbidity, and debility are far from exact. For example, in 1973 the crude death rates in Egypt and East Germany both approximated 13 per 1,000 [United Nations (61)]. But it must be presumed that morbidity was much greater in Egypt, because of the much higher prevalence of infectious and parasitic diseases there. As another example, certain forms of treatment for diabetes and cancer have the effect of prolonging life without curing the underlying condition, and the patient lives on for some years in a disabled state. Such treatments may lower the crude death rate while raising the morbidity rate.

So a satisfactory analysis of health conditions would include measures of morbidity and debility as well as mortality. The problem is that data on morbidity and debility are hard to come by. The necessary information—on the frequency of sickness and the degree of incapacitation—can only be obtained from household surveys, whose reliability is often questionable. What is more, even when mortality, morbidity, and debility are all accurately measured, there remain some important aspects of health conditions still unrecorded. In particular, there are those cases where a person adapts to an incurable ailment and pursues a full-time career, though at a rate of remuneration less than what he would have received in the absence of the handicap, like a piano tuner prevented by blindness from becoming a successful banker. Such cases do not usually enter statistics of morbidity, but clearly any picture of health conditions is incomplete without them.

An acceptable approach toward defining health for our present purposes might be as follows. From the viewpoint of social policy, two aspects of health are important: one is the frequency of deaths, and the other is the extent of infirmity among those surviving, where infirmity is meant to include morbidity, debility, and handicaps. The reduction of mortality and the reduction of infirmity are separate social objectives, which will indeed sometimes be in conflict with each other. (The debate over euthanasia is a major manifestation of this conflict.) The relationship of each objective to the economic objective of rising per capita income can be analyzed separately.

It might be noted, finally, that the literature on health economics contains some proposals for the construction of composite indexes of health like the measure of infirmity mentioned above. Culyer et al. (14), for example, propose an index reflecting degrees of pain and of restriction of activity, with each individual scored on a scale extending from "no significant discomfort or restriction" at one extreme to "unconscious" at the other.[2] The survey data necessary for such indexes do not yet exist. But as a matter of research priorities, it would seem more important to start collecting these data than to continue running correlations between per capita GNP and the number of hospital beds per capita.

A GENERAL MODEL

If we aim to investigate the links between health (defined either by the prevalence of a specific disease or in terms of an index of general health conditions) and economic development (total or per capita income), it soon becomes clear that we must take explicit account of certain other social characteristics, all of which along with income and health are jointly determined within a single social system. Three such other characteristics are obvious: nutritional status, educational attainment, and fertility. We have, then, five variables interacting with each other. Each one affects and is affected by each of the other four. The links between any two, like income and health, are influenced by the relationships between these two and the other three. A diagrammatic model incorporating these relationships is shown in Figure 1. Each arrow shows a direct causal relationship between the variables. For example, the arrow labeled 1 represents the direct or pure effect of fertility (F) on health (H), other factors held constant ($\partial H/\partial F$).

The model can be seen as applying to an individual or family, or to community-wide or national aggregates. It does not depict all relevant variables. In particular it does not show the exogenous variables which influence one or other of the five endogenous variables. The model is intended to emphasize that if one of the endogenous variables changes, perhaps as a result of exogenous influences, the effect of this change on any other endogenous variable will be the sum of the direct relationship between those two and the indirect relationships working through the other three. For example, if external factors cause an improvement in health, the effect of this on income will be the sum of the direct effect (no. 17 in the model) and the indirect effects arising from the fact that the change in health affects nutrition, education, and fertility, which in turn affect income and also produce feedback effects on health itself.[3]

The model specifies twenty direct relationships, on most of which a

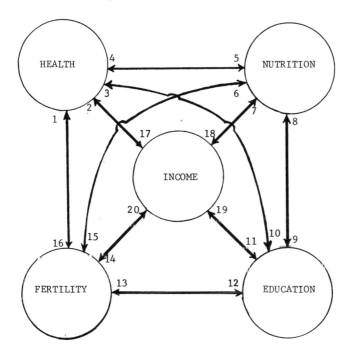

Figure 1. A General Model of Health and Development.

substantial amount of empirical research has been done. It is not our intention in this paper to review the work done on all twenty, even though all twenty affect the health-income linkage either directly or indirectly. But it may be useful at this point to give a single example of each of the twenty connections. (The examples are hypotheses which have not necessarily been confirmed empirically.) Later in the paper we return in more detail to the eight direct relationships involving health.

Examples of the direct relationships shown in Figure 1
1. Fertility → health. Later marriages and lower fertility mean fewer of the high-risk pregnancies and deliveries associated with very young mothers.
2. Income → health. Higher incomes lead to higher expenditures on medical care.
3. Education → health. Better-educated persons tend to have stricter standards of personal hygiene.
4. Nutrition → health. Malnutrition causes rickets.
5. Health → nutrition. Diarrhea involves a rapid loss of nutrients.
6. Fertility → nutrition. The larger the number of children in the family, the less care is devoted to the proper feeding of each one.

7. Income → nutrition. Higher incomes tend to lead to better diets.
8. Education → nutrition. Educated persons are better informed about nutritional requirements.
9. Nutrition → education. Well-nourished students are better able to concentrate on their work in school, and perform better academically.
10. Health → education. Sick children are often absent from school, and have inferior academic records.
11. Income → education. High-income parents place their children in high-quality schools.
12. Fertility → education. Pregnancies interrupt schooling.
13. Education → fertility. Educated women desire smaller families.
14. Income → fertility. High-income persons want to have large families, regarding children as a form of consumption.
15. Nutrition → fertility. Maternal malnutrition increases the likelihood of miscarriage.
16. Health → fertility. Malaria causes miscarriages.
17. Health → income. Healthy persons work longer and harder.
18. Nutrition → income. Well-nourished workers produce more.
19. Education → income. Educated persons get better-paying jobs.
20. Fertility → income. Women with several children are less likely to work outside the home.

It will be noted that the model is a dynamic one. Although some effects are instantaneous, others take years to develop. An immediate effect of improved health on income, for example, occurs when the treatment of a disease reduces absence from work. But other effects may be long postponed, as when improved health raises income through the indirect mechanism of improving the scholastic performance of students and raising their potential earning power.

The model can be readily extended to include utility relationships. These would be needed before normative judgments could be made about policies producing change in the system. One plausible utility function would treat as separate arguments each of the five endogenous variables specified: health (H), nutrition (N), education (E), fertility (F), and income (Y). We would then have:

$$U = U(H, N, E, F, Y)$$

where utility (U) is defined on either an individual or a community basis. A refinement would be to add leisure (L) as another argument, and to replace income by the consumption of the goods and services (C) financed by that income:

$$U = U(H, N, E, F, C, L)$$

where $C = C(Y)$.

A further possibility is to extend a suggestion offered by Berg (6), and note that health not only provides utility in and of itself but also affects the utility derived from other activities. Thus a meal or an afternoon at the beach are enjoyed more if one feels well. Health therefore may enter the utility function on its own account and also interactively with the other arguments:

$$U = U(H, N \cdot H, E \cdot H, F \cdot H, C \cdot H, L \cdot H).$$

Concerning the last item in this utility function, we might note parenthetically that the relationships between health and leisure are quite complex and deserve a lot more investigation than they have received. Initially, sickness often produces an increase in leisure, as the patient feels too ill to go to work. At the same time, the sickness reduces the utility normally derived from leisure. Later, when the sickness has gone, work effort is sometimes greater than normal, as attempts are made to make up what has been lost, and leisure is reduced. Conly (11) notices this effect with respect to malaria. Another possible outcome, noticed by Weisbrod *et al.* (67) with respect to schistosomiasis, is that when sickness worsens performance on the job, longer hours are worked in compensation.

It might be noted too that a utility function like one of those detailed above allows for both the "consumption" and the "investment" benefits of better health. Several writers have stressed this distinction, Klarman (36) being an example. As usually defined, the consumption benefits of better health are the increases in utility directly yielded by the better health itself $(\partial U / \partial H)$. The investment benefits result from any net positive effects of better health on income (dY/dH).

The model provides a framework for considering the literature on health and development. Thus used, it shows that the literature has a number of major shortcomings, examples of which appear in our more detailed review below. First, when relationships between two of the five endogenous variables are being investigated, it is often not recognized that causation typically runs in both directions. A statistical estimation of the causation in one direction often produces misleading results when no allowance is made simultaneously for the causation operating in the opposite direction.[4] Second, it is often not clear when the estimated effects of one variable on another reflect only the direct relationship between them, and when indirect effects working through the other three endogenous variables are also incorporated. Third, statistical investigations of the relationships between two variables often fail to allow adequately for the effects of other variables, both endogenous and exogenous, with the result that the correlations obtained are spurious.

BIVARIATE RELATIONSHIPS

There are twenty cause-effect bivariate relationships in the model just described. Most of the literature under review has focused on one or other of these twenty relationships, controlling in various degrees for the influence of other factors. Some other studies have dealt with a larger part of the general system, by analyzing two or more of the relationships simultaneously. In this section we review the work done on eight out of the twenty bivariate relationships, looking at the results obtained both in the general-system studies and elsewhere. In the next section a further look is taken at the general-system studies. The eight bivariate relationships discussed here are those involving health as either cause or effect.

1. Effect of health on income

An improvement in health can directly affect income through any of several different mechanisms. There may be an increase in the number of hours worked, for example, or access may be obtained to the natural resources located in regions previously shunned because of the threat of disease. Most of the studies of the effect of health on income have concentrated on one or the other of these specific mechanisms. Some, however, have looked at the total effect of health on income without trying to distinguish the separate effects operating through the different mechanisms. Correa includes health variables (measures of mortality and morbidity) among several other explanatory variables in a time-series analysis with national income as the dependent variable. The analysis is repeated for 17 countries [Correa (12), pp. 43–50]. A similar model is used by Galenson and Pyatt (22) in a cross-sectional analysis of 52 countries. Both studies find that health has little effect on income.[5] The opposite conclusion is reached in a third study of this type, a multivariate time-series analysis of Ceylonese data by Griffith *et al.* (24). A health variable (health expenditures per worker) is found to be a significant determinant of national income per worker. All three of these studies are subject to several of the difficulties noted earlier—the presence of two-way causation, multicollinearity among independent variables, or the omission of important explanatory factors.

Turning to the specific mechanisms by which health affects income, we note five as receiving particular attention in the literature:

a) Change in work hours

A reduction in mortality prolongs working lives. A reduction in morbidity lowers absenteeism. In either event, there is likely to be an increase in the number of hours worked annually, and a consequent increase in output and income. Many studies have tried to estimate the increase in income occurring through this mechanism. The standard procedure is as follows: The reductions in mortality or morbidity rates are specified for age-sex groups, and the potential increase in annual work hours is then calculated for each group; subtractions from these potential increases are made for nonparticipation in the labor force and for unemployment; and the increases in work hours thus adjusted are multiplied by an annual wage estimate. The increase in income is expressed either as an annual flow or as the present value of future flows.

A couple of studies relating to less developed countries have attempted to make these estimates for all diseases combined, along the lines of the study made by Rice (55) for the United States. One of these cited by Mejia and Paredes (46), p. 284, relates to Colombia; the other, cited by Winslow (69), p. 13, is for Ecuador. Since these estimates are predicated upon rather unlikely events, namely the reduction of mortality or morbidity or both to zero, they are of somewhat limited interest.

Another kind of study, which likewise involves handling several diseases at once, attempts to measure the effects of programs aiming at a general improvement in health conditions. Correa (12), p. 12, cites a study estimating the effects of rural health units on hours worked in Egyptian villages. Such inquiries are of more practical interest than those assuming the absence of all disease, but clearly run into severe statistical problems in their efforts to separate the effects of the health program from the effects of all other factors impinging on work hours.

A more common exercise is to estimate the work hours and income generated by the elimination of specific diseases. Some of the diseases thus analyzed in the context of less-developed countries are the following:

- malaria [Conly (11); Kuhner (38); Taylor and Hall (58); USHEW (62); Winslow (69)].
- schistosomiasis [Cohen (10); Farooq (16); Foster (18); Weisbrod *et al.* (67)]
- tuberculosis [Feldstein *et al.* (17); USHEW (62); Winslow (69)]
- yaws [Winslow (69)]
- venereal diseases [Winslow (69)]
- influenza [Griffith *et al.* (24)]
- trachoma [Karefa-Smart (32)]

All of these studies encounter two difficult problems. The first is that a correct calculation of income gains requires use of the relevant *marginal* rates (of labor force participation, of unemployment, of wages), since what the health improvement permits is an addition to existing flows. But the only data normally available relate to *average* rates. This problem is handled in various ways. Most often it is ignored, and the average rates are used, despite the fact that in less-developed countries the health improvement often takes place in a setting of widespread unemployment and underemployment. In this setting, an increase in the potential number of work hours is not likely to bring about much of an increase in output. Occasionally an attempt is made to guess at the relevant marginal rates. Cohen, for example, knowing that an estimate of the marginal product of labor rather than its average product is needed, and feeling that the marginal product is probably less than the average product in Zanzibar, uses for his calculation of the economic gains to schistosomiasis control in Zanzibar not the average wage but a "minimal wage for unskilled labor" [Cohen (10)]. The direction of the adjustment may be correct, but there is clearly much arbitrariness here.

The second problem faced in these studies is that the marginal rates, even when known, may not remain unchanged but may be affected by the health improvement itself. The studies cited so far, that is to say, are of the partial equilibrium type, whereas a general-equilibrium analysis may be called for. The appropriateness of a partial analysis depends upon the size of the analyzed change in relation to the size of a system as a whole. If we are dealing with a health program which affects only one-tenth of one percent of the labor force, it would be reasonable to assume that the marginal product of labor would not be affected by the implementation of the program. But if 80 percent or more of the labor force is affected, as may occur with some anti-malaria or anti-schistosomiasis programs, the same assumption would not be reasonable.

Some general-equilibrium analyses have in fact been used for investigating the links between health and development. A macro-model with health, demographic, and economic sectors is specified, and variables like the marginal product of labor and the unemployment rate are endogenous. A health improvement is introduced, and the model is used for simulating the effects of the improvement on the future growth of income. Examples of this approach are found in the studies of Barlow-Davies (5), Correa (12), and Vianen-Waardenburg (64).

b) Change in labor productivity

Health improvements may change hours of work, and may also change the output produced per hour of work (holding constant the stock of capital and natural resources). Such changes in labor productivity may be produced through a number of different mechanisms. Any increase in work hours due to reduced mortality or morbidity will by itself tend to lower labor productivity. With a given stock of nonhuman resources (capital and natural resources), the ratio of work hours to nonhuman resources is now more than before, and output per work hour will decline.

This negative effect of better health on productivity may be offset in a number of ways. Most straightforward is an increase in output made possible by greater physical strength and aptitude. Mental or psychological effects are also claimed. A healthy worker is said to be more ambitious, innovative, and enterprising. The achievement of better health, say through an anti-malaria campaign, is said to demonstrate to traditional communities that they can successfully control their environment. They are then more likely to carry out economic activities with a new spirit, with less fatalism. Malenbaum (43) in particular has stressed these motivational effects.

A different kind of mechanism leading to productivity increases is the reduction in labor turnover made possible by health improvements. When poor health leads to frequent absenteeism and a high degree of labor turnover, output is likely to suffer, as experienced workers continually fall ill and are replaced by others less experienced.

Several studies have purported to measure the change in income which better health produces by changing productivity. On inspection, however, several of these studies are found to obtain their results by making assumptions about the productivity changes, assumptions which are never tested against actual data. Cohen, for example, cites a study of the economic benefits from schistosomiasis control in Iraq: the productivity change was assumed to be the same as that found in an Egyptian study, which reported that an individual with the disease "would lose from 4 to 20 percent of his energy and working power" [Cohen (10)]. The differences between Egypt and Iraq in parasite strains, human immunities, work patterns, and so forth, are ignored. Other studies of the economic gains from schistosomiasis control are similarly based on sweeping assumptions, such as the estimates for China cited by Andreano (2). Certain estimates pertaining to malaria suffer from the same weakness [Mushkin (48); Winslow (69)].

When we turn to those studies which have taken the productivity change as something to be measured rather than assumed, two categories can be distinguished: the studies based on macro-data (regional or national), and those based on micro data (individuals or families). The macro-approach is typified in a study by Malenbaum (42), who uses observations for 22 countries. The dependent variable is the percentage change in agricultural output per worker over a certain period. Among the independent variables in a multiple regression analysis are two purporting to measure health conditions (the infant mortality rate and the population-physician ratio). Health is found to have a strong positive impact on productivity, the two health variables accounting for about half of the variance in the dependent variable. The favorable effect of health on productivity is attributed to the motivational influences mentioned above.

Malenbaum's results are not altogether convincing. For one thing, the direction of causation between health and output may be the opposite of what he claims. Rather than better health raising productivity, it may be that the countries with higher productivity have the means to bring about better health. Furthermore, the dating of the variables is unfortunate. Malenbaum explains the *change* in output during the period by the *level* of the health variables at some unspecified time during the period. The findings would be more persuasive if the change in productivity were related to the change in the health variables.

The micro studies of health and productivity have produced an interesting diversity of conclusions. On one side we have such studies as that reported by Winslow (69), p. 26, in which anti-malaria measures on a Malayan rubber estate resulted in an astonishing seventeenfold increase in output per worker. In contrast we have the finding in Foster's study of schistosomiasis among Tanzanian cane cutters and irrigators that "when men came to work, there was no significant difference in output between those with schistosomal infections and those without" [Foster (18)]. Sometimes contrary results appear within the same study. In an investigation of farming in eastern Paraguay, Conly (11) found in orthodox vein that crop yields per workday were lower among families with "much malaria" than among those with "moderate malaria." Yet yields among the "moderate malaria" families were *higher* than among those with "little malaria." The small size of Conly's sample goes some way toward explaining the perversity of these results.

Contrary results also appear in the schistosomiasis study conducted by Weisbrod *et al.* (67) in St. Lucia, perhaps the most sophisticated piece of field research yet undertaken in the area of health and development. A survey of banana plantation workers found that those with schistosomiasis tended to have lower daily earnings. (The infected workers then usually made up these hours by working more days per week, so that the impact of disease was more upon leisure than upon income, as we have noted above.) However, a survey of women factory workers found no association between schistosomiasis and productivity. It seems clear from all these results that the impact of disease on productivity differs substantially from disease to disease and from place to place.

c) Migration effects

A region containing rich agricultural and mineral resources may remain undeveloped because of the prevalence of certain diseases there. The elimination of these diseases may encourage workers to migrate to the region. Relocation of mobile capital may also occur. Output in the region will increase as these resources flow in.

Several descriptive accounts of such events have been provided. The eradication of malaria has been said to stimulate regional development in Nepal [Nash (49)], Ceylon and Mexico [Taylor and Hall (58)], Brazil [Perlman (51)], South Africa [Winslow (69), p. 25], and western Thailand [Griffith *et al.* (24)]. On the other side of the coin, it is reported that the spread of disease into an area has led to depopulation and a decline in output. Conly (11) discusses this effect with respect to malaria in eastern Paraguay, and Hunter (30) with respect to onchocerciasis in Ghana.

No doubt the relocation of resources encouraged by health improvements has led to some net increase in output, though the effect has generally been exaggerated. In the first place, it is often not adequately recognized that the output increase occurring in the region with the health improvement is obtained at the cost of reduced output elsewhere, namely, in those other regions from which the labor and capital migrate. The economic gain properly attributable to the health improvement is the net increase in output from all regions combined, not simply the increase taking place in the region where the health improvement occurred.

In the second place, it is customary to count the entire migration occurring in these cases as being due to the health improvement. But there are many other possible determinants of migration, and it does not seem prudent to assume that none of them had any importance at all in these particular instances.

d) Budgetary savings

A health improvement may permit a reduction in certain kinds of expenditures in private or public budgets For example, the eradication of smallpox reduces to zero the expenditures made by households or governments for smallpox vaccinations. Such reductions in expenditures do not themselves constitute an increase in income. They do, however, release funds which may be partly devoted to saving and investment, and which therefore add to future income. At the micro-level this means that a family which no longer has large medical bills is able to save a little more, and will receive a return on that extra saving in the future. At the macro-level it means an increase in the average propensity to save and in the rate of capital formation, and a more rapid growth rate of output in the future. These effects on future income have not normally been calculated in past empirical work, which has not gone beyond an estimation of the expenditure reductions.[6]

The expenditure reductions are of several types. First, there are lower costs of treatment for the particular disease brought under control. The costs of treatment include the costs of hospitalization, of outpatient services, and of medication. In more sophisticated analyses, account is also taken of the value of the time spent by the patient in waiting for and undergoing treatment. Estimates have been made for the treatment costs of malaria in British Guiana and Greece [Winslow (69)], of tuberculosis in Panama (USHEW 62)] and Korea [Feldstein *et al.* (17)], and of schistosomiasis in Iraq [Watson (65)], to name only a few examples.

Second, when a disease is eradicated, there is no longer any need to incur the costs of avoiding it. Thus in the case of malaria, eradication means that quinine or other anti-malaria drugs need no longer be taken as a prophylactic, and that mosquito netting can be dispensed with (though perhaps not entirely). The significance of avoidance costs was first stressed in a formal way by Weisbrod (66) but examples of their empirical estimation are rather rare.

Third, certain diseases cause a serious waste of caloric intake. In some of these cases, the disappearance of the disease could be expected to bring about a reduction in food expenditures. Examples are certain parasitic diseases, where many of the nutrients ingested by the human host go to sustain the parasites; diarrhea, where a large proportion of the nutrients are expelled before being fully utilized; and fevers, which create additional caloric demands. Some estimates of caloric costs have been made for tuberculosis and cholera in the Philippines, and for tuberculosis and malaria in Panama [USDHEW (62)]. The estimates of wasted calories are converted into economic terms by calculating the value of the food that would provide that quantity of calories, or the number of workdays that would utilize that same quantity. What is ignored here, however, is the likelihood that healthier people have healthier appetites, and may end up spending more on food despite any reduction in caloric waste.

In general it should be recognized that health improvements cause increases as well as decreases in expenditure (out of a given budget), and the net effect on saving is unclear. Apart from the matter of appetite just mentioned, we might consider the expenditure effects of a migration stimulated by the eradication of disease in a previously undeveloped region. Such a migration would oblige governments and households to devote extra funds to the construction of new social overhead capital (housing, roads, schools, hospitals, etc.). And it should be remembered that if the health improvement is produced by a program like insecticidal spraying or mass vaccination which costs something to run, then the expenditure on the program itself must be added to the debit side of the ledger.

e) Changes in dependency burdens

The average propensity to save and, hence, the future growth of income are determined also by the burden of dependency in a society. By this is meant the fraction of the total population who are at dependent ages, say under 15 and over 65. When this fraction is high, the average worker must support several dependents and is not able to save very much. A number of studies have suggested that there is a negative relationship between dependency burdens and saving propensities, for example Leff's (40) cross-sectional analysis of macro-data for 74 countries.[7]

Some health programs change dependency burdens and hence income prospects. Typically any change is in the direction of increasing burdens and worsening income prospects. This is particularly true of programs which reduce child mortality, like malaria eradication, measles vaccination, or the provision of drinking water. To allow for such adverse effects of health on development, it is necessary to use a macro-model of income simulation, like some of those cited above, in which dependency burdens and saving propensities appear explicitly as endogenous variables.

2. Effect of income on health

There are some obvious mechanisms by which increases in income can bring about improvements in health. Higher private incomes lead to higher expenditures on medical care—hospitalization, visits to doctors, drug purchases, and so forth. These same kinds of services can also be provided through a public health system, and the government budget increments generated by economic development are likely to be devoted in part to expanding such systems. Preventive services carried out in a public system, like mass vaccinations, are also likely to be expanded in conditions of greater affluence. (It is also true that some prevention campaigns with dramatic impact on health conditions, like malaria eradication, have been carried out in conditions of continuing economic stagnation. In such cases the campaigns have often been financed and organized to a large extent by external agencies like the World Health Organization.)

Next, higher incomes lead to certain expenditures (public or private) which are outside the medical area but which nonetheless can have an impact on health. In particular, expenditures on housing, sanitation, and food fall into this category. (In our schema, food expenditures affect health by way of changing nutritional status.) A review of the diseases which are responsible for the bulk of mortality and morbidity in low-income countries suggests that higher expenditures on housing, sanitation, and food could produce major improvements in health. For example, a study by Puffer and Serrano (53) of the causes of child mortality in South and Central America found that more than 70 percent of child deaths were caused by diseases falling into one of the following categories:

- airborne diseases (e.g., tuberculosis, pneumonia, diphtheria, bronchitis, whooping cough, meningitis, influenza, measles)
- diseases connected with human wastes (e.g., typhoid, dysentery, cholera, polio, hepatitis, diarrhea, tapeworms, hookworm, schistosomiasis)
- diseases associated with nutritional deficiencies.

It could be expected that better housing would reduce the incidence of airborne diseases by making living conditions less crowded. Better sanitation (piped water, sewers, latrines) could be expected to reduce the incidence of diseases connected with human wastes. Better diets would reduce the incidence of diseases linked with nutritional deficiencies.[8]

To establish quantitatively the effects of income on health involves looking at the general determinants of mortality and morbidity, and separating the effect of income from the effects of all other determinants. A large part of the literature in economic demography is concerned with this issue. Difficult statistical problems are encountered in the attempt to isolate the effect of income on health. An example of the difficulties is found in Krishnan's

(37) cross-sectional study of mortality determinants in Indian states. The dependent variable is the change in the crude death rate between 1951 and 1961, and there are three categories of independent variables: economic (measured by per capita income), social (literacy rate), and medical (doctors per capita, hospital beds per capita, and per capita state expenditures on health services). Per capita income and the literacy rate are reported to be important determinants of mortality, while the medical variables are quite unimportant.

Several problems exist in this analysis. In the first place, the number of observations is too small. Only 11 states are analyzed. Second, there appears to be a high degree of correlation between the independent variables (for example, between per capita income and the literacy rate), so it is difficult to isolate the true effect of each one on the dependent variable. Third, the independent variables are unfortunately dated. The dependent variable being the change in mortality between 1951 and 1961, the independent variables ought to be expressed as changes over the same period, or at least as levels at the start of the period. Instead they are expressed as levels (of per capita income, of literacy) at the end of the period, and so can hardly be said to measure prior causes of the change in mortality. Fourth, the unimportance of the medical variables is an aggregated result, obtained by combining a positive effect of doctors per capita (on mortality) with a negative effect of hospital beds per capita. These contrary effects require some explanation but get none.

The net effect of income on health is likely to be an aggregation of positive and negative influences, the separate magnitudes of which it may be impossible to determine. So far we have mentioned only the positive influences, but negative ones also exist. Higher incomes usually lead to increases in certain kinds of consumption that are deleterious for health, such as the consumption of tobacco, alcohol, and fatty foods. Economic development is normally associated with a switch from occupations involving arduous manual labor to others which are more sedentary. There is a general decline in physical exercise which in combination with richer diets produces frequent obesity and associated cardiovascular problems. Higher incomes are usually associated with industrialization, which often produces health-threatening levels of air pollution and water pollution, quite apart from creating new occupational hazards to which workers are subjected [Ciba Foundation (9)]. The building of highways increases the number of traffic accidents, a major cause of death and injury in many countries. Some projects of economic development have ecological consequences that are harmful to health. Some of the best-known examples concern the spread of schistosomiasis in areas where land reclamation projects have expanded the habitat of the water snail which acts as an intermediate host in the transmission of the disease.[9]

3. Effect of health on nutrition

Certain diseases cause a decline in nutritional status. As mentioned above, diseases involving diarrhea cause a rapid loss of nutrients. As another example, undernourishment may occur through the loss of appetite which accompanies some diseases.

An attempt to measure the quantitative importance of these relationships appears in a study by Heller and Drake (27), using a large sample of Colombian children. Since causation flows both ways between health and nutrition, the authors specify a system of simultaneous equations in order to estimate both of the cause-effect links—the effect of health on nutrition, and the effect of nutrition on health. Their analysis indicates that episodes of severe diarrhea during the first year of life tend to lower a child's height, one measure of nutritional status. A second measure, a child's weight relative to the average for its height group, is found to be adversely affected by severe diarrhea occurring in the second year or later.

4. Effect of nutrition on health

The Heller-Drake analysis also shows that nutritional status is a significant determinant of health, children of below-average weight for their height being more likely to experience days of sickness. In general, it is to be expected that undernourished persons will be more likely to suffer from those diseases which are associated with deficiencies of certain specific nutrients, such as rickets, pellagra, scurvy, and goiter. The undernourished are also likely to have lower levels of resistance to many other diseases.

The effect of nutrition on health has been the subject of numerous empirical studies. Unlike Heller and Drake, however, the authors of these studies do not always allow for the two-way causation between nutrition and health, and so their findings are sometimes rather dubious. An example is Correa's cross-sectional analysis of data for 32 countries, in which the dependent variable is infant mortality, while the independent variables include three measures of nutritional status—per capita protein consumption and average weight and height of four-year-olds—and two others: population per doctor and percentage of houses with piped water [Correa, (12), pp. 16–17]. The conclusion reached is that "the only significant reason for the high infant mortality is deficient nutritional conditions." The reverse causation, from health to nutrition, is ignored. There is also the problem that some potentially important independent variables are omitted, like the income and educational status of parents, and the extent of preventive programs like mass immunization.

Another group of studies, similarly based on aggregate data, uses an interesting non sequitur to arrive at the same conclusion about the importance of nutrition. These are the studies which demonstrate to their own satisfaction that historical declines in mortality cannot be explained to any significant degree by improvements in health services, and conclude that therefore the explanation must lie in nutritional improvements. Examples of this logic can be found in papers by Frederiksen (19, 20, 21), Howard (28), and Marshall (44). There is no rigorous attempt in these studies to measure simultaneously the relative contributions of health services, nutrition, and other factors toward reducing mortality. A study by Preston (52) which does attempt simultaneous measurement finds indeed that health services were much more important than nutrition in reducing mortality.

Several studies of the links between nutrition and health have used micro data. A notable example is the extensive piece of experimental research undertaken by Ascoli, Scrimshaw, and others (3, 57) in Guatemalan villages. The introduction of a dietary supplement in one village led to a greater decline in child mortality and morbidity than occurred in a control village without the supplements. Another example is provided by the Inter-American Investigation of Mortality in Childhood, a large-scale field study which concluded that "nutritional deficiency was the most serious health problem uncovered in the Investigation, as measured by its involvement in mortality" [Puffer and Serrano (54), p. 345].

A paper by Cravioto and DeLicardie (13) typifies a large number of micro studies which have found that malnutrition in infancy leads to mental deficiencies in later life. Correa (12), p. 18, gives several citations to this literature. Malnutrition at an even earlier stage—affecting the mother during pregnancy—has also been found to have adverse effects on the child's mental and physical development in studies by Birsch and Gussov (7) and Willerman and Churchill (68).

In the view of one leading authority, however, while research has established that nutrition has a generally positive effect on health, the magnitude of that effect remains quite uncertain. Berg writes that "although it is known that the extent of damage increases as the level of nutritional deprivation falls [sic]—as a child moves from first- to third-degree mal-nutrition—the shape of the curve relating deprivation to loss of physical, motor, and mental development, and to the severity of nutrition-related diseases, unknown" [Berg (6), pp. 26–27]. It might also be noted that the curve in question is not monotonic. As nutritional deprivation is reduced over some range, there is less sickness and disability; but when deprivation becomes sufficiently negative—that is, when nutrition reaches excessive levels—sickness and disability become more frequent as problems of obesity appear.

5. Effect of health on education

The conventional wisdom holds that better health leads to less absenteeism from school, to better motivation and greater powers of concentration for the students while in school, and therefore to superior levels of academic performance. But the empirical studies which have been carried out in this area are far from unanimous in their verdict.

On the conventional side, for example, Winslow (69), p. 22, reports that the eradication of malaria in the Philippines brought about major reductions in absences from school. Alves and Blair (1) report that a group of Southern Rhodesian students who were infected with schistosomiasis performed worse on academic tests than did those who were not infected. A study by Hassouna (25) is typical of several which conclude that students with impaired vision, hearing, or speech have relatively low levels of academic performance. Links have been found between disorders of infancy and later performance at school. Kawi and Pasaminick (33) report that prenatal and neonatal problems (complications of pregnancy or delivery, low birth weight) are associated with reading retardation at ages 10–14.

Other studies no weaker than these in methodology have found that the presence of disease has apparently no relationship at all to academic performance. This was the result of Usborne's (63) comparison using Tanganyikan data, between students with schistosomiasis and those without. The same conclusion regarding schistosomiasis and four other parasitic diseases is reported by Weisbrod *et al.* (67) in the St. Lucia study.

Some studies have even found, perhaps perversely, that diseased students actually perform better than the rest. Schistosomiasis was found to be associated with superior levels of academic achievement in a group of Tanzanian students analyzed by Jordan and Randall (31), and Loveridge *et al.* (41) report the same conclusion for a group of students in Southern Rhodesia.

6. Effect of education on health

Many diseases are avoidable, and it can be presumed that persons with more education are more likely to become informed about ways of avoiding disease. They may then adapt their behavior accordingly, for example by maintaining stricter standards of personal hygiene, taking prophylactic medication, changing their diet, or avoiding high-risk areas such as swamps. Another mechanism by which education may affect health is that children who are in school are subject to different medical risks than are those outside. Some contagious diseases like measles are perhaps more easily spread when a greater fraction of children attend school. As an opposite example,

Weisbrod et al. (67) point out that a child sitting in school will not be wading in a ditch and thus not be exposed to schistosomiasis. Weisbrod and his co-authors do not attempt to measure this relationship between education and health, in which causality flows from education to health.

Convincing studies of the relationship are in fact hard to find in the literature on low-income countries.[10] There are some pertinent findings, however, based on data for high-income countries. Auster et al. (4), for example, use an education measure as an independent variable in a cross-sectional analysis of statewide death rates in the United States. Other independent variables include personal income and health expenditures. The education variable turns out to have a significantly negative effect on death rates.

7. Effect of health on fertility

Sickness may reduce fertility by reducing sexual activity and the frequency of conception, or by increasing the probability of miscarriage and stillbirths. Newman (50) finds, for example, that the eradication of malaria in Ceylon led to a significant increase in the crude birth rate. This result is obtained by noting that increases in the birth rate following eradication tended to be larger in those districts with initially high levels of malaria prevalence than in those with initially low levels. By contrast, Weisbrod et al. (67) find no association between fertility and the five parasitic diseases studied in St. Lucia.

A mechanism by which sickness may actually increase fertility is to be found in the "replacement motive" for having children. By this reasoning, high levels of child mortality lead to high levels of fertility, as parents produce more children in an attempt to protect themselves against the loss of those already born. The demographic literature contains many empirical studies of this relationship. Examples are the studies by Gregory et al. (23) and by Heller (26).

8. Effect of fertility on health

High levels of fertility are likely to produce various health problems for both mothers and children [Kessler and Standley (35)]. High fertility among adolescents (say aged 14–16) brings special problems, since infants born to very young mothers are more likely to experience low birth weight and neonatal complications. An association between these conditions and deficiencies in motor and mental development one year later has been observed by Braine et al. (8).

When fertility is high and the typical family contains a large number of children, each child may receive less parental care, particularly those late in the birth order (i.e., with several older siblings). With less parental care, child health may deteriorate. This hypothesis is tested in the Heller-Drake study (27). In a cross-sectional analysis of individual children where the incidence of diarrhea and of other sicknesses are dependent variables, the number of young children in the family is one of the independent variables employed, and the child's birth order is another. Neither turns out to be a significant determinant of health. (The influences of other factors, like nutritional status and family income, are simultaneously allowed for.) In another part of their analysis, however, Heller and Drake find that birth order is a significant determinant of a child's weight relative to its height, an indicator of nutritional status. Later children are more likely to be below average in weight. The children of below-average weight, it will be remembered, are more prone to sickness. Thus these results suggest the existence of an indirect mechanism through which fertility affects health, namely, by way of affecting nutrition.

GENERAL-SYSTEM STUDIES

The general model proposed above contains five endogenous variables: income, health, nutrition, education, and fertility. We have reviewed several studies which attempt to measure the effect of one of these variables on another from the remaining four. Most of the studies have examined only one of the twenty cause-effect relationships in question. Some, however, have examined two or more of the relationships simultaneously. These we can call general-system studies. Their simultaneous measurement of two or more relationships is achieved in one or both of two ways. A multivariate analysis of variations in one of the five variables includes as explanatory variables two or more of the remaining four. Or the mutual effects of two variables on each other are measured by simultaneous solution of a system of two or more equations.

It is clear that an estimate of one of the twenty direct relationships which is produced by a general-system study is likely to be less biased than one produced otherwise. But it is also clear that even a general-system estimate will be suspect unless generated by a system which is truly general, namely, one including all five variables. Only one or two of the general-system studies so far completed can claim to be this comprehensive.

A classification of some general-system studies is offered in Table 1. One distinction is between the macro-studies analyzing aggregates or averages for countries or other large units, and the micro-studies based on data for individuals or families. A second distinction is between those studies which aim to estimate some of the twenty direct relationships (parameters) of the system, and those which obtain their parameter estimates from earlier studies and simulate the development of the system through time, thus allowing for the operation of indirect effects as well as direct. Parameter

Table 1. Classification of Selected General-System Studies of Income, Health, Nutrition, Education and Fertility.

		Parameter estimation		Simulation
		Cross-section	Time series	
Macro	Single equation	Galenson-Pyatt(22): Y, H, N, E Krishnan (37): Y, H, E Malenbaum (42): Y, H, E Preston (52): Y, H, N, E	Correa ((12), pp. 43–50): Y, H, N, E	
	Multi-equation			Barlow-Davies (5): Y, H, E, F Correa ((12), pp. 179–91): Y, H, N, E, F Vianen-Waarden-burg (64): Y, H, F
Micro	Single equation	Weisbrod *et al.* (67): Y, H, E, F		
	Multi-equation	Heller-Drake (27): Y, H, N, E, F		

Letters after study references show which of the following five variables are included in the study: income (Y), health (H), nutrition (N), education (E), and fertility (F).

estimation may be based on either cross-sectional or time-series data. A final distinction is between studies using a single structural equation and those involving simultaneous solution of a multi-equation system. The former type have the obvious weakness that they cannot allow properly for mutuality of causation between the dependent and independent variables. Simulation studies, it will be noted, are necessarily of the multi-equation type.

The parameter-estimation studies mentioned in Table 1 have been discussed above in our empirical review. They take account of some of the complexity of the five variables system, but are nonetheless subject in varying degrees to statistical problems which cast doubt on their findings. The three simulation studies cited in Table 1 are to be judged by their success in handling indirect effects of the five variables on each other, since in these studies the direct effects are simply assumed to have the values indicated by prior parameter-estimation studies. All three cited are based on national aggregates, the Barlow-Davies (5) model relating somewhat loosely to Ceylon, the Correa (12), pp. 179–191, model to Mexico, and the Vianen-Waardenburg (64) model to Tanzania. These models specify equations showing how the size of each age-sex group in the population is determined. Various other characteristics of each group, like its average educational attainment, are also determined within the system.[11] The population equations are linked to labor force equations, which in turn are linked to production functions determining income levels. Income then affects population size and quality through affecting health conditions, education conditions, etc., and the system is thereby closed.

In the health arena, these models are chiefly used for simulating the future growth of per capita income in response to an exogenous change in health conditions. The Barlow-Davies (5) model is used for estimating the effects of malaria eradication on per capita income. It is found that during the first eight years following eradication, per capita income is higher than it otherwise would have been, but is lower thereafter. The delayed effects of the population explosion triggered by eradication account for this result. Correa's (12) model is employed in forecasting the long-run change in per capita income produced by changing the distribution of government expenditures between the areas of food, health, education, population control, and investment. The Vianen-Waardenburg (64) model is designed to trace the demographic and economic effects of alternative deployments of personnel within the health care sector.

None of these models is fully satisfactory. The degree of aggregation is troublesome. (As is suggested in Table 1, there are as yet no large-scale micro-simulation studies in this area.) Important variables are omitted. The structural relationships assumed are often open to criticism. And the parameter values assumed, such as the effects of disease on work effort, are derived from empirical studies which have their own weaknesses, as we have had frequent occasion to observe.

SUGGESTIONS FOR RESEARCH

Our discussion leads to the following suggestions for further research into the links between health and development:

1. There is a continuing need for good empirical estimates of the twenty direct relationships in the general system. Many important diseases and populations remain unanalyzed. The analyses already conducted are for the most part of uncertain validity. Future work should aim at higher methodological standards. One might note again that a

competent study of a particular disease in a particular locality does not then remove that disease from the research agenda. The same disease may have different economically relevant effects in some other locality, and also different effects in the same locality at a later time. So the empirical results from one study are not readily transferable to another context. What should be transferable, however, is a competent methodology. This would involve obtaining a sample of adequate size, minimizing measurement error, controlling for the influence of factors other than those of principal interest, allowing for the possibility of two-way causation, and so forth.

2. In order to allow for indirect relationships in the system, work should proceed on developing models which incorporate all five endogenous variables. Simulations with such models can then measure the net effects of whatever events are of interest, whether these be events that have already occurred or others that are under consideration, such as the introduction of a new health care program. A model of this type will be usable in widely differing contexts, although it will normally be necessary to adopt new assumptions about parameter values when moving on to a different population. The model-builders should strive always for more disaggregation. They will be assisted in this by the improvements in computer technology which are likely to continue.

3. One line of inquiry which may be quite fruitful is to explore the links between health and development in a historical setting.[12] The six thousand years of human civilization, after all, provide numerous instances of prolonged economic growth. Indeed that very fact raises some doubts about whether good health is a necessary condition for development. Before scientific medicine started to have a significant impact (which happened approximately two hundred years ago), it can be presumed that health conditions were universally quite bad, at least by modern standards. Yet many societies across the world attained quite high levels of prosperity, which sometimes lasted for several centuries. On the other hand, there are clear historical examples of poor health, in the form of severe epidemics, causing major short-term disruptions in an economy, and sometimes precipitating permanent decline. A study of historical cases could lead to a better understanding of the relationship between health and development in the modern setting.

FOOTNOTES

1. As one example, a study of the economic gains from reduced schistosomiasis mortality is based on the mortality experience of a sample where four deaths out of the 22 investigated were diagnosed as being caused by schistosomiasis. The experience of this sample is then generalized to a population exceeding 300,000.

2. The scale proposed by Culyer *et al.* (14) actually extends beyond "unconscious" to "dead," states which receive scores of 9 and 10, respectively, on their disability index. The state of "no significant discomfort or restriction" at the other end of the scale receives a score of zero. Our argument in the text, however, is that it may be better to treat the reduction of mortality and the reduction of infirmity as separate objectives rather than combining them in the manner of Culyer and his co-authors.

3. The term "direct effect" in this paper is meant to describe the effect of one endogenous variable on another, *the remaining three endogenous variables being held constant.* Many such "direct" effects can, of course, be quite complicated, operating through other variables not specified in the model. For example, if better health raises income via an increase in work hours, we call this a "direct" effect of health on income even though a third variable (work hours) is involved.

4. Some studies have estimated simple correlations between two of the variables, like health and income, without trying to specify in which direction causation runs. A United Nations study, for example, reports a rank correlation coefficient of − 0.84 between per capita national income and the infant mortality rate in 45 countries [United Nations (59), p. 42]. It is doubtful whether such estimates make much of a contribution toward our understanding of how the system works.

5. Galenson and Pyatt (22), p. 114, find that a significant influence on income is exerted by calories per head, which they term a "health" variable. In our terminology calories per head would be classified as a nutritional rather than a health factor. Three other "health" variables are found to be nonsignificant in the Galenson-Pyatt analysis: population per physician, hospital beds per capita, and the infant mortality rate [Galenson and Pyatt (22), p. 114].

6. The effects on future income are allowed for in the macro-simulation model developed by Barlow and Davies (5).

7. A study by Kelley (34), however, throws some doubt on the conventional view that larger families save less.

8. Besides the mechanisms involving expenditures on medical care, housing, sanitation, and food, there are many other mechanisms — of less importance in most cases — through which development promotes health. To give one example, the replacement of draft animals by tractors in agriculture reduces the quantity of animal waste in rural areas, and may lower the incidence of certain fly-borne and other diseases. The effect is reinforced when the animals are themselves reservoirs of disease agents which affect humans (e.g., oxen in the case of schistosomiasis).

9. Hughes and Hunter (29) discuss these and other examples of development projects with unfortunate ecological and medical consequences. Weisbrod *et al.* (67), pp. 188–196, report that schistosomiasis has spread in St. Lucia as a result of the expansion of banana cultivation.

10. Puffer and Serrano (54), pp. 278–294, for example, present some tabulations relating child mortality to the education of mothers, but no attempt is made to hold other factors constant.

11. Since models of this economic-demographic type involve a detailed breakdown of the population into age-sex groups, and since there are normally several equations for each group, the total number of equations becomes very large, and the model becomes rather cumbersome to manipulate. Barlow and Davies (5) have 1,690 equations in their model, and Vianen and Waardenburg (64) have 1,255. Correa (12), p. 191, reports that twenty-year simulations for a few policy options with his model required roughly 6,000 pages of computer printout.

12. Recent examples of such historical analyses are found in studies by Laderman (39) and McNeill (45).

REFERENCES
1. Alves, William, and Dyson M. Blair. (1946) "Diagnosis of Schistosomiasis: Intradermal Tests Using Cercarial Antigens," *Lancet* 251: 556–560.
2. Andreano, Ralph L. (1976) "The Recent History of Parasitic Disease in China: The Cast of Schistosomiasis, Some Public Health and Economic Aspects," *International Journal of Health Services* 6:53–68.
3. Ascoli, W.; M. A. Guzman; N. S. Scrimshaw; and J. E. Gordon. (1967) "Nutrition and Infection in Field Study in Guatemalan Villages, 1959–64. IV. Deaths of Infants and Preschool Children," *Archives of Environmental Health* 15:439–449.
4. Auster, R.; I. Leveson; and D. Sarachek. (1969) "The Production of Health: An Exploratory Study," *Journal of Human Resources* 4: 411–436.
5. Barlow, Robin, and Gordon W. Davies. (1974) "Policy Analysis with a Disaggregated Economic-Demographic Model," *Journal of Public Economics* 3:43–70.
6. Berg, Alan. (1973). *The Nutrition Factor*, Washington, D. C.: The Brookings Institution.
7. Birsch, H. G., and J. D. Gussov. (1970) *Disadvantaged Children, Health, Nutrition and School Failure*, New York: Harcourt Brace Jovanovich.
8. Braine, M.D.S.; C. B. Heimer; H. Worlis; and A. M. Freedman. (1966) *Factors Associated with Impairment of the Early Development of Prematures*, monographs of the Society for Research in Child Development, 31.
9. Ciba Foundation. (1975) *Health and Industrial Growth*, New York: American Elsevier.
10. Cohen, Joel E. (1974) "Some Potential Economic Benefits of Eliminating Mortality Attributed to Schistosomiasis in Zanzibar," *Social Science and Medicine* 8:383–398.
11. Conly, Gladys N. (1975) *The Impact of Malaria on Economic Development: A Case Study*, Washington, D.C.: Pan American Health Organization.
12. Correa, Hector. (1975) *Population, Health, Nutrition, and Development*, Lexington, Mass: D. C. Heath.
13. Cravioto, Joaquin, and Elsa R. DeLicardie. (1973) "The Effect of Malnutrition on the Individual," in *Nutrition, National Development and Planning*, eds. Alan Berg, Nevin Scrimshaw and David Call, Cambridge, Mass.: M.I.T. Press, pp. 3–21.
14. Culyer, A. J.; R. J. Lavers; and A. Williams. (1971) "Social Indicators: Health," *Social Trends* 2:31–42.
15. Davies, A. M. (1968) "Priorities in Health and Health Services," *Israel Journal of Medical Sciences*.
16. Farooq, M. (1963) "A Possible Approach to the Evaluation of the Economic Burden Imposed on a Community by Schistosomiasis," *Annals of Tropical Medicine and Parasitology* 57:324–331.
17. Feldstein, Martin A.; M. A. Piot; and T. K. Sundaresan. (1973) *Resource Allocation Model for Public Health Planning: A Case Study of Tuberculosis Control*, Geneva: World Health Organization.
18. Foster, R. (1967) "Schistosomiasis on an Irrigated Estate in East Africa—III. Effects of Asymptomatic Infection on Health and Industrial Efficiency," *Journal of Tropical Medicine and Hygiene* 70:185–195.
19. Frederiksen, Harold. (1960) "Malaria Control and Population Pressure in Ceylon," *Public Health Reports* 75:865–868.
20. ———. (1961) "Determinants and Consequences of Mortality Trends in Ceylon," *Public Health Reports* 76:659–663.
21. ———. (1962) "Economic and Demographic Consequences of Malaria Control in Ceylon," *Indian Journal of Malariology* 16:379–391.

22. Galenson, Walter, and Graham Pyatt. (1964) *The Quality of Labor and Economic Development in Certain Countries,* Geneva: International Labor Office.
23. Gregory, Paul; John Campbell; and Benjamin Cheng. (1973) "Differences in Fertility Determinants: Developed and Developing Countries," *Journal of Development Studies* 9 : 233–241.
24. Griffith, D.H.S.; D. V. Ramana; and H. Mashaal. (1971) "Contribution of Health to Development," *International Journal of Health Services* 1 : 253–270.
25. Hassouna, W. A. (1968) "A Decision Model for School Health Services," Ph.D. thesis, Pittsburgh, Pa.: Graduate School of Public and International Affairs, University of Pittsburgh.
26. Heller, Peter S. (1976) "Interactions of Childhood Mortality and Fertility in West Malaysia, 1947–70," Ann Arbor: Center for Research on Economic Development, University of Michigan, Discussion Paper No. 57.
27. ————, and William D. Drake. (1976) "Malnutrition, Child Morbidity, and the Family Decision Process," Ann Arbor: Center for Research on Economic Development, University of Michigan, Discussion Paper No. 58.
28. Howard, L. M. (1972) "Three Key Dilemmas in International Health," *American Journal of Public Health* 62 : 73 78.
29. Hughes, C. C., and J. M. Hunter. (1970) "Disease and Development in Africa," *Social Science and Medicine* 3 : 443–493.
30. Hunter, John M. (1966) "River Blindness in Nangodi, Northern Ghana: A Hypothesis of Cyclical Advance and Retreat," *The Geographical Review* 56 : 409–410.
31. Jordan, Peter, and Kae Randall. (1962) "Bilharziasis in Tanganyika: Observations on Its Effects and the Effects of Treatment in Schoolchildren," *Journal of Tropical Medicine and Hygiene* 65 : 1–6.
32. Karefa-Smart, J. (1968) "Health and Manpower: Interrelationship between Health and Socioeconomic Development," *Israel Journal of Medical Sciences.*
33. Kawi, A. A., and B. Pasaminick. (1958) "Association of Factors of Pregnancy with Reading Disorders in Childhood," *Journal of the American Medical Association* 166 : 1420–1423.
34. Kelley, Allen C. (1976) "Savings, Demographic Change, and Economic Development," *Economic Development and Cultural Change* 24 : 683–693.
35. Kessler, A., and C. C. Standley. (1973) "Health, Family Planning, and Population Growth," *International Journal of Health Services* 3 : 561–566.
36. Klarman, Herbert E. (1963) "Measuring the Benefits of a Health Program—the Control of Syphilis," in *Measuring Benefits of Government Investments,* ed. Robert Dorfman, Washington, D.C.: The Brookings Institution.
37. Krishnan, P. (1975) "Mortality Decline in India, 1951–61: Development vs. Public Health Program Hypothesis, *Social Science and Medicine* 9 : 475–479.
38. Kuhner, A. (1971) "The Impact of Public Health Programs on Economic Development: Report of a Study of Malaria in Thailand," *International Journal of Health Services* 1 : 285–292.
39. Laderman, C. (1975) "Malaria and Progress· Some Historical and Ecological Considerations," *Social Science and Medicine* 9 : 587–594.
40. Leff, Nathaniel. (1969) "Dependency Rates and Savings Rates," *American Economic Review* 69 : 886–896.
41. Loveridge, F. G.; W. F. Ross; and D. M. Blair. (1948) "Schistosomiasis: The Effect of the Disease on Educational Attainment," *South African Medical Journal* 22 : 260–263.
42. Malenbaum, Wilfred. (1970) "Health and Productivity in Poor Areas," in *Empirical*

Studies in Health Economics, ed. Herbert E. Klarman, Baltimore: The Johns Hopkins University Press, pp. 31–54.

43. ――――. (1973) "Health and Economic Expansion in Poor Lands," *International Journal of Health Services* 3:161–176.

44. Marshall, Carter L. (1974) "Health, Nutrition, and the Roots of World Population Growth," *International Journal of Health Services* 4:677–690.

45. McNeill, W. H. (1976) *Plagues and Peoples*, Garden City, N.Y.: Anchor Press.

46. Mejia, A., and R. Paredes. (1968) "Health Planning'for Colombia: 2," *Milbank Memorial Fund Quarterly*.

47. Mushkin, Selma. (1962) "Health as an Investment," *Journal of Political Economy* 70:October Supplement.

48. ――――. (1964) "Health Programming in Developing Nations," *International Development Review* 6:7–12.

49. Nash, Helen. (1974) "Life Blooms in the Rapti Valley," *War on Hunger: A Report from the Agency for International Development*, 8.

50. Newman, Peter. (1965) *Malaria Eradication and Population Growth*, Ann Arbor: Bureau of Public Health Economics, University of Michigan Press.

51. Perlman, Mark. (1964) "Some Economic Aspects of Public Health Programs in Underdeveloped Areas," in *Economics of Health and Medical Care*. Ann Arbor: University of Michigan Press, pp. 286–299.

52. Preston, Samuel H. (1976) "Causes and Consequences of Mortality Declines in Less Developed Countries During the Twentieth Century," National Bureau of Economic Research Conference Paper.

53. Puffer, Ruth, and Carlos V. Serrano. (1971) *Inter-American Investigation of Mortality in Childhood: Provisional Report*, Washington, D.C.: Pan American Health Organization.

54. ――――, and ――――. (1973) *Patterns of Mortality in Childhood*, Washington, D.C.: Pan American Health Organization.

55. Rice, Dorothy P. (1966) *Estimating the Cost of Illness*, Health Economics Series, No. 6, Public Health Service Publication, No. 947–6. Washington, D.C.: Government Printing Office.

56. Ruderman, A. Peter. (1971) "Introduction to the Theme: Health and Socio-economic Development," *International Journal of Health Services* 1:189–192.

57. Scrimshaw, N. W.; M. A. Guzman; M. Flores; and J. E. Gordon. (1968) "Nutrition and Infection in Field Study in Guatemalan Villages, 1959–64: V. Disease Incidence Among Preschool Children under Natural Village Conditions, with Improved Diets, and with Medical and Public Health Services," *Archives of Environmental Health* 16:223–234.

58. Taylor, C. E., and M. F. Hall. (August 11, 1967) "Health, Population, and Economic Development," *Science* 157, no. 3789:651–657.

59. United Nations. (1961) *Report on World Social Situation*, Department of Economic and Social Affairs.

60. ――――. (1963, 1974) *Demographic Yearbooks*.

61. ――――. (1975) *Statistical Yearbook*.

62. United States Department of Health, Education and Welfare, Office of International Health. (1972) *Syncrisis: The Dynamics of Health*, Vol. 1 (Panama) and Vol. 4 (Philippines).

63. Usborne, Vivian. (1954) "Some Notes on Urinary Bilharziasis in Sukuma School Children Especially as Regards Scholastic Performance," *East African Medical Journal* 31:451–458.

64. Vianen, Joop G., and J. George Waardenburg. (1975) "Integration of Health Care

into a Multi-Sector Model," Rotterdam: Center for Development Planning, Erasmus University, Discussion Paper No. 29.
65. Watson, J. M. (1959) "Schistosomiasis in the Tigris-Euphrates Valley, with Special Reference to Its Economic Consequences, *Proceedings of the Sixteenth International Congress of Tropical Medicine and Malariology, Lisbon*, 2, pp. 203–210.
66. Weisbrod, Burton A. (1961) *Economics of Public Health: Measuring the Economic Impact of Diseases*. Philadelphia: University of Pennsylvania Press.
67. ———, Ralph L. Andreano; Robert E. Baldwin; Erwin H. Epstein; and Allen C. Kelley. (1973) *Disease and Economic Development*. Madison: University of Wisconsin Press.
68. Willerman, L. and J. A. Churchill. (1947) "Intelligence and Birth Weight in Identical Twins," *Child Development* 38:623.
69. Winslow, C.-E.A. (1951) *The Cost of Sickness and the Price of Health*, Geneva: World Health Organization Monograph Series no. 7.

HEALTH, NUTRITION, AND MORTALITY IN BANGLADESH

W. Henry Mosley

INTRODUCTION

Health conditions in Bangladesh are poor by any standard: 15 percent of infants die in the first year of life; 20 percent die by age five; less than 10 percent of the population have a regular supply of safe water and sanitary waste disposal; even fewer can get modern medical care [Chen (6)]. Yet, in spite of these conditions, Bangladesh is experiencing an unprecedented population "explosion," largely due to a dramatic decline in mortality rates over the past four decades. To understand the present situation, it is useful to briefly examine the historical trends in mortality in Bangladesh noting not only the

Research in Human Capital and Development, Vol. 1, pp. 77–94.
Copyright © 1979 by JAI Press, Inc.
ISBN: 0-89232-019-2

rate and magnitude of the decline, but also the major factors contributing
to the decline. This exercise will not only put the current situation into better
perspective, but will provide insights into mortality changes that may be
anticipated in the future.

HISTORICAL BACKGROUND

Separate historical records are not available for the country that is now
Bangladesh; therefore, general inferences for this area prior to independence
from British rule (1947) will have to be drawn from data on British India
and the Province of Bengal (comprising the modern states of West Bengal,
Assam, and Sikkim, as well as Bangladesh). Kingsley Davis's (14) monu-
mental work on India provides an excellent analysis of the trends and causes
of a decline in mortality prior to 1950. Some of its major points will be briefly
reviewed here.

Table 1 summarizes the major mortality trends in the India subcontinent
from 1881 to 1951 and for modern India and Bangladesh from 1951 to 1971.
Noteworthy is the extremely high mortality level prior to 1930; life expectan-
cies under 25 years imply that 50 percent of the births did not survive to
reach age 15. Beginning around 1930 there was a consistent decline in

Table 1. Trends in Mortality and Life Expectancy for British India and Bengal, 1871–
1941, and for Post-Partition India and Bangladesh (Formerly East Pakistan), 1941–1971.

Period	Life Expectancy at Birth	(Implied) Average Annual Death Rate	Life Expectancy at Birth	(Implied) Average Annual Death Rate
	British India[a]		*Bengal/Assam/Sikkim*[b]	
1871–1881	24.6	40.7	26.5	37.7
1881–1891	25.0	40.2	23.7	42.2
1891–1901	23.8	42.0	22.5	44.4
1901–1911	22.9	43.7	21.5	46.5
1911–1921	20.1	49.8	—	—
1921–1931	26.8	37.3	24.8	40.3
1931–1941	31.8	31.5		
	Post-Partition India[c]		*East Pakistan/Bangladesh*[d]	
1941–1951	33.5	29.2	—	—
1951–1961	39.0	24.1	—	—
1961–1971	45.5	18.6	48.2	16.0
1971	48.7	16.2	—	—

[a]*Source*: Davis (14)
[b]*Source*: India (17)
[c]*Source*: Ambannavar (1)
[d]*Source*: Pakistan Institute of Development Economics (29)
        (The actual period is 1962–1965)

mortality which accelerated after 1950, resulting in a doubling of life expectancy. Although detailed data are not available for the area that is now Bangladesh, it is evident from the death rates recorded in Bengal prior to 1930 and the recent records that this area participated in the general decline. The mortality rates plateaued and were relatively stable in the 1960s. Evidence now suggests not only that the mortality decline in Bangladesh ceased in the past decade, but that rises may be anticipated in the 1970s and beyond.

FACTORS IN MORTALITY DECLINE

Four factors must be considered in assessing the causes of the mortality decline from 1930 to 1960: medical (curative and preventive), political, economic, and social [Davis (14), p. 38. In attempting to define the contribution of these factors, one must take note of the fact that these mortality declines occurred in rural as well as urban populations. In Bangladesh, only 5.2 percent of the population were classified as urban in the 1961 census; the remaining 94 percent are scattered in over 60,000 villages [Census of East Pakistan (28)].

The contribution of curative medicine can generally be discounted. most really effective drugs, particularly the antibiotics, were not widely available even in the developed world prior to 1950. In rural Bangladesh, modern curative medicine remains unavailable even today to the vast majority of the population owing to lack of physicians and hospital beds. A survey in 1969 revealed a ratio of one trained physician per 50,000 persons in the rural areas [Awan (3)] and, as of 1973, there were only 2,260 public and private hospital beds in the rural areas, a ratio of one per 33,000 persons [Bangladesh (4)].

Preventive health services include environmental safeguards (pure water, food sanitation, waste disposal, and vector control), immunization, and other anti-epidemic activities. Since these measures are directed specifically toward communicable diseases, their impact on mortality in the 1930–1960 period can be best elucidated by examining some specific diseases.

The Gangetic flood plain, and Bangladesh in particular, has been the "home" of cholera from time immemorial. Annual epidemics occur with clockwork regularity, usually following the monsoon rains in the northern areas, or preceding the rains in the southern areas. Although dramatic epidemics among adults have occurred in association with religious pilgrimages or other large gatherings, the vast majority of cases and deaths are among children [Gangarosa and Mosley (15)]. Since cholera is caused by swallowing the infectious organism *Vibrio cholerae* — most often in fecal-contaminated water — transmission is effectively interrupted by provision of safe water and sanitary waste disposal. Unfortunately, only a tiny fraction of the Bangladesh population has these facilities, and most are in the urban areas. Cholera vaccination is available, but field studies have shown that injections only provide partial protection for about three months [Mosley *et al.* (26)]. This measure has thus been of almost no value in the rural population where the disease is endemic. Local sanitation efforts around reported cases and quarantine measures are also futile, since there are so many persons with mild infections that remain undetected who still transmit the disease [Gangarosa and Mosley (15)].

Fundamentally, cholera morbidity and mortality in rural Bangladesh has not been altered by the sporadic application of preventive health measures [Mosley *et al.* (26)]. It follows that there has been little, if any, change in the historical epidemiological patterns of the other enteric (intestinal) diseases in the rural areas; these would include the various diarrheas and dysenteries due to bacteria and viruses, typhoid fever, and the multitude of intestinal parasitic infestations.

Smallpox has also been a scourge of the subcontinent for centuries. Although simply controlled by vaccination, which was discovered by Edward Jenner in 1798, immunization programs were never very effectively applied in Bangladesh. Kingsley Davis (14), p. 47, notes that for British India in 1945, vaccination was compulsory for only 47 percent of the rural population. The actual vaccination rate during 1944–1945 was only 16 percent of the population. Not surprisingly, as late as 1958, Bangladesh reported 79,060 smallpox cases [Sommer (33)]. Only since 1968 has there been a major effort, spearheaded by the World Health Organization, to finally eliminate smallpox from Bangladesh. This was drastically set back by major epidemics associated with the war of 1971. Subsequent eradication efforts have been successful, and the last case was reported in Bangladesh in late 1975. Although relatively uncontrolled for many decades, in fact, smallpox has never accounted for more than one to two percent of the total deaths in any year in this century [Davis (14), p. 47], so that its control will have little effect on the overall mortality decline.

Malaria control has also contributed little to the historical mortality decline in this area. There are two reasons for this. First, the deltaic area of Bangladesh, where most of the population resides, has always been relatively free of malaria [Davis (14) p. 54]. Secondly, a national malaria eradication program did not even begin in Bangladesh until 1960, by which time general mortality had already reached relatively low levels.

For other immunizable diseases like diphtheria, tetanus, whooping cough, and polio, vaccines for general use have not been available in Bangladesh. Additionally, virtually no tuberculosis control measures have effectively reached the rural population.

To explain the mortality decline, then, we come to political, economic, and social factors. These factors, however, do not generally operate directly on mortality, but are interdependent in controlling a primary determinant:

food [Marshall (22)]. The most dramatic manifestation of food shortage is famine. The demographic history of the Indian subcontinent in the last century is punctuated by a procession of famines that have caused enormous loss of life, and resulted in slow and very sporadic population growth. To obtain a crude estimate of magnitude of mortality due to famine in the last century, Davis (14), p. 39, estimated that the actual population growth of one percent over the decade 1891–1901 was probably brought down from an expected 7.8 percent by the severe famines during that decade. The difference in growth rate represented an estimated 19 million deaths.

A substantial improvement in the general availability of food requires political stability. This developed in India in the nineteenth and early twentieth centuries, and not only did it assure public security, making storage and transport of food possible, it also led to orderly planning for agricultural productivity and management of a food distribution system. A major component of this famine control effort was the large investment by the colonial government during the early twentieth century in railroads and highways and in vast networks of irrigation systems—covering 60 million acres in the subcontinent by 1950.

Concurrent with political stability and economic investment came technological development. As technology, particularly steam transportation and later the internal combustion engine, accelerated the pace of communication, agriculture became more of a commercial rather than only a subsistence venture. Food surpluses could be sold for export, and the communication channels could be used to distribute food to deficit areas.

The overall effectiveness of these measures is shown by the fact that for the first six decades of the twentieth century, the Indian subcontinent has essentially been free of the catastrophic famines that were such a regular feature of the nineteenth century. The major exceptions have been in Bengal with the famine of 1943 and the starvation accompanying the 1971 War of Independence. In both cases the famines did not result primarily from crop failures but from political disorder. In 1943, because of the wartime conditions, there was a general breakdown of transportation and security, and extraordinary inflation due to hoarding and profiteering. An estimated 1.5 to 3 million people died [India (18)]. In 1971 the Civil War forced more than 10 million refugees from Bangladesh into India, and an additional 15 million were temporarily dislocated. This social disruption led to an estimated 1.6 to 3 million deaths, many from starvation [Greenough and Cash (16)].

A FRAMEWORK FOR FOOD/MORTALITY INTERRELATIONSHIPS

Coming to the present situation from this background, it is clear that food continues to be the major determinant of health status for the people of

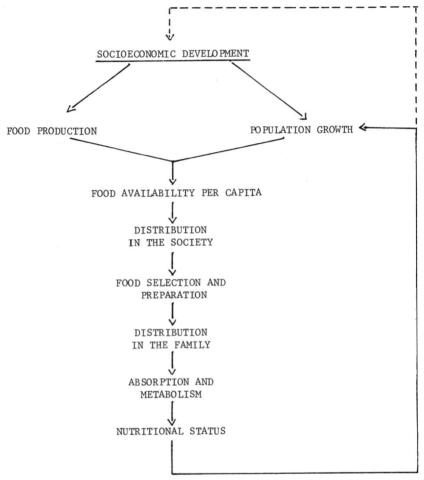

Figure 1. An Analytical Framework Illustrating the Interrelationships of Nutrition and Health to the Controlling Political, Economic, Social, and Medical Factors Relating to Food.

Bangladesh. Before examining the current health situation in detail, it is useful to present a general conceptual framework outlining the interrelationships of food supply and demand to health, and illustrating how social, economic, and political factors are involved in the food production-consumption process, and ultimately in the health and nutritional status of the population. This framework is depicted in Figure 1.

First, food availability (per capita) is dependent upon the productive capacity of the society. Production of food (including purchase of imports) is primarily a function of the political and economic institutions governing the technological inputs and the marketing system. Weather is also a factor, particularly in Bangladesh where, in fact, the technological inputs are relatively small and the major rice crop is grown in the flood season. To some degree, production is also a function of the health of the producers, although good health, in the absence of fertility control, can have the greatest and most immediate effect in decreasing availability by increasing the rate of population growth.

Which groups in society get the food—the urban versus rural areas; the military, the upper and middle classes; the students and factory workers versus the starving rural peasant; or thieves and black marketeers—is a function of the economic and political processes governing (or failing to govern) the primary distribution systems (procurement, storage, market, and rationing). In Bangladesh, distribution is largely a function of wealth, or land ownership, and is only partly governed by the market, much of which is controlled by usurious moneylenders, and (partly controlled) by rationing which is largely directed to the urban middle classes, students, factory workers, and the military [United States (37)]. It is clear that the inequities in wealth, as well as in the primary distribution system, have profound effects on the health of the poor, representing a substantial majority of the rural population.

Within the family, nutritional status is a function of social and cultural practices. First, there are culturally determined dietary habits—what people choose to eat and how they prepare it. For this reason, some nutritional deficits can be seen in all classes. Second, and especially significant for the poor families, there is the pattern of food distribution in the family. Customarily, in Bangladesh, the adult males and older male children eat first, then the older female children, the mothers, and infants. Such a pattern has apparently stood the test of time in preserving the earning power of the family in times of food crises and reflects the great value of sons to the family. Clearly, however, among the poorest groups nutritional deficiencies and starvation will be most evident in infants and young children, and females in general [United States (37)].

Not all food eaten is available to the consumer for growth and development, or work. Chronic intestinal malabsorption is frequent in the Bangladeshi population [Lindenbaum (20)]. These absorption defects can be compounded by the heavy load of intestinal parasites and recurrent episodes of diarrheal illnesses that are a feature of the unsanitary living conditions. Additionally, many febrile illnesses, such as malaria, tuberculosis, typhoid, and measles aggravate marginal nutritional states, and are often rapidly fatal under conditions of poor nutrition [Puffer and Serrano (30); Latham (19)]. To compound the problem, malnutrition actually increases the susceptibility to many of these infections as well as aggravates their course [Scrimshaw et al. (31)].

To complete the framework, it is obvious that the health of the population can determine the rate of population growth as well as its productive capacity. The linkages are more complex than given in this simple outline, but it does serve to illustrate how the nutritional status of the population is dependent on political and economic as well as social and cultural factors. Further, it serves to illustrate the compounding effects of poor health conditions.

HEALTH AND MORTALITY IN THE 1960s

A detailed analysis of the morbidity and mortality patterns in Bangladesh can highlight how the various factors outlined above actually operate on the health of the population. Because essentially no general health statistics exist for Bangladesh, most of the following discussion will be based on data from special national surveys and, in particular, from studies in a rural "population laboratory" in Matlab Thana, Comilla district, that has been under intensive epidemiological and demographic surveillance by the Cholera Research Laboratory (CRL) continuously since 1966 [Mosley et al. (25)].

Table 2 summarizes the trends in the crude death rates (CDR) and infant mortality rates (IMR) from 1962 to 1965 based on data from the national Population Growth Experiment (PGE) [Pakistan Institute of Development

Table 2. Trends in the Crude Death Rate and Infant Mortality Rate for Bangladesh (1962–1965) and for Matlab, Comilla District (1966–1972)

Year	CDR	IMR
	Bangladesh[a]	
1962[c]	16.2	138
1963	—	—
1964	17.4	160
1965	15.7	150
	Matlab Thana[b]	
1966–1967	16.0	111
1967–1968	17.2	125
1968–1969	15.7	124
1969–1970	15.1	128
1970–1971	14.6	131
1971–1972 (War)	21.3	146
1972–1973	16.4	129
1973–1974	14.6	129
1974–1975 (Famine)	20.0	167
1975–1976	18.2	150

[a]*Source*: Pakistan Institute of Development Economics (29)
[b]*Source*: Mosley et al.(25);Curlin et al.(12);Mosley et al.(24)
[c]Reporting year extends from April to March

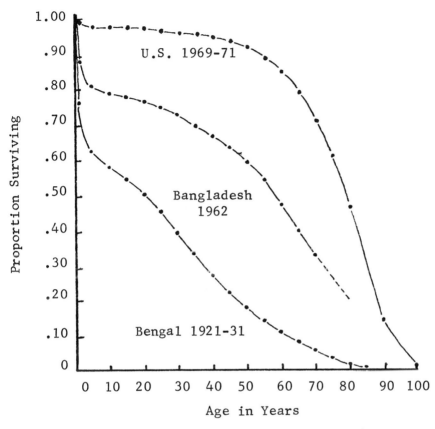

Figure 2. Patterns of Survival Based on Life Tables from Bengal 1921–1931, Bangladesh 1962 and the United States of America 1969–1971.

Economics (29)] and from 1966 to 1976 based on vital registration in the Matlab Population Laboratory [Curlin *et al.* (12); Chowdhury and Huber (11)]. Although the CRL data, being localized to a single rural geographic area, are not directly comparable to the PGE, the overall impression remains that over the decade of the 1960s mortality remained essentially unchanged. This pattern is in sharp contrast to the major declines in mortality that marked each of the three preceding decades.

To put the current mortality levels in better perspective, Figure 2 shows the survivorship curves obtained from life tables for females in Bengal during the period 1921–1931 [India (17)], and for Bangladesh for 1962 based on PGE data [Aslam, *et al.* (2)]. Also shown for comparison is the 1970 U.S. survivorship rate [U.S. Department of Health, Education and Welfare (36)]. The improvement in Bengal from the 1920s to the 1960s is impressive. Still, when compared to the United States, there remain much higher risks of death in Bangladesh, particularly in the first five years of life. In the United States, for example, 95 percent of the births may expect to reach age 30, and 80 percent will reach age 60. By contrast, barely 80 percent of the Bengali infants can expect to reach the age of five years.

Chowdhury (10) has recently completed a detailed analysis of social and demographic variables related to infant mortality in the Matlab area for the period 1966–1970. In addition to typical U-shaped patterns for both neonatal (under 1 month) and post-neonatal (1–12 months) mortality rates by birth order, he found major differentials by sex of the child. While neonatal mortality rates were higher for males than females, reflecting the universally observed higher biological vulnerability of male infants as compared to females, in the post-neonatal period where environmental factors and patterns of child care and feeding are major determinants, the female mortality rates were consistently higher than the male rates. Excluding the high birth order groups where both sexes had high mortality rates, for parities 0, 1, and 2, the female death rates were 38 percent higher than the males.

Short birth-spacing also adversely affected post-neonatal mortality rates, but not neonatal rates. If the previous infant was alive, and the next birth came in less than 26 months, the post-neonatal mortality rate for the next birth was 95 percent higher than if the next birth was delayed beyond 26 months. This differential again apparently reflects competition for food in the vulnerable post-neonatal period by the succeeding child.

Looking for other social differentials, Chowdhury (10) found that Hindus consistently had higher neonatal and post-neonatal mortality rates than Muslims. This he related to substantial differences in the traditional patterns of attending deliveries and child care for the two groups. Interestingly enough, he did not find any mortality differentials by socio-economic indicators (education, occupation and land holdings). This he attributed to the common poor environment that all families shared and the absence of health-care facilities in the area that the wealthier or more informed groups could potentially utilize.

A similar mortality differential by sex also exists in the one-to-four-year age group. For the four consecutive years from 1966 to 1970, the mortality rates for female children were 50 percent, 36 percent, 13 percent, and 29 percent higher than for the males in the Matlab study population [Cholera Research Laboratory (9); Mosley et al. (24)]. This same sex differential in mortality was evident in the national data from the PGE study; for 1964 and 1965 the one-to-four-year death rates for females were 32 percent and 24 percent higher than those for males (Pakistan Institute of Development Economics (29)].

Evidence for the direct contribution of malnutrition to mortality in these young age groups comes from studies by Sommer and Loewenstein (34).

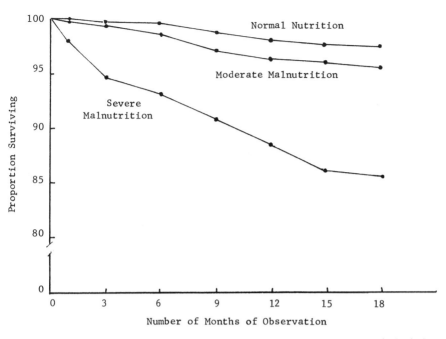

Figure 3. Survivorship of 1–4-Year-Old Children in Rural Bangladesh by Nutritional Status. Matlab Thana, December 1970– June 1972. Data from Sommer and Lowenstein.

In December 1970, Loewenstein conducted a nutritional survey of 8,292 children aged 1 to 9 in Matlab area. Nutritional status was based on a ratio of arm circumference to height (where arm circumference is an index of body weight). Based on this scale, 41 percent of the children were found to be moderately malnourished, and 9 percent severely malnourished. Eighteen months later (including the 1971 war), the fate of 98.8 percent of these children was ascertained by Sommer. Overall, 2.3 percent had died. Those classified as severely malnourished had a death rate 3.4 times higher than the normally nourished groups. A more detailed analysis of the one-to-four-year-olds by nutritional status and time of death is illustrated in Figure 3. In the younger group, 14.2 percent of the severely malnourished had died, as compared to only 2.6 percent of the normal group. For the first three months after assessment (prior to the onset of the 1971 war), 5.1 percent of the severely malnourished group died, a rate fourteen times higher than the rate of the normal group (0.36 percent).

Mortality statistics have also been revealing in studying the health aspects of childbearing. In a detailed analysis of maternal mortality in the Matlab area, Chen *et al.* found the rate to be 7.7 and 5.7 per 1,000 live births for the time periods 1967–1968 and 1968–1970, respectively [Chen et al. (8)]. These figures can be contrasted with rates below 0.3 in the developed world. Twenty-seven percent of all deaths to females in the 10–40 age group were maternity-related. In the peak childbearing ages 15–29, this ranged from 42 percent to 57 percent of all deaths. The highest death rates (12.7/1,000 live births) occurred among women having their first pregnancies, with about three-fourths of these due to eclampsia, a preventable condition. Mortality risks were also high among his parity women; in particular, women with a rapid succession of unsuccessful pregnancies often died apparently due to a depletion of their physical and nutritional reserve.

In 1962 a national nutrition survey was undertaken in Bangladesh [U.S. Department of Health, Education and Welfare (36)]. Although this was a period of relative prosperity compared to the situation in the 1970s, the survey revealed the marginal nutritional status of the majority of the population. In terms of food consumption, 46 percent of the population were reported to consume inadequate quantities of calories, and 60 percent inadequate protein.[1] Concomitant with these deficiencies were major dietary deficiencies in vitamin A, riboflavin, iron, and iodine. These deficiencies were manifest by a striking retardation in the rate of physical growth of infants and young children, such that 50 percent of the one-to-four-year-olds were classified as malnourished based on height-weight standards. Vitamin A deficiency was manifested by numerous cases of keratomalacia, an eye disease that frequently leads to blindness in young children. Among pregnant women the major clinical problems were iron deficiency anemia, found in 95 percent of this group, and low serum albumen (protein deficiency) found in 45 percent. The synergism of malnutrition and infection leading to high death rates has already been noted above.

While food availability and thus nutritional level is the dominant factor controlling current mortality rates, one should not discount the contribution of infectious diseases. In a recent analysis of the epidemiology of cholera in rural areas, based on severe, hospitalized, bacteriologically confirmed cases, Mosley and his co-authors estimated that Bangladesh actually has from 70,000 to 350,000 cases annually, with 35,000 to 150,000 deaths [Mosley et al. (26)]. Cholera, therefore, still accounts for about 2 to 10 percent of all deaths annually. Because of the concentration of cholera in the 1—44 years age group where the general mortality rates are ordinarily low, cholera can contribute to from 20 percent to 40 percent of all deaths seen in these ages.

A similar investigation of smallpox in the Matlab population was carried out by Thomas et al. (35) in 1966–1967. Obviously, with smallpox, vaccination status profoundly influences the impact of the epidemic. By 1966, 81 percent of the population in the study area was vaccinated, thus the case rate was only 1.06/1,000 with a mortality rate of 0.26/1,000. Smallpox contributed about two percent to the crude death rate for that year. As noted earlier, a global eradication program, currently in its end stages, eliminated smallpox from Bangladesh in late 1975.

Very little is known about the prevalence of tuberculosis, another major killer. Two surveys of industrial workers have reported the prevalence of active disease as 2.6 percent and 4.5 percent, respectively [Bangladesh (4)]. Based on these rates, an estimate of 100,000 tuberculosis-related deaths annually has been made.[2] Even less is known about the incidence of other epidemic diseases such as diphtheria, typhoid, whooping cough, and polio. There is indirect evidence that tetanus in the newborn due to contamination of the umbilicus at delivery may account for up to 20 percent of all neonatal deaths—or about 10 percent of all infant mortality [McCormack and Curlin (23)].

The health-care system in Bangladesh is almost totally unequipped to cope with these and a multitude of other infectious diseases. As of 1973 there were only an estimated 12,371 hospital beds, public and private; only 2,263 of these were in the rural areas (serving about 70 million people) [Bangladesh (4)]. Of these beds, 766 were for tuberculosis, and 180 for infectious diseases. None were for children's diseases. Bangladesh has an estimated 7,000 physicians, but 75 percent are in the urban areas. There is a tremendous shortage of supporting health personnel with only 700 nurses, 250 midwives, and 275 women health visitors. The eight medical colleges train 1,400 students a year while the five nursing centers train 325 nurses.

MORTALITY IN 1970–1975

The economic situation, which was generally stagnant in the 1960s [Chen (7)], has suffered catastrophic setbacks in the 1970s from natural and man-made disasters. First, there was the cyclone and tidal wave in November 1970 which inundated about 2,000 square miles and killed an estimated 250,000 to 500,000 people [Sommer and Mosley (32)]. Then in 1971 there was the War of Independence which caused massive social disruption and an esti-mated loss of 1.6 to 3 million lives [Greenough and Cash (16)]. Before the economy could recover from the war, a major drought hit Bangladesh in 1972. Because this was the year of global food shortages, as well as the beginning of the oil crisis, the country experienced unprecedented inflation, with food prices rising 50 percent over the previous year [Bangladesh Bureau of Statistics (5)].

Reports by Curlin for the CRL Matlab population [Curlin *et al.* (12)] and by MacKay (21) for a population of 48,000 tea-garden workers in Sylhet district document in some detail the deterioration of health conditions during the war and for the following year. In Matlab the crude death rate rose 40 percent from an average of 15.3 per 1,000 in 1966–1970 to 21.4 per 1,000 in 1971 (Table 2). In 1972 death rates remained higher than previously reported; the CDR was 16.2, with death rates in the 5–14-year-old children still 200 percent above prewar levels.

MacKay documented a similar deterioration of health conditions in the tea-garden population in the year following the war. Compared to 1966–1970 levels, the CDR had risen 45 percent in 1972. The greatest increases in death by specific cause were due to bacillary dysentery (24 times), anemia (5.8 times), tuberculosis (3.8 times), pneumonia (2.9 times), and malnutrition (3.1 times).

The problem of bacillary dysentery, noted above, deserves special mention. During and immediately following the war, the Cholera Research Laboratory hospital in Dacca began to document the rapid rise of a particularly virulent form of dysentery due to Shigella A (Shiga bacillus).[2] Prior to 1971 only two or three cases a year were seen in Dacca. Since 1971, the case counts have been: 35 in 1971; 395 in 1972; 311 in 1973; and 333 in 1974. Although the reasons for this epidemic are not entirely clear, general deterioration of nutritional status and living conditions must play a role. Consistent with this is the fact that the annual number of cholera cases seen at the cholera hospital in Dacca since the war has also been averaging 5 to 10 times the numbers treated prior to the war.

In 1973 good weather brought the food grain (rice) harvest almost up to the prewar (1969–1970) level and with it came a decline in the rate of inflation as well as real signs of economic recovery [Bangladesh Bureau of Statistics (5)]. A devastating flood, unequaled in the preceding 50 years, caused an abrupt deterioration in living conditions in 1974 (United States (37) pp. 111–112]. Rice production fell sharply; more significantly, because of insufficient government controls on distribution in the face of food grain shortages, the price of rice rose 250 percent between January and September 1974 [Bangladesh Bureau of Statistics, (5)]. This led to widespread hunger in the rural areas with severe famine conditions in some localities [United States (39)]. For example, in Rowmari Thana in Rangpur district, a nutrition survey in December 1974 found 58 percent of the children severely malnourished [Curry and Koster, (13)]. The Matlab area, which was not directly affected by flooding but suffered from the high food prices, experienced a 38 percent rise in mortality (Table 2). Emergency feeding centers providing for hundreds of thousands of people were established throughout the country for about three months in late 1974.

The economic situation improved substantially through 1975 and 1976. Good weather and political stability (after the changes in government in the fall of 1975) assured record harvests for two consecutive years. Food prices fell to 1974 levels and, as Table 2 indicates, mortality rates again appear to be declining.

PROSPECTS FOR THE FUTURE

This analysis has suggested that mortality trends in Bangladesh are largely determined by the political, economic, and social factors affecting the supply and availability of food. Weather could be considered a factor; however, it must be recognized that weather plays such a major role in large part because poor economic circumstances limit technological inputs (flood control, irrigation) into the agricultural sector. Further, although floods or drought may reduce annual production by 5 percent to 10 percent, it is weaknesses of the political and economic system that permit hoarding and speculation to drive food prices up to such disproportionately high levels.

The sensitivity of mortality to food supply reflects the precarious economic condition of the majority of the population. This can be illustrated in several ways. For example, although the average annual per capita income is about $80, this does not adequately depict the level of poverty of a large fraction of the population because of inequity in distribution. The top 20 percent of the population gets 75 percent of the national income, while the bottom 20 percent gets only about 12 percent [United States (39), pp. 79–108].

A better indicator of wealth in the rural population is landholdings. A 1967–1968 survey revealed that about 17 percent of the rural agricultural workers were landless (Bangladesh Bureau of Statistics, 1968). Among the landowners, 38 percent have farms of less than 1.5 acres (accounting for less than 10 percent of the agricultural land), while 15 percent have farms of greater than five acres (accounting for 50 percent of the agricultural land). There are estimates that the proportion of landless had doubled by 1975, as the smallest landowners have been forced to sell their land to survive during the recent food crises [United States (39), p. 102].

It is apparent that the landless and a substantial fraction of the landowners are at the margin of existence, and are dependent entirely or largely on the availability of agricultural work and a good harvest for their livelihood. Generally, 90 percent to 100 percent of their income will be used to purchase food, almost exclusively rice. Obviously, any inflationary increase in the price of rice will be translated directly into a proportional decrease in food intake. In the family context, as noted above, this generally leads directly to starvation of the children and women.

Given these circumstances, the future, at least over the next few decades, looks precarious and substantial fluctuations in mortality may continue for some time. There are several reasons why this may be so. First and most fundamentally, although general economic development and increasing agricultural productivity are now underway, the pace of growth in these areas is barely keeping up with population growth which has been averaging

over 2.5 percent per year. Second, the major rice crop (aman), accounting
for over 50 percent of production, is a flood crop totally dependent upon the
weather, so fluctuations in production are likely. With shortfalls, food imports may be difficult to obtain because of the rising global food demand.

The short-term prospect—over the next decade—is unlikely to show any
further decline in mortality levels below that reached in the 1960s and, in fact,
is likely to be punctuated with episodes of high mortality unless the government can maintain food price stability with the year-to-year fluctuations in
production. For improvement in the longer run, there must be both a
sustained increase in food production on a per capita basis, and an improvement in the economic conditions and thus purchasing power of the poorest
segment of society.

Bangladesh has the potential to increase agricultural productivity several-
fold to meet the food needs of the population for the next several decades.
Exploiting this potential to improve the health and welfare of the population
will require more than technological inputs; it will also require policies to
reverse a decline in the living conditions of a great proportion of society
because of inflation and increasing inequity. Overriding all these considerations is an urgent need to control the rate of population growth which is
consuming most of the gains in food production and economic development
now being achieved.

FOOTNOTES

1. It should be noted that the magnitude of "deficiency" is based on arbitrary
standards defining the various nutrient requirements. Recently these have been lowered
for protein and calories, so that the proportion with inadequate intake would be lower
by 1976 standards.
2. Personal communication, Cholera Research Laboratory, Dacca, Bangladesh.

REFERENCES

1. Ambannavar, Jaipal P. (1975) *Long Term Prospects of Population Growth and
   Labor Force in India*, Bombay: University of Bombay.
2. Aslam, M.; S. S. Hashmi; and W. Seltzer. (1967) "Abridged Life Tables of Pakistan
   and Provinces by Sex, 1962," *Pakistan Development Review* 7:66–106.
3. Awan, A. H. (1969) *The System of Local Health Services in Rural Pakistan*, Lahore:
   Public Health Association of Pakistan.
4. Bangladesh. (1973) *First Five-Year Plan, 1973/74–1977/78*, Dacca.
5. Bangladesh Bureau of Statistics. (1968) *Master Survey of Agriculture, Report No. 9*,
   Dacca.
6. Chen, L. C., ed. (1973) *Disaster in Bangladesh: Health Crises in a Developing Nation*,
   New York: Oxford University Press.
7. ———. (1974) *An Analysis of Per Capita Food Grain Availability, Consumption, and
   Requirements in Bangladesh*, Dacca: Ford Foundation.

8. ———, et al. (1974) "Maternal Mortality in Rural Bangladesh," *Studies in Family Planning* 5:334–341.
9. Cholera Research Laboratory. (1970) *Demographic Studies in Rural Bangladesh, Fourth Year, 1969–70*, Dacca: Unpublished.
10. Chowdhury, A. K. M. A. (1974) *A Study of Neonatal and Post-Neonatal Differentials in Rural Bangladesh*, master's thesis, Baltimore: The Johns Hopkins University.
11. ———, and D. Huber. (December 1976) "Fertility and Mortality—Recent Changes in Matlab, Bangladesh," paper presented at the World Population Society Meeting, Washington, D.C.
12. Curlin, G. T.; L. C. Chen; and B. Hossian. (1976) "Demographic Crisis: The Impact of the Bangladesh Civil War on Births and Deaths in a Rural Area of Bangladesh," *Population Studies* 30:87–105.
13. Curry, B., and F. Koster. (1974) *Report to OXFAM on the Nutrition Survey in Romari in December*, mimeographed, Baltimore: Johns Hopkins University, Center for Medical Research and Training.
14. Davis, Kingsley. (1951) *The Population of India and Pakistan*, Princeton, N. J.: Princeton University Press.
15. Gangarosa, E., and W. H. Mosley. (1974) "Epidemiology and Surveillance of Cholera," in *Cholera*, eds. D. Barua and W. Burrows, Philadelphia: W. B. Saunders.
16. Greenough, W. B., and R. Cash. (1973) "Post-Civil War in Bangladesh: Health Problems and Programs," in *Disaster in Bangladesh: Health Crises in a Developing Nation*, ed. L. C. Chen, New York: Oxford University Press.
17. India. (1933) *Census of India*, 1931, Vol. 1, Part 1 Report, Government of India Press.
18. ———. (1953) *Census of India*, 1951, Vol. 6, West Bengal, Sikkim, and Chandernagore, Calcutta: Government of India Press.
19. Latham, M. C. (1975) "Nutrition and Infection in National Development," *Science* 188:561–565.
20. Lindenbaum, J. (1973) "Nutrition: The Role of Malabsorption," in *Disaster in Bangladesh: Health Crises in a Developing Nation*, ed. L. C. Chen, New York: Oxford University Press.
21. Mackay, D. M. (1974) "The Effects of Civil War on the Health of a Rural Community in Bangladesh," *Journal of Tropical Medicine and Hygiene* 77:120–127.
22. Marshall, C. L. (1974) "Health, Nutrition, and the Roots of World Population Growth," *International Journal of Health Services* 4: 677–690.
23. McCormack, W. M., and G. T. Curlin. (1975) "Infectious Diseases: Their Spread and Control," in *Disaster in Bangladesh: Health Crises in a Developing Nation*, ed. L. C. Chen, New York: Oxford University Press.
24. Mosley, W. H. et al. (1967) *Demographic Studies in Rural East Pakistan, 1966–1967*, Dacca: Cholera Research Laboratory.
25. ———; A. K. M. A. Chowdhury; and K. M. A. Aziz. (1970) *Demographic Characteristics of a Population Laboratory in Rural East Pakistan*. Bethesda, Md.: National Institutes of Health.
26. ———; K. J. Bart; and A. Sommer. (1972) "An Epidemiological Assessment of Cholera Control Programs in Rural East Pakistan," *International Journal of Epidemiology* 1:5–11.
27. Mosley, W. H. et al. (1972) "Report of the 1966–67 Cholera Vaccine Field Trial in Rural East Pakistan," *Bulletin of the World Health Organization* 47:229–238.
28. Pakistan. (1961) *Census of East Pakistan*, vol. 2.
29. Pakistan Institute of Development Economics. (1971) *Final Report of the Population Growth Estimation Experiment, 1962–1965*, Islamabad.
30. Puffer, R. P., and C. V. Serrano. (1973) *Patterns of Mortality in Childhood*, Washington, D.C.: Pan American Health Organization.

31. Scrimshaw, N.; C. E. Taylor; and J. E. Gordon. (1968) *Interactions of Nutrition and Infection*, Monograph Series, No. 57, Geneva: World Health Organization.

32. Sommer, A., and W. H. Mosley. (1972) "East Bengal Cyclone of November 1970," *Lancet* 13:1029–1036.

33. ———; N. Arnt, and S. O. Foster. (1973) "Post-Civil War in Bangladesh: The Smallpox Epidemic," in *Disaster in Bangladesh: Health Crises in a Developing Nation*, ed. L. C. Chen, New York: Oxford University Press.

34. ———, and M. S. Lowenstein. (1975) "Nutritional Status and Mortality: A Prospective Validation of the QUAC Stick," *American Journal of Clinical Nutrition* 28:287–292.

35. Thomas, D. *et al.* (1971) "Endemic Smallpox in Rural East Pakistan," *American Journal of Epidemiology* 93:361–372.

36. U.S. Department of Health, Education and Welfare. (1966) *Nutrition Survey of East Pakistan, March 1962–January 1964*, Washington, D.C.: Public Health Service.

37. *U.S. Decennial Life Tables for* 1969–71. *Vol. 1, No. 1, United States Life Tables: 1969–71.* (1975) National Center for Health Statistics, Washington, D.C.: HEW Publication No. (HRA) 75–1150.

38. *World Hunger, Health, and Refugee Problems, Part VI: Special Study Mission to Africa, Asia, and the Middle East.* (1975) p. 114, Washington, D.C.: Government Printing Office.

39. *World Hunger, Health, and Refugee Problems. Summary of Special Study Mission to Asia and the Middle East* (1975) pp. 79–108. Washington, D.C.: Government Printing Office.

DISCUSSION

Ismail Sirageldin, JOHNS HOPKINS UNIVERSITY

For purposes of discussion, Khan's paper may be divided into three parts: theoretical, empirical, and the interpretation of findings. In his theoretical treatment, Khan has given us an integrated account of a number of recent contributions to the application of human capital theory to fertility decisions. He examines carefully both the static and dynamic versions of the household production model and illustrates, based on Pollak and Wachter (6), that although it is a significant extension of the conventional theory of the consumer, many of its results are based on some rather restrictive assump tions, e.g., constant returns to scale and the absence of joint production. In his development of the dynamic version of his model, Khan reviews the

Research in Human Capital and Development, Vol. 1, pp. 95–99.
Copyright © 1979 by JAI Press, Inc.
All rights of reproduction in any form reserved.
ISBN: 0–89232–019–2

problems inherent in such a model of household decision making and illustrates the lack of a general theory to adequately account for them. As an alternative solution, he follows, similar to T. P. Schultz (7), an empirical approach based on a stock-flow adjustment model.

Khan's theoretical discussion is both lucid and authoritative. There is room, however, for disagreement with what he chose to exclude from his review, especially since he applies his models to two developing countries— Pakistan and Bangladesh. Although both are relatively low on various development indices, they differ structurally in significant respects, e.g., the urban proportion in Pakistan is about four times that of Bangladesh and their rural social structures are very different. In a recent contribution, Becker introduced the concept of social income which includes a person's money income and the value to him of his social environment [Becker (1), p. 1070] concluded that "the greater the contribution of a person's social environment to his social income, the more that individual's welfare is determined by the attitudes and behavior of others rather than by his own income." This seems to be an important concept especially when studying rural fertility behavior. To what extent, for example, is the social environment responsible for a part of the social income of a sizable proportion of the rural households in Bangladesh and/or Pakistan and, moreover, to what extent are those households unable to significantly influence their social environment? More fundamentally, how responsible is the social environment for the formation and maintenance of individual or group preference? This concept of social income could be generalized to include the influence of social group membership on the demand for children.

A related topic is the possibility of a "social demand" as contrasted to parents' demand for children. In a rural setting, social demand is largely defined by local technology, implied stratification system, and the distribution of income and wealth. The existence of such social demand may complicate Khan's analysis since it may influence simultaneously both prices and preferences. Another area ignored in Khan's theoretical discussion is the biological determinants of reproduction. As Mosley's analysis in this volume illustrates in the case of Bangladesh, the main constraints on fertility could be biological in nature for a large part of the population as a result of severe malnutrition which influences both fecundity and some basic aspects of reproductive performance, e.g., average ages at first and last births.

Khan's specification of the static completed family-size model is impressive given the data limitations. A comparison of OLS with 2SLS estimates indicates the importance of simultaneity for both countries, especially for the equation for completed family size. There are, however, some unexpected results: female labor force participation has a positive sign on the number of living children in the case of Pakistan (not significant for Bangladesh);

female literacy has a negative effect for rural Pakistan, but a positive one for rural Bangladesh; and the age of wife is not significant in the case of Bangladesh. As the author indicates, there is an estimation problem related to the female labor force equation because of the dummy nature of that variable. The degree to which this influences the results is a topic for further investigation using appropriate techniques.

One should, however, be careful of possible "overinterpretation." For example, the finding that the coefficient for female education is large and relatively more significant than that for males does not imply that female education represents a price variable rather than a utility shifter as Kelley (5), p. 10, has argued. There is no *a priori* judgment that the influence of education on female preference is more or less than that for males. A similar fallacy could result from interpreting the high incidence of family planning use among high-parity women in the context of an individual economic evaluative analysis of expected costs and returns. An alternative explanation that also implies rationality may be related to the age and presence of the oldest child — the presence of social pressure or value system that makes it inappropriate for couples to reproduce when their children have reached a certain age.

In his dynamic analysis Khan's use of the probit method to estimate the demand for additional children is both novel and appropriate. It is appropriate because of the dichotomous nature of the dependent variable as well as the theoretical expectations of the nonlinear nature of the relationships. Khan's most interesting finding relates to the robust documentation of the existence of a strong preference for sons in both Pakistan and Bangladesh although this preference is almost twice as great in Pakistan. Indeed, the findings indicate that the number of living sons is the single most important explanatory factor, followed by living daughters, in both countries.

In general, Khan's analysis presents a strong case for the utility of the use of human capital theory in fertility analysis. He also explores possible extensions of his dynamic analysis of the probit model to a multi-period framework in which pregnancy intervals are the units of analysis. This is a promising area of research that combines two recent developments in the field—those by Heckman and Willis (4) and those by Ben-Porath and Welch (2).

Robin Barlow's paper has a somewhat broader orientation. In it he explores the role of health in the process of economic development and the influence of development on health. His review of the empirical evidence is organized around a general model of these relationships. Two general impressions emerge from Barlow's review: One is that the empirical studies are not generally convincing, partly because of the use of inadequate methodologies, the use of inadequate proxy variables, or the inherent difficulties in sorting out the net effects of the various factors. The other is that the presence of many conflicting findings makes it difficult to draw broad generalizations.

As a general framework, Barlow's model consists of five endogenous variables which enter as arguments into a decision unit utility function. Thus he writes

$$U = U\,(H, N\cdot H, E\cdot H, F\cdot H, C\cdot H, L\cdot H),$$

where H = health; N = nutrition; E = education; F = fertility; C = C(Y) = consumption; Y = income; and L = leisure.

This allows him to account for possible interaction effects and to identify $\partial U/\partial H$ as the consumption benefit of health and $\partial Y/\partial H$ as the investment benefit of health. Using this framework for reviewing the literature on health and development, Barlow is able to identify a number of major shortcomings in the literature. An important finding is the general lack in the literature of adequate specification, e.g., the ignoring of the simultaneity of the relationships thus leading to misleading results; or not allowing for the effect of other endogenous and/or exogenous variables when estimating the relationships between two of the endogenous variables. Barlow illustrates many such difficulties in his comprehensive review of the literature. His review is well organized and provides an excellent overview of the field. Table 1, in which he classifies the various general-system studies that deal simultaneously with three or more of the basic endogenous variables, should serve as a basic reference for the literature.

Barlow's survey raises several important issues for future research in the field. There are several points, however, about which readers might like more discussion and/or specific information than Barlow gives. No quantitative content is given to the relationships in Table 1. A comparison of the estimated coefficients or elasticities among the various models would have been very useful. Furthermore, Barlow does not include in his review a consideration of factors on the supply side. They would seem to be of importance to the extent that the quantity and quality of the health delivery system, as well as the supporting public health facilities, very greatly among countries and over time. Excluding them from the empirical survey because of space limitations does not preclude a brief mention within the theoretical framework, especially if they are probably not independent of demand considerations. Similarly, there is no mention of migration and urbanization as related to health in Barlow's basic model. This seems to be an important relationship especially in an age of high rates of urbanization and population movements. It is also a complex relationship. For example, the health effects of migration could be examined at various levels: the migrants, the population of origin, the host population, and/or on the regional, national, or international levels [Hansluwka (3), pp. 223–229]. Whether migration should be treated as an additional endogenous variable or as a control factor in Barlow's framework needs more thought—it seems, however, that such decision will depend, partly at least, on the unit and level of analysis.

Mosley's paper is more descriptive than analytical. It provides an account of recent health trends in Bangladesh and relates them to food production and population growth. His analysis suggests that mortality trends in Bangladesh are largely determined by macro-political, economic, and social factors affecting the supply and availability of food. The sensitivity of mortality to food supply and its availability reflects the precarious economic (and health) conditions of the majority of the population. This is a dismal picture indeed. In a Beckerian framework [Becker (1)], rural households in Bangladesh are faced with a double-edged handicap—the average level of their "social income" is very low and the "social environment" is responsible for most of it. Accordingly, their welfare is mainly determined by their environment rather than by their own action. One may wonder whether in such a situation an individually based analysis with a human capital framework could yield practical policy insights. Mosley's analysis should serve as a starting point for a more comprehensive study on similar lines specified in Barlow's discussion with emphasis on his interaction terms and the identification of the structural constraints.

REFERENCES

1. Becker, G. S. (1974) "A Theory of Social Interaction," *Journal of Political Economy* 82(6).
2. Ben-Porath, Y., and F. Welch. (1976) "Do Sex Preferences Really Matter?" *Quarterly Journal of Economics* XC:285–307.
3. Hansluwka, H. (1976) "Health, Population and Socio-Economic Development," in *Population Growth and Economic Development in the Third World*, IUSSP: Ordina Editions.
4. Heckman, J. J., and R. J. Willis. (1976) "Estimation of a Stochastic Model of Reproduction: An Econometric Approach," in *Household Production and Consumption*, ed. N. E. Terleckyj, New York: National Bureau of Economic Research.
5. Kelley, A. C. (1976) "Interactions of Economic and Demographic Household Behavior," preliminary paper presented at the N.B.E.R. Conference on Population and Economic Change in Less Developed Countries, New York: National Bureau of Economic Research.
6. Pollak, R. A., and M. L. Wachter. (1975) "The Relevance of the Household Production Function and Its Implications for the Allocation of Time," *Journal of Political Economy* 83:255–278.
7. Schultz, T. P. (1976) "Determinants of Fertility: A Microeconomic Model of Choice," in *Economic Factors in Population Growth*, ed. A. J. Coale, London: Macmillan.

PART II
EDUCATION AND
MANPOWER

COLLEGE QUALITY AND EARNINGS

James N. Morgan and Greg J. Duncan,
UNIVERSITY OF MICHIGAN

INTRODUCTION

Investigations of the economic returns to education have focused on quantity of education, and only recently has attention turned to the quality of education, the intensive rather than extensive margin. Work has had to be done where data were available, usually with specific age groups of special populations.

Questions added to the eighth interviewing wave of the Panel Study of Income Dynamics enabled us to add three measures of the quality of colleges attended by husbands, wives, and unmarried household heads in the sample.[1]

Research in Human Capital and Development, Vol. 1, pp. 103–121.

This initial presentation of data is limited to asking how each of these three quality measures relates to the current earnings of adults in our sample. We do not attempt to fit a proper model of the whole process of investment in human capital, nor to estimate rates of return to educational quality.

ANALYSIS

Past Research

There have been three recent studies using the NBER-Thorndike sample of veterans to assess the effects of college quality on earnings:

1. Terence Wales used the Gourman academic ratings of undergraduate colleges, interacted with the amount of college education, in regressions which standardized for various socio-demographic, background, and mental ability characteristics. He concluded:

> Earnings of individuals in the top fifth of the undergraduate school quality distribution and in the top two-fifths of the graduate distribution are significantly and substantially higher than the earnings of others. However, it is unclear to what extent the quality variable is reflecting educational quality as opposed to individual scholastic abilities by measuring selection of entrance to college [Wales (9), pp. 306–317].

In looking at the "returns to education" Wales found they differed depending on quality of college, and that the differences were substantially larger for college dropouts and for those with advanced degrees than for college graduates only.

2. Paul Wachtel used a path analysis to focus on the effects of quality of secondary schooling and of direct investment costs of college in the form of years attended times the college expenditures per full-time-equivalent student. He found that "the earnings function ... reveals that both school and college expenditure levels have strong effects on earnings in 1968" [Wachtel (8), pp. 502–536].

3. Lewis Solmon focused on quality of college and compared ten different measures of college quality, some reflecting student quality, some instructional quality, and two subjective measures derived by Gourman which proved to be related to size of college. He concluded:

> We have found that the quality of institutions of higher education has an important impact on lifetime earnings of those who attend. A subjective evaluation of institutions (the Gourman Index) was used to measure quality in many of the estimated equations, but it

appears that certain objective traits that contribute to these evalua-
tions can be isolated. In particular, average student quality as
measured by the S.A.T. scores of entering freshmen, and faculty
salaries, are strongly related to the Gourman Index and are the
most important of the measurable institutional traits in the
earnings functions of former students.

The importance of college quality does not appear to vary significantly with years of college (and graduate school) attended. We
have only weak evidence of an interaction between college quality
and student ability. Quality does affect later incomes more than it
influences incomes immediately on entering the labor force.
These results hold even after controlling for certain occupational
choices, individual ability, and socioeconomic background
[Solmon (6), pp. 537–587].

These three studies are based on a single age cohort of veterans in the upper
half of the IQ range and in good health (in 1942), who entered the labor
market at a particularly favourable period of history. They are also based on
annual earnings. An annual measure may mask some quality effects if high
wages are partly invested in leisure, low ones offset by long hours, or if the
quality and quantity of education affects unemployment as well as earnings.
They do, however, have a good measure of ability,[2] earnings (at two points
in time), and family background. The analysis is careful and exhaustive.
The panel data used here have the advantage of being representative of *all*
household heads and wives in the United States and of covering a much
wider range of age groups who have been to college at various times. Our
cognitive skills measure is only a brief sentence completion test given almost
concurrently with the measure of earnings.

There are, of course, serious measurement problems with any assessment
of college quality. Expenditures and freshmen student test scores measure
inputs, prestige may measure an output. Some people go to more than one
college. The effects of college quality may take some time to appear, as
Solmon's findings indicate, but with our sample of people who graduated at
various points in the past, the longer since graduation, the more likely college
quality rankings are to be inappropriate. The rankings are mostly based on
recent data, but some of our respondents graduated from college much
earlier.[3]

The Role of College Quality

Solmon and Wachtel view college quality in a human capital context
where quality confers skills on graduates (and dropouts) and those skills
increase productivity and earnings. But if college education is purely invest-

ment in human capital, then one might expect the effect of quality to be similar regardless of the number of years completed.[4] Solmon finds no significant difference in separate functions fitted to those with less than 16 years and those with 16 years of school, but a significantly different function for those with advanced education (17 or more years) where he used a separate indicator of the quality of the college where the graduate work was done.

A positive association between college quality and earnings can also be explained by two other interpretations. First, because colleges select whom they admit, college quality may merely be a proxy for level of personal ability, high school achievement, and family background. In this case, merely being admitted indicates ability and would predict higher earnings later. Second, colleges confer a highly visible set of credentials, giving each student, in effect, credit for the *average* college quality. In this case, getting the degree might be more important than the actual learning which takes place.

It is probably impossible to discriminate among these three possibilities with nonexperimental data. We might argue that if mere admission to a high-quality college predicts higher earnings later, regardless of the number of years attended, then the selection factor is at work. But we do not have a sample of those who were admitted but never went at all.

We might rely, as Wales, Wachtel, and Solmon do, on regression adjustments for measured ability to take care for the selection factor, but so long as they are measured incompletely or with error, they will fail to eliminate the estimated effect of individual differences, even those restricted to test-passing abilities.

Similarly, the credentialist argument about a degree from a high-status college cannot be answered by comparing graduates with dropouts. Although dropouts were also selected into the same colleges, the act of completing college may reflect important traits of personality—such as finishing things—that interact with the quality of the college experience to affect later earnings.

Our purpose is less ambitious, namely, to look at the relationships between three measures of college quality, on the one hand, and later earnings, on the other, both before and after adjustment by regression for other factors affecting earnings. We introduce all three quality measures into the regression simultaneously to see which one dominates.

PROCEDURE

We have three measures of the quality of colleges attended by the husbands, wives, and unmarried heads of household in our sample:[5]

1. The average ACT test scores of freshmen classes in the last college attended (SAT scores translated into their ACT equivalent),

2. The expenditure per pupil in that college, and
3. A prestige ranking of that college, prewar for those 45 and older, postwar for those under 45.

Our sample covers a wide range of ages, work experience, and job tenures, so estimates of the effects of college quality need to be adjusted for correlations with such factors.

Our procedure is to attempt to explain the natural logarithm of 1974 hourly earnings by regression with categorical predicators, adding each of the three college quality measures separately, and then all three simultaneously. We start with those individuals with at least some college education who worked 500 hours or more in 1974. Because the effects of college quality may well be substantially different for men and women, we look separately at these two subgroups. We then follow with analyses of successively smaller subgroups of men. First, we eliminate those who are new heads of households since 1972 in order to be able to use the 1972 test scores as one of the control variables. Then we look separately at college graduates and those without a four-year college degree, since original selection, college experience, and the prestige of the degree are all potentially involved in affecting later earnings.[6]

We have not attempted a full explanation of earnings, including detailed family background and the various paths through which background and education might affect earnings, but we do control for the effects of the following variables: years of work experience since age 18, years on the present job, size of the largest city in the area, father's occupation, amount of college completed, and for the men, the score on a sentence-completion test administered in 1972. We also ran the regression without occupation, since it is one of the paths by which college quality can affect earnings. For the women we substituted father's education for his occupation which was not available, and added a classification by hours worked in 1974. We also adjusted men's earnings up by 5 percent for those covered by an employer pension plan for the analyses that did not use pension coverages as an explanatory variable

RESULTS

The relative explanatory power of the three measures of college quality is given in Table 1 for a variety of subgroups with the other control variables specified. Since an apparently insignificant variable can have a pattern of effects that is significant with a more precise test that specifies rank order; and since apparently significant characteristics can have effects contrary to the theory, we present the estimated effects (adjusted by regression) in Table 2 and in the figures which follow.

Table 1. Power of Three Measures of College Quality in Explaining Hourly Earnings, Unadjusted and Adjusted by Regression.[1]
(For Various Subgroups Who Have Had Some College
and Who Worked 500 or More Hours in 1974)

		Measure of College Quality		
Subgroups	Number of Observations	ACT Scores	Dollar Expenditure per Student	Prestige Rank
Women	517			
Unadjusted		.014	.012	.029**
Adjusted (for education, experience, age, city size, hours worked, father's education)		.003	.009	.004
Men	881			
Unadjusted		.081**	.020	.052**
Adjusted (for education, experience, job tenure, city size, pension coverage, commuting hours)		.017	.006	.014
Men—Household Heads Since 1972 (no missing data on quality measures)	592			
Unadjusted		.086**	.032**	.039**
Adjusted (for test score, education, experience, job tenure, city size, father's occupation)		.025**	.011	.013
Adjusted also for other quality measures		.028**	.035[2]	.017
Men—Household Heads Since 1972, College Dropouts Only	244			
Unadjusted		.109**	.024	.036*
Adjusted (for test score, experience, job tenure, city size, father's education)		.063**	.020	.027
Adjusted also for other quality measures		.051*	.019	.014
Men—Household Heads Since 1972, College Graduates Only	231			
Unadjusted		.061**	.037*	.019
Adjusted (for test score, experience, job tenure, city soze, father's occupation)		.011	.016	.011
Adjusted also for other quality measures		.006	.017	.017

(Notes to Table 1)

1. For unadjusted (gross) effects, the number given is the square of the correlation ratio (Eta^2); for adjusted (net) effects, it is an analogous measure, using the adjusted subgroup means (Beta^2). See Andrews *et al.* (1), pp. 47–49.

For the unadjusted effects and those adjusted for factors other than the other quality measures, the tests are proper F-tests using the increment in R-squared, but without allowance for sample design effects. For adjusted effects taking account also of the other college quality measures, an approximate test is used, since the Beta-squared is an approximation to the partial R-squared when intercorrelation among predictors is not too serious relative to the explanatory power of the predictors. See Duncan and Morgan (4), p. 439, and Andrews *et al.* (1), p. 49.

2. Significant, but effects not as hypothesized; see Figure 3.
*Significant at .05 level, ignoring design effects.
**Significant at .01 level, ignoring design effects.

Table 2. Earnings by ACT Scores of Freshmen, Adjusted by Regression for Other Background Characteristics.*

ACT Scores	517 Women	881 Men	592 Men— Heads Since 1972	415 Men— 25–44 Years Old Heads Since 1972
4–18	$4.10	$5.10	$5.70	$5.70
19–20	5.22	5.58	6.23	5.87
21–22	4.31	5.81	6.11	5.87
23 24	4.26	6.11	6.96	6.17
25–26	4.14	6.55	7.69	7.17
27–98	3.74	6.82	7.61	6.42

ACT Scores	592 Men— Heads Since 1972	244 Men— Heads Since 1972 College Dropouts	231 Men— Heads Since 1972 College Graduates
4–19	$6.11	$5.53	$6.62
20	6.30	5.00	6.42
21–22	6.11	5.05	7.32
23–24	6.89	6.82	6.62
25–98	7.69	6.75	7.61

*These are adjusted geometric means since the regression used log earnings.

Women

For women with any college, none of the quality measures has a significant effect after adjustment. The prestige rank does have a significant unadjusted effect, and an interesting nonmonotonic effect pictured in Figure 1. One might think that taking account of father's education fails to allow for the

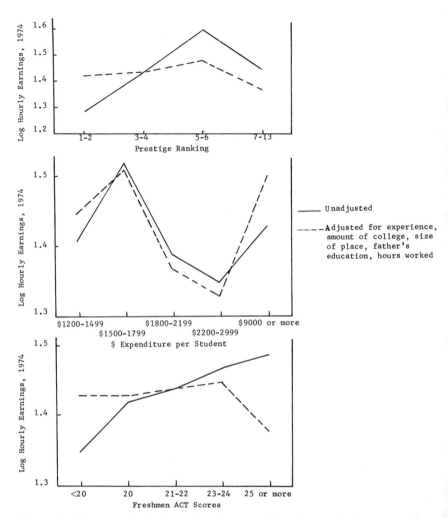

Figure 1. Effects of College Quality on Earnings of Women—Three Measures, Unadjusted and Adjusted by Regression (517 Wives or Female Household Heads with Some College Who Worked 500 Hours or More in 1974).

possibility that it operates *through* the daughter attending a high-prestige college, but earlier runs without that predictor produced similar results. It is, of course, possible that society is changing, and that in the future women will be able to profit financially from quality education. The evidence is that they do not now, even taking account of how many hours they work.

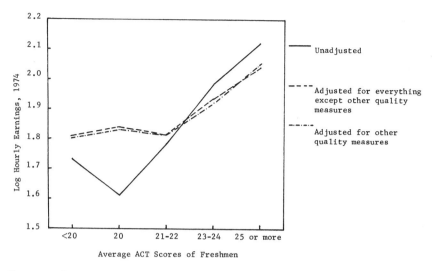

Figure 2. Log Hourly Earnings in 1974, by Average ACT Scores of Freshmen in College Attended. (For 512 Men with Some College, Heads Since 1972, and Worked 500 + Hours in 1974)

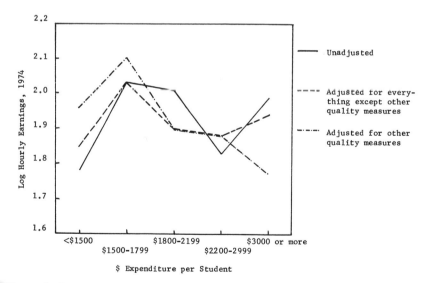

Figure 3. Log Hourly Earnings in 1974, by Expenditure per Student in College Attended. (For 592 Men with Some College, Heads Since 1972, and Worked 500 + Hours in 1974).

Men

For men, all three of the measures appear to have a significant bivariate relationship with current hourly earnings, although the expenditure-per-pupil measure does not give a monotonic pattern of effects. After adjustment for other background characteristics, however, only Freshman ACT score remains significant and exhibits the hypothesized pattern of effects. This is true even after we eliminate new heads since 1972 and add the 1972 test score as a control variable. Figures 2, 3 and 4 give the estimate effects for average ACT score, expenditure per student, and college prestige rating, respectively.

Given the relatively high correlation between the three measures of college quality, it is all the more impressive that the ACT score measure stands out in Table 1. This superiority reinforces the findings of Solmon. It remains if we look separately at those under 45 years old (results not shown), on the assumption that the college rankings are less out-of-date for them, even though the effects of college training may have had less chance to reveal themselves. Selecting only unchanged heads since 1972 in order to have the test scores also made little difference, except to produce a significant effect of expenditures per student counter to the hypothesized pattern when all three highly correlated measures of college quality are introduced into the same regression.

However, the amount of college has a substantial effect even though the quality of the undergraduate college may not be an adequate measure for graduate work. Attendance at a high-quality college may indicate a select group by personal characteristics and ability, and graduating from one may indicate credentials that could pay off regardless of what was learned. Hence, we look separately at college dropouts and at college graduates. The results are startling and at variance with those of Solmon, though they agree with Wales. It is college dropouts for whom the college quality measure (ACT scores) seems to matter. Figure 5 shows the patterns.

An examination of what the adjustments by regression do shows that they tend to make the effects of college quality weaker, but smoother and more monotonic. In the case of the ACT score measure, job tenure and test scores seem to have more effect on college graduates than on dropouts, and hence presumably attenuate the estimated effect of college quality more severely for college graduates.

Correlations Among the Quality Measures

A question arises as to why we should find such different patterns with three measures which are relatively highly correlated, one of which (prestige rank) presumably includes some of the information in the other two. Table A.1a shows the patterns of correlation among the three measures. The colleges

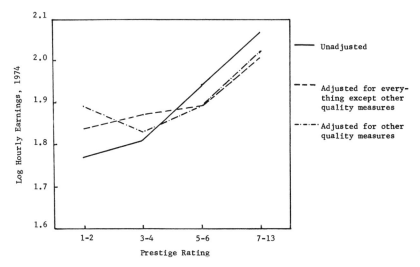

Figure 4. Log Hourly Earnings in 1974 by Prestige Rating of College Attended. (For 592 Men with Some College, Heads Since 1972, and Worked 500 + Hours in 1974).

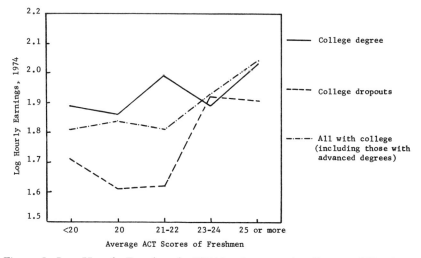

Figure 5. Log Hourly Earnings in 1974 by Average Act Scores of Freshmen Attended. (For 592 Men with Some College or More, 244 College Dropouts, and 231 College Graduates).

ranked 3 or 4 on the prestige ranking, "teachers' colleges and their social equivalents among private colleges," include a substantial number with relatively low expenditure per student (less than $1,800) and a substantial number with freshman ACT scores of 21 or higher, though few above 25. This may account for the high earnings of those who went to colleges with low expenditure per student. When we remember that this is a distribution of people who went to college rather than of colleges as such, it may still be that there are economies of scale in public colleges that specialize, and/or that the explosion in the school population benefited those who specialized in education. The sample does not contain enough people from the highest-ranked colleges to study the educated elite, nor those with advanced degrees.

Both for policy analysis and for individual decision making, once it is clear that the quality of college has some effect, the crucial question is how much effect? In terms of hourly earnings, the range from colleges with the lowest freshmen ACT scores to those with the highest seems to be somewhere over $1.00 an hour but less than $2.00. This ignores effects on ability to secure steady work, pleasant jobs, or control over one's own work. Economic interpretation would require also calculating the extra cost of going to the better colleges. The finding that it is the freshman ACT score rather than the expenditure per student that seems to matter would indicate that there were some "better buys" in college choice.

SUMMARY AND IMPLICATIONS

We have related earnings to three measures of college quality and have found, as Solmon did, that the ACT scores of the student body have a much stronger association with earnings of men than do per-pupil expenditures. In addition, the ACT quality measure was found to be more important than a prestige measure, which presumably takes ACT scores into account. The ACT measure retains its explanatory power even when the effects of the other two quality measures have been taken into account.

As mentioned earlier, it is impossible to test among competing explanations of this ACT effect. The panel respondents who attend high ACT colleges may themselves have above-average ability or other characteristics and thus the earnings may be relating to *individual* ability rather than overall ability of the student body. We were able to adjust for individual differences with scores of a crude test of cognitive skills, but the adjustment is obviously imperfect. Solmon, on the other hand, was able to adjust for ability with scores from a much more detailed battery of IQ tests, and his finding that the student body average ACT quality measure retained its explanatory power casts doubt on the hypothesis that earnings do not react to quality of the student body. Both this analysis and that of Solmon found the ACT effect to be weaker for earnings measured soon after entry into the labor market, which cast doubt on the hypothesis that employers use college quality to screen job applicants.

It is most tempting to view the ACT-quality result directly: men from higher-quality schools earn more because they learn more from their classmates and because the standards set by their classmates are higher. The notion that the quality of the student body is more important than other school measures is certainly not a new one, since it was the principal conclusion of the so-called Coleman Report (6) on elementary and secondary schooling. But the data also support the notion that quality of college attended largely indicates selection by ability, background, or motivation.

APPENDIX
Measures of College Quality and Other Explanatory Variables

The variable we call "Average ACT Score of Freshman Class" is actually an estimate based either on American College Test composite scores, a translation from Scholastic Aptitude verbal plus mathematical scores, or estimates of these scores. The procedure is described by Astin (2).

The variable we call "expenditure per student" is education and general expenditures per resident, degree-credit student. It includes expenditures for instruction and departmental research, sponsored research, extension and public service, libraries, physical plant maintenance, organized activities related to education departments (activities related to instructional departments and conducted primarily to provide instructional or laboratory training) in the numerator. The denominator includes extension students and those not receiving credit toward a degree. The information was made available through the courtesy of the Higher Education Research Institute, Los Angeles, California, and is from the U.S. Office of Education's Higher Education General Information Survey.

The variable we call prestige ranking of college was created by Richard P. Coleman of the Joint Center for Urban Studies of the Massachusetts Institute of Technology and Harvard University, once for the 1935–1954 period and then for the period 1970–1974. We have used the latter for those under 45 years of age in 1975. It is intended to suggest the social prestige of having been a student at the particular institution and makes use of the information in the other two measures, plus other things. Table A.1a gives the verbal description of the ranks, but Table A.1b indicates a high correlation with ACT scores even with expenditure per student, and a somewhat lower correlation between ACT scores and expenditure per student.

Where more than one college was mentioned, the one coded and ranked was the final one (from which the highest degree was received), even though

Table A.1a. Category Descriptions for Prestige Ratings of Colleges Attended.

01. Lowest-prestige, two-year public schools and four-year unaccredited schools; lower prestige accredited schools administered by lower status religious groups, such as Assemblies of God, the Nazarenes, and Seventh Day Adventists

02. Higher prestige, two-year public schools and four-year unaccredited schools; higher prestige accredited schools administered by lower status religious groups

03. Lower prestige public teachers' colleges and their social equivalents among private colleges

04. Higher prestige public teachers' colleges and their social equivalents among private colleges

05. Lower prestige land-grant agricultural and mechanical colleges and their social equivalents among private colleges, as well as other public schools

06. Higher prestige land-grant agricultural and mechanical colleges and their social equivalents among private colleges, as well as other public schools

07. Lower prestige state universities and their social equivalents among the private colleges

08. Higher prestige state universities and their social equivalents among the private colleges

09. Lower prestige upper-to-middle quality private colleges and a few very prestigious public institutions

10. Higher prestige upper-to-middle quality private colleges and a few very prestigious public institutions

11. Lowest quality upper-class private colleges

12. Medium-quality upper-class private colleges

13. Highest quality upper-class private colleges

99. NA; DK college; foreign college or university; no rating for that college

the ratings, except perhaps the prestige one, were more appropriate for the four-year college work.

The test score results from the administration in the 1972 interview of a sentence completion test specifically designed for the purpose of discriminating in the lower-middle range and with as little bias from the sex or race of interviewer or respondent as possible. It uses thirteen sentence completion items where the respondent selects one of five words to make sense of a sentence. For more detail see Appendix F of Morgan (5), pp. 381–385, and Appendix C of Duncan and Morgan (4), pp. 447–458. For detailed documentation of the development, see Joseph Veroff *et al.* (7).

Job tenure is the reply to the question: "How long have you had this job?" rather than a cumulation of answers to the question from 1967 on. Work experience is the reply to the second of two questions: "How many years have

Table A.1b. Relations Between College Quality Measures for 592 Men, Household Heads Since 1972, Who Worked 500 Hours or More in 1974 and Had Some College or More.

Average ACT Score	Expenditure per Student						Rank Correlation Coefficient (Kendall's Tau-B)
	Less Than $1,500	1,500–1,799	1,800–2,199	2,200–2,999	$3,000 or More	All	
Less than 20	13%	3%	1%	1%	1%	19%	
20	7	1	0	0	0	9	
21–22	5	4	2	4	1	15	.54
23–24	4	6	6	6	6	27	
25 or more	2	2	3	2	20	30	
All	30%	15%	12%	14%	28%	100%	

ACT Score	Prestige Rank					Rank Correlation Coefficient (Kendall's Tau-B)
	1–2	3–4	5–6	7–13	All	
Less than 20	10%	9%	0%	0%	19%	
20	3	6	0	0	9	
21–22	2	8	4	1	15	.67
23–24	0	8	11	8	27	
25 or more	0	3	6	21	30	
All	15%	33%	22%	30%	100%	

Table A.1b (Contd.)

Expenditure per Student

Prestige	Less Than $1,500	1,500–1,799	1,800–2,199	2,200–2,999	$3,000 or More	All	Rank Correlation Coefficient (Kendall's Tau-B)
1–2	11%	2%	1%	1%	1%	15%	
3–4	17	9	4	2	0	33	
5–6	2	3	5	6	5	22	
7–13	0	1	3	5	21	30	
All	30%	15%	12%	14%	28%	100%	.65

you worked since you were 18?" "How many years of these years did you work full time for most of the year?" (For male heads the two do not differ enough to matter.) The questions were asked in 1974 and of new heads only in 1975. Size of the largest city in the area (county or group of counties forming a primary sampling unit) is intended to reflect both the extent and variety of the job market, and the cost-standard of living and related wage levels.

Table A. 1c. Relative Power of Various Predictors in Explaining Hourly Earnings of Men with Some College.

All 592 Men with Some College	Eta^2	$Beta^2$				
Years of Experience	.141	.098	.080	.096	.080	.076
Job Tenure	.104	.041	.044	.040	.045	.043
Father's Occupation	.096	.041	.041	.041	.044	.039
Size of Largest City in Area	.071	.040	.030	.039	.039	.032
Test Score	.003	.007	.010	.006	.008	.008
Amount of College	.044	.047	.037	.042	.038	.034
ACT Scores	.087		.025			.028
Dollar Expenditure per Student	.032			.011		.035
Prestige of College	.039				.013	.017
R^2 Adjusted		.278	.294	.283	.286	.304

240 Dropouts Only	Eta^2	$Beta^2$				
Years of Experience	.089	.067	.057	.081	.058	.061
Job Tenure	.067	.055	.045	.060	.058	.044
Father's Occupation	.064	.078	.075	.086	.082	.065
Size of Largest City in Area	.093	.046	.035	.047	.045	.030
Test Score	.001	.011	.017	.011	.015	.013
ACT Scores	.109		.063			.051
Dollar Expenditure per Student	.024			.020		.019
Prestige of College	.036				.027	.014
R^2 Adjusted		.181	.224	.191	.195	.215

231 *College Graduates Only*	Eta^2	$Beta^2$				
Years of Experience	.162	.081	.069	.079	.066	.061
Job Tenure	.210	.090	.094	.089	.105	.099
Father's Occupation	.087	.049	.053	.051	.050	.051
Size of Largest City in Area	.124	.053	.046	.051	.055	.051
Test Score	.008	.021	.024	.025	.026	.026
ACT Scores	.061		.011			.006
Dollar Expenditure per Student	.037			.016		.017
Prestige of College	.019				.011	.017
R^2 adjusted		.318	.316	.319	.320	.311

Two other predictors used in the first few regressions were eliminated in the main analysis: whether covered by a pension plan, and time spent commuting to work. They were thought of as corrections to the hourly earnings. In fact, however, pension coverage may reflect nonmoney compensation, but those covered usually receive more take-home pay as well, even considering all the other factors we can measure. Consequently, in most of the analysis, hourly earnings are simply adjusted upward 5 percent for those with employer pension coverage. Commuting hours are positively correlated with hourly earnings, but may well be considered not a cost of getting a better job, but a way of consuming higher earnings by living in a pleasanter place farther away. In any case, it has Beta-squareds of .02 so would not affect other estimates much.

The inclusion of cases where college quality was not ascertained makes competitive evaluation of the three quality measures unsafe, since the "missing information" group tends to be the same individuals on all three measures. Hence, we provide such estimates only for the subgroups that exclude missing information cases.

It is also impressive that both the ACT score of fellow students in the college attended, and the individual's own sentence completion test score in 1972, are more highly correlated with 1974 earnings for college dropouts than for those with college degrees.

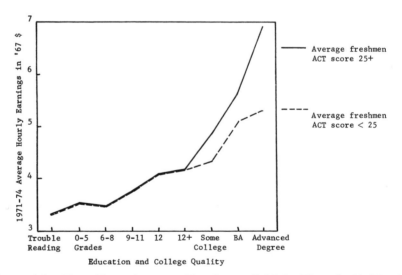

Figure A.1a. Four-Year Average Earnings of Male Household Heads, Adjusted by Regression for Experience, Test Score, Farm Background, and Eight Other Factors, by Education and College Quality. (For 2,549 Unchanged Heads Since 1972 Who Worked 500 + Hours Each Year).

Since most of the college quality differences can be accounted for by a single dichotomy—whether the college attended had average freshman ACT scores of 25 or higher—we add one final figure (Figure A.1a) giving four-year average earnings for males who were heads since 1972, adjusted by regression for a large number of other factors. The combination of education and college quality was the most important predictor in a regression which had an adjusted R-squared of .35.

FOOTNOTES

1. The addition of the college quality information was made possible by the assistance, financial and otherwise, of Christopher Jencks, Richard Coleman, and Lee Rainwater.

2. Their ability measure is an IQ estimate based on the Air Force Qualifying Test, which was administered before many of them completed their schooling.

3. Solmon did look at some data on intertemporal correlations of college rankings and found them comfortably high.

4. Assuming that the equation is properly specified.

5. See Appendix for details.

6. There were not enough with advanced degrees to justify separate analysis, and it is doubtful that our college ratings apply to graduate schools adequately.

REFERENCES

1. Andrews, F. M. *et al.* (1973) *Multiple Classification Analysis: A Report on a Computer Program for Multiple Regression using Categorical Predicators*, rev. ed., Ann Arbor, mich: Institute for Social Research.
2. Astin, A. W. (1971) *Predicting Academic Performance in College*, New York: Free Press.
3. Coleman, James S. *et al.* (1966) *Equality of Educational Opportunity*, Washington, D.C.: Government Printing Office.
4. Duncan, Greg J., and James N. Morgan, eds. (1975) "Some National Norms for a Sentence Completion Test," in *Five Thousand American Families—Patterns of Economic Progress*, vol. III. Ann Arbor, Mich.: Institute for Social Research.
5. Morgan, James N. *et al.* (1974) "Measures of Achievement Motivation and Cognitive Ability," in *Five Thousand American Families—Patterns of Economic Progress*, vol. 1, Ann Arbor, Mich.: Institute for Social Research.
6. Solmon, Lewis, C. (1975) "The Definition of College Quality and Its Impact on Earnings," *Exploration in Economic Research* 2: 537–587.
7. Veroff, Joseph; L. McClelland; and K. Marquis. (1971) *Measuring Intelligence and Achievement Motivation in Surveys*, Ann Arbor, Mich.: Institute for Social Research.
8. Wachtel, Paul. (1975) "The Effect of School Quality on Achievement, Attainment Levels, and Lifetime Earnings," *Explorations in Economic Research* 2: 502–536.
9. Wales, Terence. (1973) "The Effect of College Quality on Earnings: Results from the NBER-Thorndike Data," *Journal of Human Resources* VIII: 306–317.

THEORETICAL ISSUES IN MANPOWER AND EDUCATIONAL PLANNING

Mohiuddin Alamgir, BANGLADESH INSTITUTE OF DEVELOPMENT STUDIES

EDUCATION IN DEVELOPMENT

The emergence of interest among economists and other social scientists in manpower and educational planning is a recent phenomenon. Classical economists, in spite of some differences of opinion, by and large recognized the importance of the concept of human capital and the role of education in the production of human capital, although there was no formal articulation of the concept of planning as such. J. S. Mill and Marshall were thought to have shied away from applying the concepts of "wealth" and "capital" to human beings [Schultz (83), pp. 1–2]. It has, however, been pointed out

Research in Human Capital and Development, Vol. 1, pp. 123–148.

that "Marshall's problem with human capital was definitional, not conceptual" [Blandy (18), p. 874]. Reference to this concept can be found in the writings of pre-Smithian authors like Sir William Petty [Johnson (65), pp. 129–144]. Of course, a more clear exposition and bold recognition came from other classicists such as Adam Smith [Schultz (83), pp. 1–2] and H. Von Thunen [Kiker (70), pp. 339–343]. Later Irving Fisher used an all-inclusive concept of capital [Schultz (83), p. 2].

Among modern writers, the contribution made by T. W. Schultz (83) in drawing the attention of economists to the need "to include the acquired abilities of man that augment his productivity as a form of capital, as a product of investment" is most noteworthy. According to him [(86), p. 48] again, "the concept of capital ... consists of entities that have the economic property of rendering future services of some value. ... The distinctive mark of human capital is that it is a part of man. It is *human* because it is embodied in man, and it is *capital* because it is a source of future satisfactions, or of future earnings or of both." Notwithstanding some criticisms leveled against the concept of human capital by Schaffer [(82), pp. 1026–1035] and Weisman [(94), pp. 1–12] it has been found useful to explain some of the puzzles about long-term growth of an economy. Various empirical studies [Abramovitz (2), pp. 5–23; Solow (91), pp. 312–320] attempting to explain the growth of the U.S. economy over the first half of the twentieth century came across a relatively large residual which could not be explained by the growth in capital and labor as conventionally measured. It was later recognized that the growth of human capital, as reflected in the increase in the amount of education of the labor force and therefore in its productivity, accounts for a substantial portion of additional output. A few of the pathbreaking studies in the field are: Schultz [(84), pp. 46–88] and Denison (30) for the United States, Denison (31) for Western European countries, Harberger and Selowsky (54) for Chile, and Griliches [(49), pp. 331–346] for U.S. agriculture.

Alternative techniques have been adopted in order to assess the contribution of education to economic growth. Bowen [(23), pp. 67–100] describes the simplest of all approaches as the correlation approach which "consists of correlating some overall index of educational activity."

A second approach, the more popular one, is the residual approach. Estimation of the residual was based on the neoclassical marginal productivity theory. The implicit production function allowed for smooth substitution between different factors. In their studies, Kendrick (69) and Denison (30) did not introduce the concept of production function directly, but Solow (91) introduced a linear homogeneous production function with "neutral" technical change. A more direct method of measuring the contribution of education consists of introducing education as an independent variable in estimating the production function. Griliches [(51), pp. 2–20] discusses a number of hypotheses developed with respect to the role of education in the aggregate production function. In his own work on U.S. agriculture [(49), p. 424] he succesfully tested the hypothesis that when education is introduced as an independent variable the least squares estimate of the coefficient associated with it is of a magnitude similar to that associated with labor. Welch [(95), pp. 17–25] suggests that this procedure may understate the role of education if one does not take account of both the "worker effect" and the "allocative effect" of education; the latter refers to managerial contribution (better allocative ability with respect to other inputs). In order to capture both, one has to estimate the value-added production function.

One other important problem is to find a measure of the education variable. Usual practice is to use the average number of school years completed [Griliches (48), p. 423]. In one of his studies, Griliches [(50), p. 969] measured the education variable "in dollar per year that a comparable average education mix would fetch in the nonfarm sector."[1] However, doubts have been raised as to what these variables actually measure [Judge (66), p. 431]. For cross-country analysis a common index used by many [Singh (90)] is that proposed by Harbison and Meyers [(55), chapter 3]. Their composite index is a weighted average of the enrollment at second level of education as a percentage of the age group 15 to 19, adjusted for length of schooling, and enrollment at the third level of education as a percentage of the age group 20 to 24.[2]

While the problem of obtaining a satisfactory measure of education remains, reliance on the aggregate production function approach to formulate policies for educational development is also subject to controversy. For developing countries the use of a Cobb-Douglas production function to indicate the contribution of education to growth has been criticized by Blaug and Streeten [(21), p. 384].[3]

Drawing upon the evidence from developed countries, it may be argued that developing countries should pay due attention to accumulation of human capital. Some doubts are raised, however, from the experience of a country like Greece, which is underdeveloped in relation to other Western economies. It was found that increasing the educational level of the labor force did not contribute significantly to the observed rate of growth [Bowles (25)]. What this implies is that careful consideration should be given as to how resources are allocated between education and other sectors of the economy. Planning in this context will consist of comparing productivity of scarce factors of production in education with that elsewhere in the economy in order to determine investment priorities. The problem is a dynamic one, since the effect of educational expenditure is realized after a time lag and is spread over a period of time.[4]

The importance of education as a contributing factor to growth is confirmed by empirical findings on the relationship between schooling and earnings, although Bowles [(28), p. 14] and others have pointed out that "schooling is only one of the many influences on earnings." Most of these studies [Houthakker (58), pp. 24–28; Becker (14), chapter VII; Hanoch (53), pp. 42–47; Gounden (36), p. 69; Bowles (28), p. 15] are based on cross-sectional data on age, earnings, and educational level which are available either from census documents or from sample surveys. The main emphasis is on changes in earnings over time. The influence of education is observed through the nature of the shift in curves depicting the relationship between age and earnings. The analysis is usually done for the labor force as a whole and no attempt is made to classify labor by occupational category. The general conclusion is that education is positively correlated with higher mean income and, for a given educational level, annual earnings rise up to the age of 50 and then start declining.[5]

Recently, attempts [Arrow (12), pp. 193–216] have been made to promote the so-called screening hypothesis which says that earnings (productivity) differentials cannot be explained by differences in education (after other related factors have been taken into account) and that the major function of education is only screening. Thus, education is conceived to be "a device for signaling preexisting ability differences" [Layard and Psacharopoulos, (71), p. 985].[6]

The significance of the relationship between education and earnings lies in the fact that it is often taken as a surrogate for the relationship between education and productivity. Such an assumed relationship would be meaningful if it helped determine the optimum level of education for each skill (occupation) and thereby helped determine the optimal level of total investment in education. The crucial question, how far the differences in earnings represent the differences in productivity, remains to be settled clearly. Some theoretical and empirical work has been done with respect to individuals' behavior regarding investment in human capital. It is recognized that "the producer of human capital has a choice between producing additions to his stock or renting his stock in the labor market or both" [Haley (52), p. 929; Ben-Porath (17), pp. 352–365] presents a theoretical model explicitly incorporating a production function of human capital to derive the optimal path of accumulation of human capital and the life cycle of earnings. Within this framework, the individual is assumed to maximize the discounted future earnings stream. Some improvements and slight modifications are to be found in the work of, among others, Haley [(52), pp. 929–944] and Blinder and Weiss [(22), pp. 449–472].[7] In their present form, these exercises have little relevance for manpower and educational planning as such, particularly in the context of developing countries.

An important dimension of the research on human capital is the relationship between distribution of income and distribution of education. Pioneering work in this area by Mincer [(73), pp. 281–302] and Becker and Chiswick

[(15), pp. 358–369] was carried out within an individual welfare maximization framework. Oulton [(78), p. 387] presents a critique observing that "the human capital approach seems incomplete since the distribution of income is made to depend on the distribution of education but the latter is not explained." The author considers more general models in which the two distributions are simultaneously determined.

While debate will continue over the appropriate analytic framework to examine the relationship between the two distributions, the impact of public and private investment in human capital on the distribution of income (or well-being) in developing countries has become a lively social and political issue. It is suspected that the pattern of investment in human capital is reinforcing the underlying trend of increasing disparity between the level of well-being of different classes in the society. Educational planning in developing countries, with weak transfer mechanisms, must take note of this phenomenon.

MANPOWER AND EDUCATIONAL DEVELOPMENT

The importance of education in growth and distribution highlights the need for social intervention in the educational process. Bowles [(28), pp. 33–36] correctly points out that while decisions regarding social intervention are political, there are also good economic reasons behind them. The most important, of course, is the efficient allocation of scarce resources, especially in the context of developing countries where it is also necessary to strike a balance between economic planning and social planning. The term "social planning" is used here to imply the mobilization of human resources in a manner so that the active part of the population is trained and gainfully employed.

It is necessary to formulate a comprehensive plan for education and gainful employment of the available labor force. Accordingly, in the process of planning for education and training, one should move a step further and inquire about the ultimate use to which the output of various educational processes can be put. The latter stage requires that the products of the first stage should be distributed in the form of different types of skill among various sectors of the economy. The actual process of distribution will depend on two things: (1) the relationship between education and skill, and (2) the relationship between various skills and production techniques.

What needs to be emphasized is that planning for a meaningful solution to the problem of educational development does not necessarily solve the problem associated with the development of skilled manpower. The latter has to be formulated explicitly and the solution of the two must be sought simultaneously.

In the literature, quite often the distinction between the two aspects of human resource development mentioned above is forgotten. For example, the rate of return to investment in education is calculated separately for various levels of education usually defined in terms of number of years of schooling. This fails to bring out the proper relationship between education and economic activities (expressed in terms of various techniques of production), because no attempt is made to integrate into the analysis the intermediate step, which defines the process of formation of skills. More specifically, the rate of return approach can do no more than indicate the direction along which further investment may be socially desirable, while effective policy making, aimed at sectoral development, would demand that the planning technique throw adequate light on the relationship between education, occupation, and productivity.

The need for such integration of manpower and educational planning, as suggested above, indicates that any exercise in development planning should involve a three-stage optimizing procedure: (1) optimum levels of production of goods and services; (2) optimum levels of production of various skills; and (3) optimum levels of educational output, i.e., graduates from different levels of education [Alamgir (6), pp. 28–33; (7), pp. 200–204]. Correspondingly, the process entails decision making at three levels. However, in reality such optima can be reached only through an iterative procedure. At any point in time, the output of any stage mentioned above may be out of line with others, in which case an adjustment (upward or downward as the case may be) is warranted in the next iteration. Given the iterative solution of the problem, it follows that whatever the outcome of the decision-making process at each level may be separately, there must be an underlying mechanism through which these decisions are synchronized in order to achieve various implicit social objectives. The interdependence of various elements in development strategy has been incorporated in a number of studies [Adelman, (3), pp. 385–412; Benard (16), pp. 267–344; Gallady (34); Geier (35); Alamgir (6)].

Alamgir [(6), chapter 2] stresses the point that formulation of a comprehensive development plan incorporating the educational process must be preceded by a clear understanding of the three production processes: physical output, skill production, and educational output. Alternative specifications of the analytic form of the production function depend on the nature of the restrictions put on certain theoretical entities, e.g., the elasticity of substitution between different factors or production, the shape of the marginal productivity curve, the nature of the implied returns to scale. In the literature on education, emphasis has been placed on the concept of elasticity of substitution as between physical capital and labor, and as between various types of labor. Two extreme assumptions about the magnitude of these elasticities are known to be zero and infinity.[8] In a technical production function which may be related to physical output, one can strike a compromise between the extremes while conceptualizing the overall planning process in a developing country. One such possibility would be to allow for zero substitutability between physical capital and various types of labor, and unlimited substitutability over a limited range between various types of labor [Alamgir (6), chapter 2]. What needs to be underlined here is that labor input should be classified by levels of skill.

An analysis of the concept of the skill production function will help the understanding of the process of formation of skill and also the nature of interdependence between manpower and educational planning. Here, too, there are the extremists (particularly those who follow the fixed requirement approach in educational planning) who define a one-to-one correspondence between occupation or skill and the level of education. According to them, there is a particular level of education that is necessary to perform a given skill satisfactorily.

In general, one looks for some average or modal level of education to relate to a particular skill. Empirical evidence indicates that there is considerable dispersion in educational attainment within a particular occupational or skill category [Bowles (28), pp. 52–54]. The basic question is, can one be sure that the demand for education based on such a concept as the average or the mode would be optimal? One could work out the proportion of people with various qualifications within a skill group and project the future on the basis with the question of optimality remaining in the background. In essence, these methods tend to perpetuate the existing imbalance.

In empirical estimation of manpower supply and demand, the labor force is usually classified by years of schooling, thus avoiding the issue of specifying the skill production function. This actually conceals a lot of information. Years of schooling do not usually reveal differences in the nature of the job done by persons belonging to different occupational groups. On the one hand, it ignores the influence of factors other than education, and on the other hand, no distinction is made concerning the type of education received.

Among scholars who contributed to the field of manpower and educational planning, only Adelman (3) allowed for a separate skill production process, although she did not develop the concept rigorously. The same is true of the work done by two of her students [Gallady (34); Geier (35)]. Using basically Adelman's assumption regarding the elasticity of substitution between different educational inputs in the production of a skill, Alamgir [(6), pp. 45–46; (7), pp. 204–209] provided an analytic framework to articulate the concept of skill production function to be used in a manpower and educational plan.[9]

In order to formulate a plan for the development of the educational system, it is also necessary to have a clear understanding of the concept of the educational production function. After quantitative forecasts are made regarding the required number of graduates from each level of education, it will be necessary to determine the optimal production strategy for these graduates.

An educational production function should be helpful in this respect. But what is its form and what are the independent and the dependent variables? In general one can express number of graduates from a particular level as a function of the number of teachers, amount of physical facilities and their respective quality indexes, and a host of other factors. This creates two immediate problems on the output side. First, what does an educational level represent? Apparently, one usually aggregates several grades and labels them as a level although the basis of aggregation of different grades into one level is not always very clear. Second, how is the qualitative difference among graduates taken care of? The issue is, should the number of graduates be the dependent variable in an educational production function?

The question about the aggregation of different graduates into a single educational level is extremely important for a planner. The planning strategy usually covers the entire educational system. It is necessary to be able to formulate precise policy measures affecting the growth of education. In general, it is easier to provide a guiding framework in terms of the groups of levels of educational processes. The group concept here is analogous to the concept of industry in the economic system. But contrary to the economic system, there is no effective criterion for defining a group. On the one hand, one can stratify the entire spectrum of education by years of schooling; thus, the number of graduates in a group will refer to those with, say, one to six, seven to twelve, and above twelve years of schooling. Alternatively, a further dimension, based on the nature of the courses and training offered, can be added. This will render the graduates within a group a certain degree of homogeneity, although perhaps not to the most desirable extent. The second alternative is more desirable than the first and policies should be expressed in terms of projected enrollment in, say, primary, secondary, or teacher training education.

In empirical implementation of various educational planning models, a Leontief-type production function for the educational process has been specified [Adelman, (3), pp. 385–412; Bowles (26), pp. 189–219; Alamgir (6), pp. 56–59] and only observable and controllable inputs (e.g., teacher, building, equipment, etc.) have been taken into account. Bowles (27) attempted to estimate a more generalized form of the educational production function with score on a verbal achievement scale as the dependent variable and with various independent variables reflecting nonschool environment, general school environment, teacher quality, teacher quantity, school facilities, and student attitude. This direction of research awaits further work, especially in operationalizing its proxy variables, to be integrated into an overall planning framework. One cannot, however, deny that it throws further light on the complexities of educational processes and can prove useful in supplementing one's knowledge for policy formulation.

EDUCATIONAL PLANNING IN DEVELOPING COUNTRIES

Clearly, a sound factual basis of the underlying educational, skill production and material production processes must be developed before one can conceive of a plan for educational development. However, analytic exercises of the type mentioned above are necessary before one can choose among alternative approaches to educational planning available in the literature, or evolve a new one. More importantly, quantitative forecasts, in order to be realized, should be backed by a consistent policy package. It needs to be appreciated, particularly in the context of developing countries, that there are many substantive components and parameters related to an educational plan which are neither controllable nor measurable. No wonder, as Shamsul Huq [(62), chapter 1], points out, that developing countries are characterized by crises and tension arising from disequilibrium in the educational system due to imbalances in different markets.

One should distinguish between two markets, the education market and the labor market [Blaug (19), pp. 171–178]. Demand for education is both derived demand and direct demand, but demand for various types of labor (skills) is only derived demand. Therefore, the private and social demand for education is derived from the need of the individual and the society to acquire knowledge, broaden mental horizons, preserve the traditional cultural values, and improve upon them. Admittedly, some of these benefits to the society are largely subjective and difficult to measure. Problems arise because there is no useful way to distinguish between the consumption and the investment component of education.[10]

A situation of crisis and tension develops from three sources: (1) imbalance between demand and supply in the labor market; (2) imbalance between private demand and social demand for education; and finally, (3) imbalance between social demand for education and supply of education. The first source is the most important source of crisis and this should be the starting point for formulating a plan for manpower and educational development of developing countries. This is not to suggest that (2) and (3) should be relegated to the background; rather they should be accommodated (in the sense that corrective measures be taken) within the overall planning framework.

The different components of the labor and the education market are influenced to a varying degree by the different policy instruments which are available to the decision making authority. The matching of the policy instruments with targets is possible after the dynamics of interaction among variables operating in the two markets are clearly understood. As mentioned before, this is possible within a comprehensive plan for manpower and educational development. Need for such planned development has been felt in most developing countries where the financing and administration of education are largely concentrated in the hands of the state, particularly those related to primary and higher education [Huq (62), chapter 7].

Educational planning has been looked at from two different points of view. One view sees it as an integral part of economic and manpower planning [Adelman (3); Benard (16); Houthakker (58); Alamgir (6)]. The other treats educational planning completely independently of other elements of planning; the economic elements, particularly total budgetary allocations, are considered exogenous to the system [Correa and Tinbergen (29); Parnes (80); Bowles (25)]. The latter is quite a common practice in some of the developing countries. Almost without exception, each new government of the country appoints an education commission to formulate educational policies for the country. It is only after recommendations are made to the government that it undertakes to work out the financial implications of the suggested policies. Hardly ever do the terms of reference of such a commission include the analysis of the economic and manpower consequences of their plan.

In some countries (e.g., Nigeria and India), educational plans were formulated on the basis of manpower forecasts [Ashby (13); Government of India (44), pp. 94, 99; Hunter (60), p. 23, Huq (62), p. 59]. However, such attempts failed to take into account all variables that affect the growth of the educational system. Apart from its consistency with the development of the economy and manpower, an educational plan must provide answers to a number of complex socio-political questions. Unfortunately, most of the existing approaches fail to do so and as such the framework suggested turns out to be inadequate to ensure a synchronized growth of the economic and the educational systems. A critical appraisal of educational planning techniques reveals this fact.

Evaluation of alternative methods of educational planning should be done applying some basic criteria. (1) How far are the underlying assumptions of the different approaches realistic for the countries concerned? (2) What are the questions that can be answered by the alternative methods? How important are these questions for the region concerned? (3) Can the policy measures suggested by different methods be easily implemented? (4) What are the data requirements and are they easily met in these countries? In the literature, the tendency has been to compare different planning methods without any particular reference to the environment in which they are being applied. Alternatively, Blaug (20), pp. 262–287, asserts that it may be useful to consider different methods of educational planning as complementary rather than competitive. But neither of the above approaches puts the role of educational planning in its proper perspective. Given the criteria (1) to (4) above, it is not possible to use more than one method for a particular situation without suitably modifying the basic assumptions Alternative approaches differ from one another in very fundamental ways and applicability of each depends on the actual state of the world. Any attempt to combine different methods with the given assumptions is likely to be illegitimate [Alamgir (8)]. Existing techniques have been evaluated by many [Sen (87), pp. 188–197; Bowles, (24), pp. 412–417; Hollister (56); Blaug (20), pp. 262–287; Bowles (28), pp. 134–175; Sen (89); Alamgir (6), pp. 63–92; (8), pp. 37–79]. Therefore, only a few general remarks will be made here:

1. Relatively more popular approaches (e.g., manpower requirement approach, social demand approach) do not lend themselves to optimization analysis except that the internal rate of return approach renders itself amenable to a semi-optimization procedure.

2. Most of the approaches are either vague or make extreme assumptions regarding processes involving production of skill and educational output.

3. The approaches which have so far been considered for policy formulation in different countries (e.g., manpower requirement approach, rate of return approach, and social demand approach) do not take account of the interdependence between manpower, educational, and economic development.

4. Whatever approach is adopted to suit a particular situation, a number of important questions remain unanswered. (1) Alternative approaches fail to take note of the risk and uncertainty associated with manpower and educational planning which necessarily involves a long gestation period. (2) Methods are not clear about the adjustment mechanism in response to major socio-political and structural changes. (3) None of the methods provides for evaluation of the consumption component of education. (4) Questions about distributional considerations are altogether ignored.

Needless to say, educational planning has a significant role to play in economy-wide planning. An integrated framework can determine, among other things, how resources should be allocated with and between education and other sectors. Two links between the economy and education can be identified. The first is what has already been highlighted, that the development of the educational system needs to keep pace with that of economic sectors so as to satisfy the demand for skilled labor. The second is that expansion of educational facilities requires resources that, given their general scarcity, compete with the demands of other sectors.

Most of the economy-wide planning models for developing countries fail to recognize that a skill shortage can emerge as a bottleneck to the process of growth. The main emphasis in planning was on efficient utilization of foreign exchange and capital. The fallacy of ignoring the skill constraint in a planning model originated from the treatment of labor as a homogeneous factor of production. The existing evidence of unemployment and underemployment was taken to be an indication of a surplus labor economy with a zero opportunity cost of all types of labor. A further assumption, implicit in the treatment of the skills mentioned above, was that the process of skill formation was completely exogenous to the economic system. Thus it was not clear how the demand for various skills originating from the economic activities would transmit itself to the educational system in a manner which would insure a balanced supply of graduates and dropouts in order to produce the necessary skills. It is no wonder that many of the developing countries are finding themselves in the paradoxical situation of abundance of unskilled labor and shortage of specialized skills.

The interdependence between educational planning and economy-wide planning has an important longitudinal dimension. The structure of education and manpower suggested by the optimum structure of output given by the planning exercise is likely to change over time in response to two factors. First, changes in the structure of demand as tastes and preferences for various commodities change due to changes in income and its distribution, thus leading to increased demand for those skills in which the new and more demanded commodities are intensive. Second, the labor force changes in terms of basic educational and training content of each skill. Over time, the average educational level of the population is likely to go up as greater opportunities will be available for a child to attend school. For example, in the United States, the educational attainment of workers within each occupational group has gone up over time without any reference to the minimum requirement for such a job [Folger and Nam (32), pp. 19–33]. Technical progress and its rate of diffusion [Nelson (76), pp. 1219–1248] among sectors as well as among individual firms will affect the structure of the labor force. To the extent to which developing countries rely on tied foreign aid, which implies production with imported technology, the skill structure will be exogenously determined and in that case the existing educational system or its projected development may be completely out of line with the pattern of economic development. In any case, a certain amount of structural change in the labor force is inevitable in countries moving from a very low level of education and technology to a more sophisticated technology.

OTHER ISSUES RELATED TO MANPOWER AND EDUCATIONAL PLANNING

An important issue which needs to be emphasized here is the disparity in distribution of educational opportunity. It is very closely linked with other forms of inequity in the society. The basic problem is one of conceptualizing the phenomenon of inequality in the distribution of educational benefit. The concept is clearly analogous to inequality in the distribution of income and wealth. But while there are relatively well-defined criteria in relation to measuring the degree of inequality in income and wealth, the situation is not as clear in the case of educational opportunity. In particular, there is some confusion as to what constitutes equal educational opportunity especially in the context of developing indices to measure the extent of inequality of educational opportunity.

The Organization for Economic Cooperation and Development conference on "Social Objectives in Educational Planning" [OECD (77)] attached three different meanings to the concept of equality of educational opportunity: (1) equal access to noncompulsory education for all youngsters of equivalent measured ability regardless of sex, race, place of residence, social class or other irrelevant criteria; (2) equal rates of participation in noncompulsory education by members of all social classes; (3) equal opportunity to acquire academic ability for youngsters of all social classes.

The emphasis on noncompulsory education is understandable to the extent that compulsory education necessarily implies an obvious attempt to establish a minimum degree of equality of educational opportunity. There are problems, however, with these definitions. One still needs to put some operational content into such expressions as "equal access," "equivalent measured ability," and "equal opportunity," which may not be very easy in the context of a developing society. Only the second definition renders itself to unambiguous interpretation, although it would perhaps have made more sense if reference had been made to equi-proportionate rates of participation with respect to school age-group populations. In this case, one could have derived an index of inequality analogous to the index of decile inequality in income distribution [Alamgir (9), p. 510].

A slightly different interpretation of equality of educational opportunity is given by Anderson and Bowman (11), pp. 359–360. They present the following four criteria and indicate that each one of them calls for a different set of policies: (1) an equal amount of education for everyone; (2) education sufficient to bring every child to a given standard; (3) education sufficient to permit each person to reach his potential; (4) continued opportunities for schooling so long as gains in learning per input of teaching match some agreed norm. The first concept is difficult to implement while the others require elaborate operational content. What emerges clearly from the above criteria is that the concept of equality of educational opportunity should contain a quantitative and a qualitative dimension. The quantitative dimension should refer to proportional representation on the basis of number. The qualitative dimension, however, does not have a unique ordinal scale since it refers to equal access after the prospective candidates have been normalized for differential socio-economic environment.

Discussions in the literature [Alamgir (9), pp. 510–511; Huq (62), chapter 7)] point out a number of manifestations of inequality in the distribution of educational facilities. (1) In general, in secondary and higher education, the student participation rate from higher social strata is greater than that from lower social strata. The narrowing of this gap seems to be a very slow process as seen from the experience of even a country like the United States. (2) The dropout rate is higher among students from economically disadvantaged classes as compared with other classes. (3) Selective schooling systems seem to favor upper income groups compared with lower-income groups. (4) For all comparable age groups and educational levels, the dropout rate is higher and student participation rate lower in rural areas as compared with urban areas. (5) At all levels of schooling, the female participation rate is much lower than the male participation rate. (6) Per student facilities (teachers, building space, equipment and other resources) are better in urban as compared with rural areas, and in government and private grammar schools as compared with other private schools within the same area. While many have shown concern with these apparent manifestations of inequality of educational opportunity, very little has been done by way of suggesting realistic policies for correcting the imbalances.

The distribution of educational opportunity is not independent of the distributions of income, wealth, and political power. Planning models have so far failed to take explicit account of the distributional aspects of development. Theoretically, the problem of integration is quite involved. Available techniques are not flexible enough to introduce distributional considerations within the structural framework. Programming models are somewhat more useful than others in this respect since under restrictive assumptions distributive components can be entered either into the objective function [Bowles (28), pp. 207–214] or into the set of constraints.

Another aspect of the educational process of considerable importance to developmental planning is the staggering problem of wastage in education faced by the developing countries. Huq (62), p. 143, defines wastage in terms of dropouts and repeaters adding a qualitative dimension "represented by the degree of retardation in intellectual and educational development due to an unfavorable environment within or outside the school, or in other words by the difference between the potential for educational development and the actual development." He does not present a specific measure of wastage in education. A generalized concept of wastage was earlier proposed by Nageshwara and Tikkiwal (75), pp. 229–236, who define it by $W_0 = (V + Z + V)/(X_1 + X_2 + Y + Z)$ where

X_1 = the number of fruitful years in the case of students,

X_2 = the number of fruitful years in the case of delayed students,

Y = the number of unfruitful or additional years spent in the course by the delayed successful students,

Z = the number of years spent in the course by students who are unable to complete the course,

V = the number of successful and delayed successful students where knowledge is not utilized in their jobs and takes care of wastage through inappropriate placement.

Kamat (67), pp. 5–12, proposes an unbiased sample estimate w_0 of the corresponding population estimate W_0. A number of problems associated with the measurement of the components of wastage are pointed out by Kamat.

An equally important task is to identify the determinants of wastage. The problem is both theoretical and empirical. Some of the factors which may affect dropout rates have been mentioned in the literature [Manzoor Ahmed (5), pp. 101–105; Alamgir (6), pp. 99–101; Huq (62), chapters 1 and 7], but no attempt has yet been made to specify a complete analytic form of the wastage function which could be meaningfully incorporated in an educational planning model (except for a crude attempt made by Alamgir (6), pp. 396–418. Reference may be made here to the fact that perhaps it will be worthwhile to establish a link with the more generalized version of an educational production function [Bowles (27)].

A GENERALIZED VIEW OF EDUCATIONAL PLANNING

Panitchpakdi (79), pp. 3–4, quotes resolution of a meeting of Latin American educators about the content of educational planning:

> a. comprehensive coverage, embracing all levels and parts of the educational system both in terms of quantity and quality; b. long-term perspective reaching beyond a single year to at least several years and, where possible, covering a period comparable to the length of formal education itself; c. complete integration of the educational plan with the planning of economic and social development.

The above presents a very generalized view of educational planning, the task of the planner now being to provide an analytic and operational (empirical and policy) content to it. It is difficult to incorporate all relevant factors within a single planning framework. A reasonable approach is to carry out planning in a number of stages. New questions can be raised at each stage and appropriate answers found. Once the social objectives are set, preferably through a process of political arbitration, the first task of planning would be to obtain a macro-economic allocation of resources between sectors. However, as a preparation for this stage, previous exercises must be carried out at a more disaggregated level so that regional peculiarities and potentials can be taken note of. As an analytic framework, either an input-output model or a programming model depending on the availability of data and of computational facilities can be adopted. Sectoral allocation of resources in some of the developing countries (e.g., Bangladesh, India,

Pakistan) is known to have been based on input-output exercises.

The second stage will involve detailed micro-project analysis within each sector including education. It is likely to bring out some of the inconsistencies hidden in the results of the more aggregated model. Depending on the outcome of the sectoral and project planning exercises, one may have to revise the computation of the original model. In essence what one needs as an operational document is a "rolling" plan, reviewed continually and at least annually, and adapted to new information [Blaug and Streeten (21), p. 393]. Any single exercise (calculate a few rates of return, forecast manpower demand on the basis of fixed requirement approach, or solve a programming model) is not enough to produce the policy package which will ensure a continuous socio-economic balance.

At the sectoral planning stage, the influence of all complex socio-political variables on the educational sector must be carried out in as much detail as possible. For example, the curriculum of each educational level should be so chosen that it provides a balanced teaching of technical, cultural and political aspects of skill formation [Suchodolski (92), pp. 516–522]. The idea is that an individual will not only be an economic agent of production, he/she must also be a social agent of production. Furthermore, an estimate of the social demand for education should be made in order to avoid the kind of imbalances referred to above. The planner has to derive a policy package insuring that supply matches demand. As a final general note on educational planning in developing countries, the following quote from Blaug and Streeten (21), p. 393, appears very relevant.

> Because of the narrow margins of tolerance and the closeness of many underdeveloped countries to misery and starvation, it is crucially important that minimum needs are estimated and that the required combination of measures is planned and executed. Failure to execute complementary measures can spell disaster. The isolation of "educational" expenditure distracts attention from the urgent need, not only to select the right type of education, but also to combine it with the provisions of better seeds, drainage, and fertilizers, with land reform and price stabilization, with improvements in transport and birth control, with the improvements of rural amenities, with a reform of recruitment to the Civil Service and business management. The waste involved in not planning for the required complementarities and pushing education too far, can be detrimental to development.

EDUCATIONAL PLANNING IN BANGLADESH

Research on manpower and educational planning has been relatively neglected in Bangladesh. Several planning models were developed to analyze the process of economic growth of Pakistan (including Bangladesh) and to derive policy conclusions for future development. Alamgir (6) developed a separate model for Bangladesh (then East Pakistan) where the growth path of the country was projected over a 20-year planning horizon and its implication for manpower and educational development was worked out. The study revealed that higher-level skills emerge as binding constraints over time. This reinforces the earlier assertion that the assumption that the opportunity cost of all types of skill is zero is likely to be grossly misleading. In that model the adjustment to skill scarcity was carried out by changing the educational composition of the new labor force. Interestingly enough, it appeared that the process of adjustment through the educational distribution of the new labor force could be carried out only up to a limited extent. Beyond a certain point, the structure of education itself became an important bottleneck, implying that adjustment in the structure will be necessary in order to ease the skill scarcity situation.

As expected, primary education came out as the most important component of the educational system of Bangladesh. Another important finding was that investment in the reduction of the dropout rate was very profitable since it led to a reduction in wastes in education and also in the relative scarcity of all skills. However, these and other conclusions derived from the study refer to pre-independent Bangladesh.

Between the pre-liberation and post-liberation Bangladesh four different commissions [Government of Pakistan (45, 46, 47); Government of Bangladesh (37)], were appointed to analyze problems related to the education sector and to make recommendations. These documents discuss at length some of the fundamental problems which are particularly relevant to different educational processes as well as personnel (teachers and students) attached to them, but unfortunately they fail to emphasize a unified strategy for the development of education as a source of skilled manpower. Different reports came out in favor of different types of education without any particular reference to the ultimate needs of the economy over time in terms of various types of skill.

The first Education Commission Report of 1959 [Government of Pakistan, 45)] put greater emphasis on secondary and higher education at the cost of elementary education. On the whole, the Report emphasized the role of education in national development without elaborating the economic consequences of educational development. The Report of 1969 takes the above report to task [Government of Pakistan (47), p. 20] for such an unbalanced emphasis on one aspect of education and points out that higher priority should be attached to elementary education on the one hand, and technical and vocational education on the other. This, it says, provides the proper answer to the present problem of widespread unemployment among the educated youth. The question as to exactly how it is accomplished with actual reference to supply and demand for various types of skills within the economy is not raised at all.[11] The fourth Education Commission (Government of Bangladesh (37), p. 293) emphasizes universal primary education (the concept of primary education being extended to cover the first eight years of schooling instead of six) to be attained over a ten-year period. The other important recommendations include introduction of science and agricultural education at the primary level, upgrading of their quality at all levels, and making education work-oriented. The latter has also been highlighted in the recently published draft report of the National Curriculum Committee [Government of Bangladesh (39) 1976].[12] All of these recommendations, while philosophically quite well taken, are somewhat empty in the sense that they are not related to the demand for skills. More importantly, they generally imply a substantial growth of formal education within a short period of time without regard to its already distorted structure.

The different economic development plans being concomitantly formulated lagged far behind the recommendations of the Education Commission reports in the sense that they neither attempted to critically evaluate these recommendations nor did they attempt to integrate them into the main stream of planning so that a meaningful manpower and educational plan could emerge. The First Five-Year Plan of Bangladesh [Government of Bangladesh (40), p. 441] presents a critique of earlier plans because of their emphasis on a linear expansion strategy for the education sector without a commensurate manpower plan. But the proposals in the First Plan itself do not go beyond what is said above. Although the Plan carries out a very crude exercise on employment projection, it does not present a manpower plan as such and the suggested framework for educational development appears to be inconsistent with the projected economic growth. The planners do not seem to have had a proper appreciation of the basic issues in economic, manpower, and educational planning to which extensive references have been made earlier in the paper. Bangladesh probably is not an exception; a similar trend is observable in a number of other developing countries.

The absence of comprehensive planning for manpower and educational development has been reflected in: (1) imbalance in educational development; (2) high wastage in education; and (3) high overall rates of unemployment and underemployment. Imbalance in education can be seen from the relative enrollments in different levels as well as in the relative rates of growth. On the one hand, at the second and third level only a small proportion of the age group population is enrolled; on the other hand, the rate of growth in higher education is much higher than primary education—the result being a very high absolute increase in enrollment at higher secondary levels and above [Huq (63), pp. 3–4]. In a country where age-specific enrollment rates are very low, this emphasis on higher education at the cost of primary education should have adverse distributional effects, especially when also considering the high adult illiteracy rate, where investment in nonformal education should be given serious consideration.[13]

We now turn to a brief examination of the efficiency of the education system in Bangladesh. Available data on the wastage in education present a staggering picture. The rate of failure is very high, particularly in higher education [Huq (63), pp. 4–5]. A substantial portion of new entrants at the primary level drop out of the system. Manzoor Ahmed [(5), p. 100] quotes a UNESCO study of the late 1960s which places Pakistan (including Bangladesh) in the medium enrollment (30–69 percent) and high wastage (over 56 percent) category with respect to lower grades (I and II) of the primary level. A study by the Planning Department of the Government of East Pakistan [Government of East Pakistan (43), Tables 4–1–1] revealed that during the early 1950s more than 75 percent of students enrolled in grade I dropped out before they completed even three years of school. Although this study and a later one [Rabbani and Arif (81), p. 63] indicated some improvement, the situation by and large remains very alarming. The dropout rate is much higher among female students than male students and in rural areas than in urban areas. Available evidence from different studies [M. Ahmed (5), pp. 101–103; Islam (64), p. 117] indicates the following as causes of the high dropout rate in Bangladesh: poverty, parental neglect, scattered location of schools, cultural prejudice, marriage, quality of school facilities, and quality of teaching. Furthermore, the rate of failure among those who survive beyond the secondary level is also very high [Huq (63), pp. 4–5]. It is evident that the allocation of resources within the education system in Bangladesh needs reconsideration.

Finally, there is evidence of considerable unemployment and underemployment in Bangladesh. One estimate by Alamgir (10), p. 35, places the figure at 32 percent for rural areas in 1973–74. Scanty evidence for selected urban areas for the mid-1960s [Ahmed (4), p. 247] gives figures between 29 percent and 48 percent for the proportion of unemployed in the labor force. A fairly exhaustive account of unemployment among the educated is given in a recent publication of the Bangladesh Planning Commission [Government of Bangladesh (37)]. The central finding of this study is that, as of 1973–1974, 44 percent of the educated labor force (i.e., all economically active persons with secondary school certificate or above degree) in Bangladesh are unemployed. While debate will continue over the reliability of alternative estimates, the following will probably be acknowledged as the relatively important causes of the phenomenon of unemployment and underemployment; (1) rapid growth of population and labor force; (2) slow growth of the economy and its deformed structure; (3) inappropriate technology reflected in the capital intensity of some Bangladeshi industries which is partly due to structural dependence on imported technology through foreign aid; (4) inequality in the distribution of asset ownership, particularly land, and the existing tenurial practices; (5) rural-urban migration; (6) imbalance in the educational structure; (7) high rate of growth of formal education; and (8) high rate of dropouts. The size of the problem is obviously very large and a massive effort will be necessary to tackle it. Bangladesh exemplifies a case where total synchronization of the economic, manpower, and educational planning is essential and an appreciation of the underlying theoretical and policy issues is necessary.

FOOTNOTES

1. Schultz (86), pp. 124–131, points out that years of school completed understates changes in the stock of education because no adjustment is made for length of schooling. Such adjustment produces a measure in constant school years completed which also understates changes in the stock of education as equal weights are given to different levels of education. To overcome this, Schultz suggested a third measure which is to use the cost of different levels of education as weights and obtain a combined estimate in terms of total cost of education. However, he himself points out that a "measure based on costs of schooling is also an incomplete estimate of the stock of education. It does not distinguish between the younger and older workers in the labor force in measuring their education" (85), p. 130. The alternative measure suggested by Griliches does represent an improvement because, if properly estimated, it can correct for the deficiencies mentioned above.

2. The relative weights used for the two components are 1 and 5, respectively. Use of these weights has been rightly questioned by Sen (87), pp. 69–70. His more substantive criticism is directed to the meaning of the index. In his words, "for them the index seems to stand for some kind of a guide to the stock of human resources, whereas as far as I can see, it tells us nothing more than the rate at which people are making additions to stock" [Sen (88), pp. 70–71].

3. They prefer to call the coefficient associated with the human factor in the aggregate production function the "coefficient of our ignorance" [Blaug and Streeten (21), p. 384].

4. Uzawa (93) and Aarrestad (1) have attempted, on a theoretical level, to determine the optimal level of investment in education in an aggregative model, but without empirical validation.

5. Becker (14), chapter VII, analyzed the U.S. data and made the following general observations about the age earnings profile: (1) education brings about an upward shift in the profile; (2) it tends to increase the slope of the profile; and finally (3) the profile is moved to the right, that is, the peak is reached later. The last point reflects the fact that better-educated persons have a greater capability to learn from experience and from training received. Related to this, the influence of on-the-job training has been studied extensively by Mincer (74).

6. The authors point out that the three predictions that follow from the screening hypothesis are not borne out by fact. The predictions are: (1) private returns are to certificates and not to years of schooling; (2) private returns to education fall with work experience; (3) education will not be demanded if (privately) cheaper screening methods exist [Layard and Psacharopoulos (71), pp. 989–995].

7. An important contribution relevant for developed countries involving the relationship between age, experience, earnings, and investment in human capital is made by Kelmarken and Quigley (68), pp. 47–72. They take issue with the conventional practice

of measuring experience by calendar age and establish convincingly "the necessity for distinguishing between experience and age in analyses of investment in human capital" (68), p. 47.

8. Three well-known forms of production function are fixed coefficient, Cobb-Douglas, and CES which are derived by putting restrictions on the implied elasticities of substitutions. Singh (90) derives a very general form of production function of which the above three are special cases.

9. Various types of skills are measured in efficiency units as opposed to absolute numbers [Adelman, (3), p. 388; Alamgir (6), pp. 50–54; (7), pp. 205–208]. Elasticity of substitution between different educational inputs in the skill production function is assumed to be infinity. To be more precise, skill in efficiency units is represented as the weighted average of educational inputs (measured in absolute units), the weights reflecting the relative productivity of different inputs. It was assumed that observed earnings represent the marginal productivity of a factor input.

10. As a consumption item, analysis of demand for education is analogous to demand for any other goods and services. Education should, however, be treated as a consumer durable item. Its utility is not derived only at a point of time, rather it is distributed over time. Besides, unlike many other commodities, it may not be subject to diminishing marginal utility. As an individual obtains more education, the utility derived from additional units of education may be increasing. Clearly, if account is not taken of this component while formulating an educational development plan, it may be very difficult to obtain a balance between the supply and demand for various types of educated personnel.

11. For technical education, the Report recommends that "the educational policy should aim at raising the proportion of those enrolled in vocational and technical subjects at the secondary stage to 60 percent of the total enrollment at that stage" [Government of Pakistan (47), p. 23]. This implies a fundamental shift in the structure of education. It was recommended without any analysis of the capacity of the economy to absorb these graduates. Had this policy prescription been adopted, by now the problem of the educated unemployed would have assumed an even greater proportion than what it already has today. One is reminded of the vocational school fallacy as experienced in Ghana [Foster (33), pp. 396–423].

12. In this context one can refer to the pilot "open air school scheme" introduced by the Ministry of Education at grades I through V in rural school since the beginning of 1976 [Government of Bangladesh (38)]. The experiment involves introduction and involvement of students outside the classroom to various activities of everyday life. Preliminary evaluation carried out after the first phase of the program indicated considerable success in terms of raising the awareness of the students and teachers regarding value of work-oriented education although it is too early to specify further direct benefits to the society. One may also refer here to the concept of community schools suggested by Mahtab (72). In this experiment, academic curriculum is integrated with work experience in development projects.

13. Nonformal education, as popularly understood, refers to that component of learning that is imparted outside the formal schooling system. In Bangladesh, attempts at spreading nonformal education have been carried out only on an experimental basis. An evaluation of a number of selected projects was carried out by a committee appointed by the Planning Commission [Government of Bangladesh (38)]. The committee's findings were mixed. It recommended among other things integration of the nonformal education program with other development programs at the local and regional level.

REFERENCES

1. Aarrestad, Jostin. (1975) "On the Optimal Allocation of Labour to the Education Sector," *Swedish Journal of Economics* 77:303–317.
2. Abramovitz, Moses. (1956) "Resource and Output Trends in the U.S. Since 1870," *American Economic Review* 46:5–23.
3. Adelman, Irma. (1966) "A Linear Programming Model of Educational Planning: A Case Study of Argentina," in *The Theory and Design of Economic Development*, eds. Irma Adelman and Erik Thorbecke, Baltimore: The Johns Hopkins University Press, pp. 385–412.
4. Ahmed, Iftikhar. (1974) "Employment in Bangladesh: Problems and Prospects," in *The Economic Development of Bangladesh*, eds. E.A.G. Robinson and Keith B. Griffin, London: Macmillan, pp. 238–259.
5. Ahmed, Manzoor. (1969) "The Problem of Educational Dropout in East Pakistan," in *Education is Progress*, ed. Abdullah Al-Mati Sharafuddin, Proceedings of the Symposia, East Pakistan Education Week, 1968. Dacca: The Star Press, pp. 93–111.
6. Alamgir, M. (1971) "A Planning Model for East Pakistan with Special Emphasis on Manpower and Education," unpublished doctoral dissertation, Cambridge, Mass.: Harvard University.
7. ———. (1973) "Some Theoretical Issues in Manpower and Educational Planning," *Bangladesh Economic Review* 1:199–212.
8. ———. (1974) "Alternative Approaches to Educational Planning—Their Relevance to a Developing Economy," *Economic Echo*, Chittagong University, Bangladesh, pp. 37–79.
9. ———. (1975) "Education, Manpower and Development in South and Southeast Asia," *Bangladesh Development Studies* III:505–524.
10. ———. (1976) "Bangladesh: A Case of Below Poverty Level Equilibrium Trap," Bangladesh Institute of Development Studies, mimeo.
11. Anderson, C. A., and M. J. Bowman. (1968) "Theoretical Considerations in Educational Planning," in *Economics of Education I*, ed. M. Blaug, Baltimore: Penguin Books, pp. 351–382.
12. Arrow, K. J. (1973) "Higher Education as a Filter," *Journal of Public Economics* 2:193–216.
13. Ashby, Sir Eric. (1960) *Investment in Education: The Report of the Commission on Post School Certificate and Higher Education in Nigeria*, Nigeria: Federal Ministry of Education.
14. Becker, Gary S. (1964) *Human Capital*, New York: National Bureau of Economic Research.
15. ———, and Barry R. Chiswick. (1966) "Education and Distribution of Earnings," *American Economic Review* 61:358–369.
16. Benard, Jean. (1967) "General Optimization Model for the Economy and Education," in *Mathematical Models in Educational Planning*, Paris: OECD, pp. 267–344.
17. Ben-Porath, Yoram. (1967) "The Production of Human Capital and the Life Cycle of Earnings," *Journal of Political Economy* 75:352–365.
18. Blandy, R. (1967) "Marshall on Human Capital: A Note," *Journal of Political Economy* 75:874–875.
19. Blaug, M. (1966) "An Economic Interpretation of Private Demand for Education," *Economica* 33:171–178.
20. ———. (1967) "Approaches to Educational Planning," *Economic Journal* 77:262–287.
21. ———, and P. Streeten. (1968) "The Planning of Education in Poor Countries,"

in *Economics of Education I*, ed. M. Blaug, Baltimore: Penguin Books, pp. 383–395.
22. Blinder, Alan S., and Yoram Weiss. (1976) "Human Capital and Labour Supply: A Synthesis," *Journal of Political Economy* 84:449–472.
23. Bowen, W. G. (1963) "Assessing the Economic Contribution of Education: An Appraisal of Alternative Approaches," *Higher Education Report of the Committee under the Chairmanship of Lord Robbins* 1961–63, London, H.M.S.O., Appendix IV, pp. 73–96, reproduced in *Economics of Education I*, ed. M. Blaug, Baltimore: Penguin Books, pp. 67–100.
24. Bowles, Samuel. (1966) "Comments on Irma Adelman's Programming Model of Educational Planning," in *The Theory and Design of Development*, eds. Irma Adelman and Erik Thorbecke, Baltimore: The Johns Hopkins University Press, pp. 412–417.
25. ———. (1967) "Sources of Growth in the Greek Economy 1951–1961," Memorandum No. 27, Development Advisory Service, Center for International Affairs, Harvard University, mimeo.
26. ———. (1967) "The Efficient Allocation of Resources in Education," *Quarterly Journal of Economics* 81:189–219.
27. ———. (November 1968) "Towards an Educational Production Function," paper presented at the NBER Conference on Income and Education, mimeo.
28. ———. (1969) *Planning Educational System for Economic Growth*, Cambridge, Mass.: Harvard University Press.
29. Correa, Hector, and Jan Tinbergen. (1962) "Quantitative Adaptation of Education to Accelerated Growth," *Kyklos* 15:776–785.
30. Denison, Edward F. (1962) *Sources of Growth in the U.S. and the Alternative Before Us*, New York: The Committee on Economic Development.
31. ———. (1967) *Why Growth Rates Differ: The Post War Experience in Nine Western Countries*, Washington, D.C.: The Brookings Institution.
32. Folger, John K., and Charles B. Nam. (1964) "Trends in Education in Relation to the Occupational Structure," *Sociology of Education* 38:19–33.
33. Foster, P. J. (1968) "The Vocational School Fallacy in Development Planning," in *Economics of Education I*, ed. M. Blaug, Baltimore: Penguin Books, pp. 396–423.
34. Gallady, F. L. (1969) "A Dynamic Linear Programming Model for Educational Planning with Application to Morocco," unpublished doctoral dissertation, Chicago: Northwestern University.
35. Geier, Marshal Lee. (1969) "An Educational Planning Model for Chile," unpublished doctoral dissertation, Chicago: Northwestern University.
36. Gounden, Nalla A. M. (1965) "Education and Economic Development," unpublished doctoral dissertation, India: Kurukshetra University.
37. Government of Bangladesh, Ministry of Education. (1974) Bangladesh *Shikhya Commission Report*. Dacca: Bangladesh Government Press.
38. ———. (1975) *Muktangan Shikhya Kram*, Dacca: Bangladesh Government Press.
39. ———. (1976) "Draft Report of the National Curriculum Committee, Part I," Dacca: Bangladesh Government Press.
40. ———, Planning Commission. (1973) *The First Five Year Plan 1973–78*, Dacca: Bangladesh Government Press.
41. ———. (1974) *Employment Market for the Educated in Bangladesh*, Dacca: Bangladesh Government Press.
42. ——— (1975) *The Report of the Committee on Nonformal Education*. Dacca: Bangladesh Government Press.
43. Government of East Pakistan, Bureau of Statistics. (1969) *Manpower Planning in East Pakistan*, Dacca: East Pakistan Government Press.

44. Government of India, Ministry of Education. (1966) *Report of the India Education Commission (1964–66) Education and National Development*, New Delhi: Government of India Press.
45. Government of Pakistan, Ministry of Education. (1959) *Report of the Commission on National Education*, Karachi: Government of Pakistan Press.
46. ———. (1966) *Report of the Commission on Student Problems and Social Welfare*, Karachi: Government of Pakistan Press.
47. ———. (1969) *Proposals for a New Educational Policy*, Karachi: Manager of Publications.
48. Griliches, Zvi. (May 1963) "Estimates of Aggregate Agricultural Production Function from Cross-Sectional Data," *Journal of Farm Economics* 45, No. 2 : 419–428.
49. ———. (August 1963) "The Sources of Measured Productivity Growth: United States Agriculture, 1940–60," *Journal of Political Economy* 71 : 331–346.
50. ———. (December 1964) "Research Expenditures, Education and the Aggregate Agricultural Production Function," *American Economic Review* 54 : 961–974.
51. ———. (November 1968) "Notes on Role of Education in Production Functions and Growth Accounting," paper presented at NBER Conference on Income and Education.
52. Haley, William J. (December 1973) "Human Capital: The Choice Between Investment and Income," *American Economic Review* 63, No. 5 : 929–944.
53. Hanoch, Giora. (1965) "Personal Earnings and Investment in Schooling," unpublished doctoral dissertation, Chicago: University of Chicago.
54. Harberger, Arnold C., and M. Selowsky. (June 1966) "Key Factors in the Economic Growth of Chile: An Analysis of the Sources of Past Growth and of the Prospects for 1965–70," Report 6611, Center for Mathematical Studies in Business and Economics, University of Chicago, mimeo.
55. Harbison, F. H., and C. A. Meyers. (1964) *Education, Manpower and Economic Growth*, New York: McGraw-Hill.
56. Hollister, Robinson G. (1966) *A Technical Evaluation of the First State of the Mediterranean Regional Project*, Paris: Organization for Economic Cooperation and Development.
57. Horvat, B. (December 1958) "The Optimum Rate of Investment," *Economic Journal* 68 : 747–767.
58. Houthakker, H. S. (February 1969) "Education and Income," *Review of Economics and Statistics* 41 : 24–28.
59. Hunter, Guy. (1963) *Education for a Developing Region, A Study in East Africa*, London: George Allen & Unwin.
60. ———. (1966) *Manpower, Economy and Education in the Rural Economy of Tanzania*, Paris: UNESCO, International Institute for Educational Planning.
61. ———. (1967) *Higher Education and Development in Southeast Asia, Volume III, High Level Manpower*, Paris: UNESCO.
62. Huq, Shamsul. (1975) *Education, Manpower and Development in South and Southeast Asia*, New York: Praeger.
63. ———. (1975) *Higher Education and the Dilemmas of Poor Countries: A Search for New Paths in Bangladesh*, Dacca: The Foundation for Research on Educational Planning and Development.
64. Islam, Taherul. (1973) *Social Justice and the Education System of Bangladesh*, Dacca: Bureau of Economic Research, University of Dacca.
65. Johnson, E. A. J. (1964) "The Place of Learning, Science, Vocational Training and 'Art' in Pre-Smithian Economic Thought," *Journal of Economic History* 24 : 129–144.

66. Judge, George G. (1963) "Discussion: Estimates of the Aggregate Agricultural Production Function from Cross-Sectional Data," *Journal of Farm Economics* 45:429–432.
67. Kamat, A. R. (1968) "Estimating Wastage in a Course of Education," *Sankhya*, Series B, Vol. 30:5–12.
68. Kelmarken, Anders, and John M. Quigley. (1976) "Age, Experience, Earnings and Investment in Human Capital," *Journal of Political Economy* 84, No. 1.
69. Kendrick, John W. (1961) *Productivity Trends in the United States*, Princeton, N.J.: Princeton University Press.
70. Kiker, B. F. (1969) "Von Thunen on Human Capital," *Oxford Economic Papers* (New Series) 21:339–343.
71. Layard, Richard, and George Psacharopoulos. (1974) "The Screening Hypothesis and Returns to Education," *Journal of Political Economy* 82:985–998.
72. Mahtab, F. U. (1975) "Community School—An Education for Development," Dacca: mimeo.
73. Mincer, Jacob. (1958) "Investment in Human Capital and Personal Income Distribution," *Journal of Political Economy* 64:281–302.
74. ———. (1962) "On-the-Job Training: Costs, Returns, and Some Implications," *Journal of Political Economy* 60, No. 5, Part 2, Supplement:50–73.
75. Nageshwara, Rao G., and B. D. Tikkiwal. (1966) "An Integrated Approach to the Study of Wastage in a Given Course of Education," *Shakhya*, Series B, Vol. 28, Parts 3 & 4:229–236.
76. Nelson, Richard R. (1968) "A Diffusion Model of International Productivity Differences in Manufacturing Industry," *American Economic Review* 58:1219–1248.
77. Organization for Economic Cooperation and Development. (1967) *Social Objectives in Educational Planning*, Paris: Organization for Economic Cooperation and Development.
78. Oulton, Nicholas. (1974) "The Distribution of Education and the Distribution of Income," *Economica* 41:387–402.
79. Panitchpakdi, S. (1974) *Educational Growth in Developing Countries*, Rotterdam: Rotterdam University Press.
80. Parnes, H. S. (1962) *Forecasting Educational Needs for Economic and Social Development*, Paris: Organization for Economic Cooperation and Development.
81. Rabbani, Ghulam A. K. M., and Abu Ahmed Arif. (1971) *Education and Employment in East Pakistan*, Dacca: Bangladesh Government Press.
82. Schaffer, Harry G. (1961) "Investment in Human Capital: Comment," *American Economic Review* 51:1026–1035.
83. Schultz, T. W. (1961) "Investment in Human Capital," *American Economic Review* 51:1–17.
84. ———. (1961) "Educational and Economic Growth," in *Social Forces Influencing American Education*, ed. Nelson B. Henry, Chicago: University of Chicago Press, pp. 46–88.
85. ———. (1963) *The Economic Value of Education*, New York: Columbia University Press.
86. ———. (1971) *Investment in Human Capital*, New York: The Free Press, p. 272.
87. Sen, A. K. (1964) "Comments on the Paper by Messrs Tinbergen and Bos," OECD Study Group in the Economics of Education, *The Residual Factor and Economic Growth*. Paris: Organization for Economic Cooperation and Development, pp. 188–197.
88. ———. (1968) "The Index of Human Resource Development," in *Economics of Education I*, ed. M. Blaug, Baltimore: Penguin Books, pp. 67–75.

89. ———. (1969) "Models of Educational Planning and their Applications," Mimeo.
90. Singh, S. K. (1969) "Models of Production Relation," unpublished doctoral dissertation, Cambridge, Mass.: Harvard University.
91. Solow, Robert M. (1957) "Technical Change and Aggregate Production Function," *Review of Economics and Statistics* 39 : 312–320.
92. Suchodolski, Bogdan. (1966) "Balance between Cultural and Technical Education," in *The Economics of Education*, eds. E. A. G. Robinson and J. E. Vaizey, London: Macmillan, pp. 516–522.
93. Uzawa, H. (1965) "Optimum Technical Change in an Aggregative Model of Economic Growth," *International Economic Review* 1 : 18–31.
94. Weisman, Jack. (1965) "Cost-Benefit Analysis in Education," *Southern Economic Journal* 32, Part 2 : 1–12.
95. Welch, F. (1968) "Education in Production," Southern Methodist University: mimeo.

BARRIERS TO EDUCATIONAL DEVELOPMENT IN UNDERDEVELOPED COUNTRIES: WITH SPECIAL REFERENCE TO VENEZUELA

Kristin Tornes, UNIVERSITY OF BERGEN

INTRODUCTION

Educational ideologies of developed societies are now "exported" by private and public development programs to underdeveloped countries where they serve as a panacea for development and industrialization, and as requirements for qualifying for loans from international financial agencies. Furthermore, such ideologies are increasingly adopted by large sections of the population of developing societies as the main road to economic success and personal prestige. The main point to be underlined in this article is that these ideologies may turn out to be an obstacle to development given

Research in Human Capital and Development, Vol. 1, pp. 149–167.
ISBN: 0–89232–019–2

the dependent nature of the economies and class structures of the countries to which they are exported.

This line of reasoning will be supported first by discussing educational development in general, and the function of educational institutions in underdeveloped societies in particular. We will then try to detect how the educational ideologies of developed societies may function as barriers to educational development at the societal level and to educational achievement at the individual level. We then discuss in some detail educational development in Venezuela as an example of our general thesis.

DEFINING EDUCATIONAL DEVELOPMENT

The main functions of the socializing agents in a society can be seen to be "(1) the provision of a mode of childhood currently thought proper for the culture as a whole; (2) the provision of facilities for certain aspects of child unbringing thought to be necessary; and (3) the inculcation of skills, knowledge, and ideas thought of as necessary life-enablements for society later on" [Levitas (21), p. 17]. Educational institutions mainly take care of the last of these functions.

Educational development will be defined here as changes in the educational institutions of a given society so that these contribute to an increasingly more equal distribution among the population at large of skills, knowledge, and ideas thought of as necessary for a prosperous life. Herein are also included knowledge and ideas which enable members of a society to participate in the political decisions that determine the quality of life and the level of living in general in that society.

In the history of Western ideologies of education, two major arguments have predominated during the last hundred years or so about how educational institutions should function in order to secure for the population at large a greater share of the fruits of economic progress. These ideologies are also clearly related to changing needs of the economy which have mainly centered around the need for mobilizing talents in order to increase production and profits through the increasing technological sophistication and rationalization of the process of production. We may distinguish among arguments centering around equal formal access to educational institutions and schooling, and equality of educational resources [Hernes (16)]. Arguments for general educational reforms were not voiced very strongly until labor became a relatively scarce resource in the production process. As long as labor was considered brawn power and not brain power, schooling was accepted as the exclusive privilege of the ruling classes serving as a means by which they could preserve their upper-class culture and manners and keep themselves distinct from the rest of the population. There were rules defining which schools the various social classes were admitted to, upholding a strict class barrier also when it came to curricula and values transmitted to the pupils. It was almost unheard of for the son of a worker to go through more than basic schooling. Even for the up-and-coming industrialists' sons it proved difficult to gain admittance to the upper-class schools before the industrial/capitalist structure had a stronger hold in societies which hitherto had been mostly agricultural. In such societies, social standing had been judged on the basis of land owner-ship. Transmission of qualifications needed in the production process was accomplished by apprenticeships and on-the-job training, which was how merchants, farmers, and those in handicrafts learned their trades [Vaughan and Archer (36); Tornes (34)].

I have gone into some detail on this because it bears importance to the argument that demand from the socio-economic structure has been basic in calling forth changes in ideologies pertaining to schooling and education. For Western societies it is clear that the political claim of equal formal access to education for all males did not become a public issue until there had been a rising demand for an increased level of general education due mainly to economic reasons. The increasing demand for new technology and the consequent increasing level of automation in the economy called for a change. A lack of qualified persons to fill jobs was seen as due to res-trictive educational laws and practices which had their basis in a pre-capitalist social order. This put heavy pressure on established institutions to break the existing social hierarchy and allow an increasing amount of social mobility in order to recruit and educate technological talents and expertise.

Apart from the purely economic reasons for this new ideology, one should not overlook the humanistic ideas as well, which certainly were an important force in securing new educational laws. These laws defined basic education as the right of every child, often prescribing a minimum amount of schooling as compulsory. For the first time, the state was also held to bring responsible for promoting the level of schooling among the population. This can be seen as a beginning in the development of the welfare state, resulting partly because the government was now voicing the interests of new groups in society, as against those of the traditional elites.

It became clear, however, that formal rights to enter educational institu-tions did not accomplish their intent of increasing the mobility of talents and thereby of increasing distribution of the benefits of industrialization to larger sections of the population. Equality of educational resources, therefore, gradually became the new ideology. Basic to it was the idea that talents and educational accomplishments depend on IQ and individual abilities which were seen as being equally distributed among children from the various social classes. Only by offering the same kind and scope of educational facilities to all children at the same educational level, however, would their abilities find the proper climate for growth. Increasing investments in education thus became an important public duty. Given the fact that all children now theoretically had equal access to the same resources in school, the responsibility for educational failure was no longer laid to lack of educational facilities but to meager talents and low IQs in the children themselves. Educational failure was thus defined as personal failure because formal barriers to educational achievement no longer existed.

In order to get a better understanding of how these ideas of educational development have come to function within the context of underdeveloped societies, we will have to relate them more closely to their socio-economic structure. Only in this way can we become aware of how these ideas which have promoted educational participation in developed societies may work as barriers against such a development in underdeveloped ones. We will therefore discuss at some length the function of education and schooling in societies in general, and underdeveloped societies in particular.

THE FUNCTION OF EDUCATION AND SCHOOLING IN UNDERDEVELOPED SOCIETIES

Educational institutions in underdeveloped societies equip children with the skills, knowledge, and ideas they need to function in the future in a way which is defined as proper within existing social structures. Viewing the role of education in this light implies two basic assumptions. First, educational institutions are seen as functioning mainly to uphold the existing culture of a society by passing on ideals and values that support the structure on which the culture is based. These values legitimize both existing power and class structures as well as the mode of production and consumption in the society. Secondly, educational institutions have as another of their main functions the provision of those skills and knowledge most in demand from the economy of the society. These are also the kind of qualifications which are said to receive the highest economic and social rewards within that socio-economic order. This serves to reinforce the cultural basis of that order by "proving" it successful through the success of those who function on its premises. Achievement and success are essentially the winning of positions which guarantee wealth and power. Social mobility via education has thus become the main function of education. We will return to this discussion after first presenting some views as to how educational institutions function within underdeveloped societies.

In the words of Levitas, institutions operate in the following way: "Societies, wherein exploitation is part of the culture, part of the ongoing behavior, generate institutions whose special task it is to maintain the form of exploitation in practice. Those who are in an economically advantageous position create special organizations of persuasion, judgment, punishment and repression in order to perpetuate the structure" (21), p. 14. Educational institutions are no exception. The dependent economies of underdeveloped societies and their consequent class structures call for educational institutions which, along with other institutions, uphold the existing relationships between the dominating classes of the Metropole and the Periphery Nation as well as their mutual exploitation of the underprivileged classes within the underdeveloped Periphery Nation [Galtung (15)].

In discussing how educational institutions in these societies function according to the two main objectives mentioned above, we distinguish between explicit and implicit educational policies [Herrera (18)]. Explicit policies refer to the aims and ideals stated in educational programs, official plans, etc., intended as legal rules and guidelines for activities within the educational sector. Implicit policies are those which are *actually* carried out in order to realize the main functions of education, i.e., passing on the culture and the economic system from one generation to the next. This kind of policy can be detected through budgets and various kinds of educational investments in curricula or material facilities; through number of students enrolled or those actually getting through the compulsory years of basic schooling, etc. In underdeveloped societies there will be a lack of fit between explicit and implicit educational policies, mainly due to these societies' dependence on a financial and cultural Metropole which determines the state of exploitation which characterizes most of these societies.

In every society there will be a lack of fit between the ideals voiced in the explicit educational policies of the state by private groups having a say as to educational ideals, and the implicit policies actually carried out in the more day-to-day activities of school administration, decisions on curricula, teaching methods, investments, etc. There may, however, be varying degrees of lack of fit, as well as differences in the subsequent effort to correct for it. In underdeveloped societies the educational aims as stated in their explicit policies will have little chance of being realized given the existing socioeconomic structure. Their implicit educational policies—by fulfilling the function of legitimizing existing structures in the name of order and development—are therefore actually working against the realization of explicitly stated goals. Let us go into some detail on this subject.

Explicit educational policies of dependent nations have increasingly become copies of educational policies found in the industrialized, Western societies, especially those based on the ideology of equality of educational resources. Partly this is a consequence of the diffusion of the humanitarian ideal of education as the right of all. Such a stand is advocated by UN agencies, among others. These policies also stem from the adoption of the belief that education is the most efficient means by which to distribute the wealth of a society, a belief rather widespread in industrialized societies, as mentioned above.

The newly acquired political independence of many underdeveloped societies, with its corollary of national development as well as a changing international market, has led them to place a greater emphasis on economic development through industrialization. Among other things, this has focused attention on the extreme lack of educated and technically qualified manpower in these societies. This in turn has given a great impetus to explicit educational policies which emphasize the importance of general education as well as specialized skills, especially within technical fields. The change from a basically feudal economic structure—where positions were allotted on the basis of family and wealth—to a capitalist economic structure in which (according to its ideology) positions are acquired via rational allocation of talents and resources, has implied increasing opportunities for structural as well as geographic mobility with corresponding social mobility. Social mobility, however, is contingent upon individuals' acquisition of the "right" skills and talents.

For education to function as a steppingstone to skill acquisition and social mobility, there must be a demand for educated manpower from the economy. If such a demand does not come about, the result of an increasing level of education in general, and of the amount of qualified manpower in particular, will be either an increasing number of unemployed with higher education or an overall increase in the number of people who are overqualified for their jobs, thereby squeezing out those with little or no education at all. In either case, the social and political costs of an increasing number of frustrated people who find that education did not open doors to prosperity as expected or promised may lead to serious social unrest. Demonstrations by university-educated people without jobs or with low-paid jobs during the Olympics in Mexico are cases in point, as are the violent student riots at both secondary-school and university levels in Venezuela in 1969.

The lack of such a demand for skilled manpower occurs far too often in underdeveloped societies, given their frequently lopsided economic and social structures. We use economic structure here in reference to a society's production basis. Most underdeveloped societies are characterized by an economy based mainly on the production and export of raw materials such as agricultural products and minerals. Their economies are mostly of the mono-product kind, and the product is little if at all refined. The secondary sector is generally of little importance compared to the primary and tertiary sectors which carry the load of production. Foreign markets and export are crucial, often representing the major source of income for the central government. These markets also furnish the country with whatever is needed of industrial and advanced consumer goods. Foreign capital generally controls the export activities, often the import as well, thereby representing a crucial link between the raw-materials-producing dependent economy and the industrial markets. Internal consumption is limited to the relatively few families who control the means of production, be it land or natural resources — middlemen, merchants, and civil servants. Thus, the market will demand only a limited number of skills from among the spectrum available.

These characteristics implant themselves in the labor market, and thereby serve to perpetuate the existing class structure. This structure is generally characterized by a sharp division between the upper classes, who control the economic, political, and social life, and the majority who have little or no say in the economic and political life of the nation. Latin American societies, in particular, have seen a rapid growth of the middle classes. This growth is due in part to the economic and political foothold of the middle class in national policies such as import substitution, construction of communication networks, and modernization of agriculture during the populist governments of the 1950s and 1960s. The widening expansion of central and local bureaucracies also contributed to the growth of the middle class. Along with this, mounting number of people moved from the stagnant geographical periphery to the relatively prospperous centers. The labor market of these centers, however, geared to raw-material export, quickly became saturated.

Another characteristic of the labor market in underdeveloped countries has been structural unemployment. This is of main importance in the tertiary sector which, apart from administration, comprises both public and private series. Such activities often disguise a large number of petty vendors and domestic servants. This implies that an increase in tertiary sector activities in the underdeveloped societies can in no way be compared to a similar development in the tertiary sector of the industrialized ones. In the former, this sector must rather be seen as an "underdeveloped" tertiary sector, whereas in the latter a large tertiary sector reflects the increasing productivity of the other sectors. Along with the secondary sector, the tertiary has therefore become the main sector from which has arisen the demand for an increasing level of education and specialized skills among the population at large.

The fact that labor markets of the underdeveloped societies are quickly saturated, given the economic basis on which they function, implies limited opportunities for social mobility. Those already in relatively secure positions, therefore, become all the more conservative in the effort to preserve their privileges, thus barring new groups from achieving social mobility. Governments, consequently, have to strike a balance between, on the one hand, explicit policies which underline equality of educational opportunity as well as education as the legitimate road to success and, on the other hand, the structural realities which set severe limits upon the amount and kind of educated manpower actually demanded, as well as the lack of political will to distribute their resources and wealth more equally and justly than at present. This is accomplished by what Bourdieu (6), p. 42, has called "the confidence trick" and Carnoy (10) "the myth of schooling." We propose to discuss these mechanisms as devices that legitimize barriers to educational achievement and development. It is this kind of implicit educational policy which shapes the basic educational achievements of children as well as their possibilities for further education which in a decisive way determine their chances for betterment.

EDUCATIONAL BARRIERS

We distinguish between three kinds of barriers: material, structural, and socio-psychological. Material barriers refer to the material structure of a society, such as buildings, geography, communication networks, etc. In relation to education, material structure represents barriers if, for instance, buildings and books are lacking or the geographical distance to a school makes regular attendance difficult. We propose, however, that except for cases of clear physical features of the landscape with which little can be done, material barriers are mainly an indication of lack of investment and planning due to structural barriers.

Structural barriers have their basis in the socio-economic structures of a society, and operate through norms regulating educational priorities and investments in that society. These norms function as barriers to educational development via dominant classes and interest groups (both national and foreign), who also control the educational policies through which they intend to uphold and legitimize existing structures and their own positions within it. This may manifest itself in a lack of interest in defining a policy which goes beyond the mere formal equal access to educational institutions or an unwillingness to accept the explicit educational policy of equality of educational resources by not furnishing facilities and personnel without which the policy cannot be realized.

We see these barriers as operating through three kinds of norms: (1) cultural norms which emphasize certain values and ideals as more worth striving for than others; (2) social norms which define what behavior is regarded as proper for the various social classes, thereby limiting the sphere of action and interaction among the classes. This helps stabilize the social hierarchy; (3) political norms which regulate the right to power and resources, and legitimize inequalities in the distribution of wealth in the society. Given the dependent economic structure and the class structure of underdeveloped societies referred to above, these kinds of norms will all act in limiting educational development in spite of explicit educational policies to the contrary. Implicit educational policies will work to discourage young people from aspiring to education above the basics. This is mainly accomplished by material and structural barriers working through socio-psychological ones.

Socio-psychological barriers stem from children's limited expectations as to their own educational achievements. This is tied to the position of the family in the socio-economic structure which will define what claims are seen as legitimate on the part of the family as to their share of the wealth of the society. Such expectations are internalized by the child and in turn become the child's own expectations. Unless there is a strong societal ideology of allocation of positions and resources on the basis of achievement and talents, the experiences of children from less-privileged families may limit their belief in their own educational opportunities, thereby holding the expectations of the children at the same low level as their parents'.

Even in societies that stress educational achievement as the road to social mobility, and in which equality of educational resources is hailed as the aim of educational policies, want of educational success helps legitimize the system by lowering the expectations of students who are ranked as personal failures. Let us go into some detail on the mechanisms of this process. In a society with such an explicit educational policy, lack of educational success will be defined as lack of abilities, motivation, and interest in the student. What is actually a social or cultural attribute tied to the social background of the pupil is thereby taken to be a personal one [Bordieu (6), p. 32]. Those who lack schooling or fail in educational achievement will thus accept their social standing in the belief that they have no right to claim a larger share of the societal wealth, seeing themselves as not sufficiently qualified to participate in the process of development [Carnoy (10), p. 12]. Schooling will thus accomplish its function by helping to "prove" that equality of educational resources rewards those who have the best abilities because those who succeed in school win the highest positions and the greatest share of the wealth once schooling has ended. This further legitimizes an unequal distribution of resources in the society at large and the existing class structure, helping to preserve a state of underdevelopment.

Children from the lower social classes who fail at school internalize the rationalization, i.e., the defense mechanisms of the dominant classes [Freire (14), p. 29] which is not to deny the facts of the structural barriers, but to see them differently. The barriers lose their objective base, and become a myth claiming a lack of abilities and motivation among children from the lower classes, the group least likely to succeed given the existing barriers. This myth is created by the dominant classes in defense of their interests and will be internalized by the children through their educational failures. Let us illustrate how this interplay between the various kinds of barriers may function by referring to some major lines in the educational development of Venezuela during the last thirty years.

BARRIERS TO EDUCATIONAL DEVELOPMENT
IN VENEZUELA

In presenting some main themes in the educational picture of Venezuela, we limit ourselves to the very general aspects of this development. Our data will be mostly from already published sources, and although no single educational project has yet offered data covering all the dimensions touched upon by our theoretical discussion, an increasing number of educational reports, taken altogether, present a varied set of facts that can be used to illustrate our main points and their interrelatedness.

Venezuela spelled out her first educational plans in the middle of the last century. That period also saw a tremendous upsurge in coffee as a new product for export, furnishing the central government with financial means to carry out its objectives. Educational plans were based on liberal ideas adopted mainly from Europe, emphasizing public responsibility for educating the population in order to promote a just social order. Explicitly, these policies were also intended to curb the influence of the Catholic Church in matters of education. However, institutions at that time favored education as a clear privilege for only the wealthy and the elites. In Venezuela, as in most other Latin American societies at that time, liberal educational policies remained mostly ineffective given a socio-economic structure which in no way favored full participation by the population at large in the economic and political life of the republic. Independence from Spanish rule had merely shifted the economic dependence from the mother country to the industrializing centers of Europe—mainly England—which represented prospering markets for their primary products. Thus, the demand for qualified labor remained the same, except for some changes in personnel. Instead of Spanish merchants and representatives of the Crown, German and British companies and their representatives became middlemen between the landowners (first the producers of cocoa, then of coffee) and their European markets. These same middlemen also dealt with the demand for luxury products from the indigenous elite. It was not until the power of the traditional *latifundia* oligarchy and of the coffee producers began to crumble that efforts were exerted to make educational plans into something other than mere paper decisions. This did not take place until the middle of the 1930s, after the death of President Gomez, whose military regime kept the nation almost inert for more than thirty years.

Strong pressure for change in the economic and political structure was put on the new government from a growing middle sector who saw the state of affairs as mainly favoring the interests of the landowners. Foreign oil investments, which had started in Venezuela by the end of 1800, led to an acceleration of public investments and a greater diversity of small-scale industries, trade, etc. They were also a driving force behind the changing class structure. The new governments, therefore, had to seek support from these groups in order to secure their basis of power. At the same time, there was also a evident change in economic policy toward emphasizing the need for industrialization, development of national industry, and regional development—in short, a compulsion toward the Western ideology of development which has come to be associated with the populist regimes of Latin America. In the case of Venezuela, enormous oil revenues have given the various governments a solid financial basis for carrying out these policies.

The first government which tried to realize such a program was that of President Rómulo Betancourt after his election in 1945. The explicit educational program of this government heavily emphasized both the humanitarian aspect of the right to basic education and the need for educated manpower in a country bent upon modernization, as well as education as an important means by which to prepare the population for participation in a democratic political system. Under the slogan "*sembrar el petróleo*" (to sow the oil), social mobilization through education was hailed as a major way to achieve a more equal distribution of oil income [Cuadernos (13)].

However, as the first impetus of this "new deal" passed, partly because of a military coup by Pérez Jiménez intended to curb these new economic policies which were seen as threatening to the elite, the period of industrialization through import substitution and national priorities developed into a policy based on close cooperation between national and foreign capital, dominated by giant multinational corporations—chiefly the oil companies and U.S. corporations.

When the stagnating tendencies of this kind of dependent capitalism and moreover the limited demand for qualified human resources became obvious

Table 1. Venezuelan Labor Force[1] by Economic Sectors 1950–1970

Year	Primary	Secondary	Tertiary
	%	%	%
1950	47	19	35
1955	44	19	37
1960	39	19	42
1965	35	21	44
1970	23	23	52

[1]Not including Persons unemployed.
Sources: 1950–65. Banco Interamericano de Desarrollo.
Datos Basicos y Parametros Socio-económicos de Venezuela 1950–65. Washington: División de Desarrollo Económico y Social, 1967.
1970. Banco Central de Venezuela. *Informe Económico* 1971. Caracas: 1972, p. A-119.

(see Table 1), it became increasingly important to limit access to educational institutions. Only by avoiding a great number of unemployed with education above a few years of basic schooling could the myth of education as the steppingstone to greater shares of the wealth of the society be preserved, while at the same time preserving the belief that lack of education among the majority of the population was the main reason for their low level of existence. Implicit educational policies came to diverge more and more from explicit ones, these continuing to voice the need for educated manpower and the opportunities for social mobility for all under an ideology of equality of opportunity [Martel Peñate (22)].

During the first period, education functioned to channel people from a rural pre-capitalist hierarchy based on agriculture to a hierarchy of a capitalist order in the urbanized centers. With an ideology, first, of equal formal access to educational institutions and later of equality of opportunity, schooling during this period appeared to further social mobility for a limited number of the poor. The rapidly growing enrollment testifies to this (see Table 2) as do favourable changes in level of income. Schooling in the 1950s and 1960s thus helped curb a beginning institutional crisis caused by the development of a capitalist system of production with an broadening demand for qualified labor, and the growth of a new and potentially powerful middle class. Schooling in the 1960s and 1970s began to function more and more as a means for legitimizing the established dependent economic structure against demands for a greater share of the benefits of industrialization from the masses of people who had been left out of the lopsided industrial development.

Table 2. Educational Enrollment 1957–1974.

Year	Total	%	Primary	%	Secondary	%	Tertiary	%
1957–58	844,988	100.0	751,561	88.9	82,811	9.8	10,616	1.2
1960–61	1,451,053	100.0	1,243,948	85.8	180,628	12.4	26,477	1.8
1965–66	1,760,028	100.0	1,481,333	84.3	231,870	13.1	46,825	2.6
1970–71	2,274,271	100.0	1,769,680	77.9	417,367	18.3	87,224	3.8
1973–74	2,674,923	100.0	1,941,498	72.7	597,756	22.2	138,669	5.1
Interannual rates of growth	7.5%		6.2%		13.5%		17.9%	

Sources: 1957–66. Ministerio de Educación (24), *Mas y mejor Educación.* Caracas, pp. 15, 23, 88.
CORDIPLAN (11). *Estudio de los recursos humanos de Venezuela.* Caracas, pp. 78, 135.
1970–74. Ministerio de Educación (27). *Memória 1973.* Caracas, pp. 9, 39, 41, 65.

Table 3. Public Educational Expenses in Percent of Total Public Expenses. (millions of Bs.)

Year	Total public educational expenses (A)	Total public expenses (B)	$\frac{A}{B}.100$
1957–58	342	2,780	12.3
1959–60	817	5,069	16.1
1965	1,271	7,260	17.5
1970	2,280	9,886	23.1
1973	3,459	13,858	25.0

Sources: 1957–65. Ministerio de Educación (24), *Mas y mejor Educación* Caracas, p. 94, Table 19. IDES. *Educación— La gran urgencia.* Caracas: 1968, p. 76.
1970–73. Ministerio de Educación (27). *Memória 1973.* Caracas, p. 72.

As a consequence, the overall picture of Venezuelan education in the middle of the 1970s is a rather dismal one, considering the steadily swalling oil revenues which the central government has received for more than 70 years, and the lofty educational programs which the elite, however, have never considered wise to realize. The relative size of educational investments compared to total public expenditure is beginning to stabilize, in spite of an official figure of illiteracy still as high as 20 percent in 1973, down from 57.2 percent in 1941 [Ministerio de Educación (23); see Table 3].

Furthermore, when it comes to the allocation of these public investments, there has been a tendency opposed to what we see in industrialized societies. Whereas "normal" development most likely would be an increasing share of the investments toward improving the educational standard through the acquisition of modern materials, the construction of new buildings, the setting up of funds for educational research etc., the tendency in Venezuela has been the opposite. In 1971, 86 percent of total public expenses of primary and secondary levels went to cover teachers' salaries. Of the increase in public educational expenses between 1969 and 1971, 40 percent was due to a rise in teachers' salaries. A declining percentage goes to capital investments with the far-reaching consequence that educational standards will be decreasing as more and more students are enrolled, although educational materials were not being increased accordingly. At the primary level, educational investments per pupil dropped from Bs. 15 in 1969 to Bs. 6.00 in 1971, representing a 40 percent decrease [Ministerio de Educación (26), pp. 2, 11 and 15].

Some of the short-term consequences of this policy can already be seen from data on dropouts and educational standards. In spite of compulsory primary education of six years, only 56 percent of those starting primary school in 1968 finished at the regular time in 1973 (compared to only 20 percent for the 1952 cohort—an improvement which should not be overlooked) [Ministerio de Educación (24), p. 26, and (27), p. 21]. The number of dropouts, as well as those older than normal students within the educational system on all levels, is also substantial, the latter being as high as 48 percent during 1969–1970 at the level of primary education. Budgets of the Department of Education were increasing at a rate of 8.5 percent during the years 1965–1968, while enrollment was up to 12.9 percent during the same period [Cuadernos (13), pp. 64, 67]. There are thus enormous differences among, for instance, a laborer in the countryside who generally has little more than one year of schooling, a dweller in the urban slums with three years of schooling, a small merchant or tradesman with five years, and a high government or oil company employee with 12 to 15 years of schooling.

Considering the social background of those who succeed within this system, several studies show that while education in Venezuela has been an important road to social mobility as measured by a comparison of children's education to that of their parents, the groups which have been best able to utilize educational opportunities are often families with a social position and level of education which were relatively advanced for their time, although they may seem low compared to standards of today (12), p. 59. Grades, educational achievement, and social background of the students also correlate in a way familiar to us from studies of industrialized societies, i.e., the higher the social background of the student, the greater his or her chances of educational success [see, for instance, Ministerio de Educación (25), pp. 45–51].

When it comes to the expectations of various groups as to the function of educational institutions and their own success within them, an investigation on conflict and consensus in the Venezuelan society revealed that executives of the larger industrial and oil companies saw education especially as furnishing the economic sectors with needed qualified manpower. The same groups were also relatively satisfied with the education they had received themselves, as opposed to inhabitants of urban slum areas, who considered the main function of education to be the creation of a national and civic conscience among the population. These groups were, furthermore, dissatisfied with the education they had received—an average of three years—although for reasons which did not question the system. Between these two extremes were found the middle sectors—merchants, small-scale industrialists, teachers, etc.—who also underlined mainly the political function of education, and were fairly satisfied with their education, although not to the extent of the executives. It should also be stressed that a majority in most groups did agree on the level of secondary education as a minimum necessary "to succeed in life," although there was no clear profile among the various social classes. Among those groups who see primary education or less as sufficient, there seems more likely to be a division along the urban/rural dimension cutting across social classes, which probably mirrors the vast differences between educational opportunities in the countryside compared to the cities, even for the poor [Cuadernos (13), p. 79, Table 8]. To this picture could be added the opinions of what Bonilla has called "the invisible elites," i.e., members from the North American community and the military, groups who make their power felt through extralegal or extra-parliamentary channels. These groups strongly emphasize the functions of educational institutions as mainly to prepare individuals for productive labor and to make sure that these individuals are not "ideologically contaminated." This last aim they have tried to accomplish through close cooperation with the Catholic Church [Bonilla (5)].

It should also be mentioned that in another study regarding the Venezuelan elite, it was found that few of the sample considered the great mass of the population as a positive force in the development of the society in the sense of being able to realize its own destiny. Either they saw the masses as a dead weight on the system or as victims of the same [Cuadernos (13), p. 83]. If we add to the above fact that most of the members of these groups are satisfied with the educational institution as it exists, there seems to be little chance of the leading groups' capability of advancing basic changes in the system. As a matter of fact, this has already been brought out in various attempts to change educational laws in the 1960s. What was accomplished was instead a closer adaptation of the educational institution to changes in the socio-economic structure which had already taken place rather than laws which set out to change the serious educational imbalances found at present [Martel Peñate (22), p. 17].

Another feature which is increasingly brought out in various studies is the relative conservatism of the teachers. In the study mentioned above concerning the educational expectations of various occupational groups, there were more teachers both at primary and secondary levels who thought primary education or less, as well as vocational training, sufficient to succeed in life than those who favored a secondary or university education [Albornoz (2), p. 83, and (3), pp. 35–37; Bronfenmajer (7), pp. 5–11; Cuadernos (13), p. 79]. This could be taken both as an indication of the social background of most teachers in Venezuela coming from the lower social classes, or as an indication of realism on the part of teachers, seeing that few of their students really have a chance of getting past the basic level. Whatever the reasons, these values may work as barriers to educational motivation for students for whom the teacher is the only role model regarding the activities and values of educated persons.

As for the students themselves, various studies show that Venezuelan youth have a strong notion of education as a means to success, with secondary school students being somewhat more clear on this point than the primary students [Silvert and Reissman (32), p. 35]. For the secondary school student, this is generally tied in with a world view stressing individual achievement within the existing social structure (32), p. 51. Among these students, a deep concern with the lack of educational facilities and the lack of opportunities for technical and vocational training has been reported, even ranked above other main problems of industrial and economic development in the society at large [LaBella (20), p. 639]. This in spite of the fact that they themselves mostly want to work at academic careers or secondary schools as teachers. Given the concern mentioned above, and the extent to which the need for technically qualified human resources is being underlined in the explicit educational policies, there are surprisingly few secondary school students who consider vocational training and technical education equally important compared with secondary, humanistic education. What we see here, then, is an apparent contradiction among the students who, on one side, argue for technical and vocational training, whereas, on the other, they opt for rather traditional educational careers themselves. This contradiction will be better understood if we relate their choices to our terms of explicit and implicit educational policies.

In accordance with a basic premise in the explicit policies, these students see the need for technically qualified people in an industrializing economy. Furthermore, as successful students—getting to the secondary level already defines them as such—it seems likely that they also have internalized another basic of the explicit policies, *viz.*, the idea of their success based on individual achievements made possible through equal educational resources for all. Thus, they have become strong supporters of the basic ideology of the explicit educational policy. The fact that they nevertheless prefer an academic or humanistic education to a technical or more practical one has sometimes been taken as an indication of the continued importance in the Latin culture of "the man of letters" as the gentlemanly ideal. On the more implicit level, however, the students have, through their educational career, also internalized norms which actually direct the system, through what we have labeled structural and socio-psychological barriers. Defining education as the road to success, they know they have to take into consideration these implicit educational determinants in order to succeed. Their preference for a secondary education is therefore most likely due to the fact that they realize there is little demand for technically qualified people within the existing structure. Those with a general educational background, however, can be fitted into the various branches of the tertiary sector, both public and private, which is the most dynamic sector. Also, humanistic education is the only kind which opens doors to the university, and the university is still the highest educational achievement and key to societal prestige as well as the "good life." At the university level, there is likewise a heavy emphasis on traditional fields like the humanities and education, law, the social sciences, and medicine [Tornes (33)]. This must be taken as an expression of rational choices on the part of students, and not seen as unwillingness to "modernize." Rather, it is a consequence of the dependent road to industrialization which Venezuela, like so many other underdeveloped societies, has decided upon.

These students will, through their continued success, not only justify the existing system to those who are excluded; they will also in their turn probably become staunch supporters of the existing educational system and the social structure of which it is a part. Their social positions and privileges are tied in with the continued existence of this structure. Those who did not reach the top of the educational pyramid will be defined by others, as well as be defined by themselves, as personal failures given the explicit ideology of equality of educational resources. In its essence, then, an educational institution based on the ideology of equality of educational resources will, within such a dependent socio-economic structure, not function as a promoter of development and a more equitable distribution of the societal wealth, but rather will be a chief mechanism through which the prevalent underdevelopment is upheld and legitimized.

CONCLUSION

Educational research, then, both on developed and underdeveloped societies, makes it increasingly clear that family and class background, geographical location, not to mention sex, are some of the factors which decisively influence the school accomplishments of children [Silver (31); Jencks (19); Hernes and Knudsen (17); Tornes (35)]. These factors are in no way compensated for by supplying equal resources for every pupil. In order to achieve the goal of a greater equity of life chances after schooling, one has therefore to focus on equality of educational results. This could either imply that any member of one social class, ethnic group, sex, etc., shall have the same expectation as any member of another class, group, etc., of reaching the various status positions in a society, or that every member of a society is to achieve the same educational standards which would lead to different but equal life chances [Hernes (16)].

Equality of educational results in the first sense would not necessarily imply a change in the existing class structure of a society, whereas the second would call for radical changes. To realize such an educational goal, it would be necessary to differentiate among kinds and number of resources spent on every student in order to compensate for differences in background variables so that children with different backgrounds would really reach the same standard in school. In cases where a majority of students from the working classes, of a certain sex, ethnic group, or geographical area were not successful, the responsibility would be on the school and the society for not furnishing facilities which could have compensated for their background. To the extent that the educational policy of a society explicitly aims at furnishing everyone with more equitable life chances through education, this will also have to involve changes in the socio-economic structure so that there would be a demand for educated human resources. In Venezuela, as in any other under-developed society with a similar dependent socio-economic structure, investment in education will therefore most likely have little effect on educational development unless a program of equality of educational standards is realized, within a new policy of independence from existing national and international structures of dominance.

I would like to thank Helga Hernes and Knud Knudsen for valuable comments during the preparation of this manuscript, and Eva Siversten for typing assistance. Grants from the Norwegian Council for the Sciences and Humanities and the Meltzer Fund, University of Bergen, made the collection of data possible.

REFERENCES

1. Alberti, Giorgio et al. (1974) Educación y Desarrollo Rural, Lima: Instituto de Estudios Peruanos.
2. Albornoz, Orlando. (1962) "Valores Sociales en la Educación Venezolana," Boletín Bibliográfico 111, No. 18.
3. ———. (1965) El Maestro y la Educación en la Sociedad Venezolana, Caracas: DIPUVEN.
4. Barkin, David. (1975) "Education and Class Structure: The Dynamics of Social Control in Mexico," Politics and Society 5:185–199.
5. Bonilla, Frank. (1969) Las elites invisibles, Caracas: CENDES.
6. Bourdieu, Pierre. (1974) "The School as a Conservative Force: Scholastic and Cultural Inequalities," in Contemporary Research in the Sociology of Education, ed. John Eggleston, London: Methuen, pp. 32–46.
7. Bronfenmajer, Gabriela. (1969) Consideraciónes Sobre Educación Como Instrumento de Cambio," Caracas: CENDES.
8. ——— et al. (1969) "Algunas Consideraciónes para logar una Población Crítica, Creadora y Participante," in Dos Trabajos sobre el Proyecto de Ley Orgánica de Educación. Caracas: CENDES, pp. 23–54.
9. Cardoso, Fernando Henrique. (1974) Ideologías de la Burgesia Industrial en Sociedades Dependientes, Mexico: Siglo XXI.
10. Carnoy, Martin. (1974) Education as Cultural Imperialism, Stanford, Calif.: Stanford University Press.
11. CORDIPLAN. (1968) Estudio de los Recursos Humanos en Venezuela, Caracas.
12. D'Aeth, Richard. (1975) Education and Development in the Third World, Farnborough, Eng.: Saxon House.
13. Equipo de Educación y Recursos Humanos de la CENDES. (1972) "Participación de la Communidad en la Educación," in Cuadernos de la Sociedad Venezolana de Planificación No. 96–99:35–176.
14. Freire, Paulo. (1972) Pedagogy of the Oppressed. Harmondsworth: Penguin.
15. Galtung, Johan. (1971) "A Structural Theory of Imperialism" Journal of Peace Research 2:81–117.

16. Hernes, Gudmund. (1975) *Om ulikhetens reproduksjon*, Copenhagen: Christian Ejlers Forlag.
17. ———og Knud Knudsen. (1976) "Utdanning og ulikhet," Oslo: NOU: 46.
18. Herrera, Amilcar. (1972) "Social Determinants of Science Policy in Latin America. Explicit Science Policy and Implicit Science Policy," *The Journal of Development Studies* 9:19–37.
19. Jencks, Christopher. (1975) *Inequality. A Reassessment of the Effect of Family and Schooling in America*, Batlimore: Penguin Books.
20. LaBella, Thomas. (1973) *The New Professional in Venezuelan Secondary Education*, Los Angeles: University of California Press.
21. Levitas, Maurice. (1974) *Marxist Perspectives in the Sociology of Education*, London: Routledge.
22. Martel Peñate, Armando (1969) "La Ley de Educación Vigente y el Proyecto de Ley de Educación presentado al Congreso Nacional," in *Dos Trabajos sobre el Proyecto de Ley Organica de Educatión*, Caracas: CENDES, pp. 1–23.
23. Ministerio de Educación. (1966) *El analfabetismo es Derrotado en Venezuela*, Caracas. Dirección Primaria y Normal, División de Educación de Adultos
24. ———. (1967) *Mas y mejor educación*, Caracas.
25 ———. (1970) *Conocimientos Generales de los Educandos*, Serie 1, Informes preliminares. Matemática y Lenguaje Sexto Grado, Caracas.
26. ———. *Analisis Comparativo del gasto por Alumno y la estructura del gasto en los programas de primaria y media del Ministerio de Educación en Venezuela. Para los años 1969 y 1971*, Caracas: Dirección de Planeamiento, Departamento de investigaciónes Educacionales.
27. ———. (1974) *Memória 1973*, Caracas.
28. Musgrave, P. W., ed. (1970) "The Definition of Technical Education 1860–1910," in *Sociology, History and Education*, London: Methuen, pp. 65–71.
29. ———. (1970) "A Model for the Analysis of the Development of the English Educational System from 1860," in *Sociology History and Education*, London: Methuen, pp. 15–29.
30. Piñedo Brigé, Lucia. (1976) "Un Estudio de las Estructuras de Ocupación y Educación de la Mano de Obra en Venezuela," *Cuadernos de la* Sociedad Venezolana de Planificación 128–129:221–242.
31. Silver, Harold, ed. (1973) *Equal Opportunity in Education*, London: Methuen.
32. Silvert, K. H., and L. Reissman. (1976) *Education, Class and Nation. The Experiences of Chile and Venezuela*, New York: Elsevier.
33. Tornes, Kristin. (1971) *Human Resources and Socio-Economic Development: The Case of Venezuela*, unpublished thesis, Oslo: Peace Research Institute of Oslo.
34. ———. (1975) *Is Education the Crucial Factor It is Claimed to Be?* Bergen: Institute of Sociology, mimeo, p. 35.
35. ———. (1977) *Hvorfor bruker ikke jenter sine gode karakterer?* Bergen: Institute of Sociology, mimeo.
36. Vaughan, M., and M. S. Archer. (1971) *Social Conflict and Educational Change in England and France 1789 1848*, New York: Cambridge University Press.

MANPOWER PLANNING AND THE CHOICE OF TECHNOLOGY

S. C. Kelley, CENTER FOR HUMAN RESOURCE RESEARCH, OHIO STATE UNIVERSITY

The importance of human resource endowments to the process of accelerated economic growth and the consequent importance of human capital formation as a policy variable is a universal article of faith. Yet the specification of this relationship in operational form as criteria for social actions is still the object of significant controversy concerning the appropriate theoretical paradigm for the interpretation of the construct.

Since the perception of developed human attributes as human capital was restored to economics in 1960, it has been expressed in two quite different operational forms. One is the market form in which it was first expressed by Adam Smith, an explanation of the presence of wage differentials in a compe-

Research in Human Capital and Development, Vol. 1, pp. 169–189.

titive labor market—the rate of return to investment in human capital. The other is a set of technical relationships between human ends and human means combined in a planning structure.

Paradoxically, the market expression has dominated the literature of human resources for twenty years but it has had no important role as an instrument for policy formation. In contrast, the planning expression has had little impact on economic theory or recognition in formal economic literature but it is the dominant form in the development of policy criteria.

The reasons for the paradox are obvious, although its consequences seem less apparent. Human capital theory has developed in a market form because neoclassical economic theory has dominated Western economics in the past twenty years for reasons internal to the discipline. In the same period, the dominant problems of both highly industrialized and developing economies have been associated with growth and structural change. Both the static and restrictive assumptions of labor market theory and disciplinary boundaries that exclude the most critical variables in the development process have limited its role as a policy instrument to a peripheral set of allocative decisions.

Rapid economic development involves, by definition, extreme shifts in economic and social parameters with consequent great structural imbalance. The radical shifts in human aspirations that have characterized the past twenty years have demanded equally radical change in the rate and structure of economic activity, in the techniques of production and in institutional and cultural forms. The resulting structural disequilibrium has many dimensions but it is particularly marked by the gap between the society's human resource endowments and its needs for human capacities and attributes to implement and sustain appropriate social change. These attributes include technical skills and knowledge, behavioral characteristics, role perceptions and values that are not congruent with traditional, agrarian culture or produced by traditional institutions.

One consequence of this condition is that the society is constrained in responding to its changing and expanding goals by critical scarcities of technical and behavioral skills. Another is that an important part of its membership becomes redundant to the economic system and is excluded from participation in the process of growth and from its rewards. Both conditions have produced a universal commitment to human resource development as a priority area of social action, and to human resource planning as the primary source of policy criteria.

Unfortunately, no unified theory of economic growth and development has evolved to compete with the market paradigm, and the gap between the dominant theoretical construct and the decision environment has forced planners and policy makers to rely on limited empirical specification of functional relationships and partial specifications of systems and process.

The current state of the art of human resource planning is a reflection of the pragmatic nature of planning experience and of the tremendous variance in the economic, social, and political contexts in which it has occurred.

The importance of this condition to the present discussion of manpower planning is twofold. One is that much of the critique of manpower planning in the formal literature derives its criteria from the formal market model, and that model has limited relevance in the context of economic development [Ahmad and Blaug (1) or Bowles (3)]. It has focused almost totally on a non-issue: the presumed assumptions of planning models about the elasticity of substitution of factors as a function of changes in their relative supply price. We believe, in the first instance, that this issue has very limited meaning in the presence of rapid technical progress. Secondly, one objective of this paper is to demonstrate that there is nothing generic in manpower planning models that requires an assumption of zero elasticity of substitution.

A second consequence of the gap between the practice of planning and its theoretical base is that the products of planning experience are usually policy documents or at best published monographs and do not enter the formal literature. They are known generally to a limited number of practitioners and are not readily synthesized as a statement of the state of the art. The simplicity of the conventional critique is attributable in part to the fact that the critique relates to the initial methodological statement of a manpower model that has been developed and modified subsequently in hundreds of applications in the past fifteen years. The second objective of this paper is to reduce the information gap by discussing or describing some methodological aspects of recent experience that relate, on the one hand, to the policy value of manpower planning and, on the other, to the methodological argument noted above.

Manpower policy is concerned with three basic problems of development. One problem is the obvious structural inequality between the technical and behavioral attributes of the current labor supply and the role and performance requirements of an industrial society. Another is the ubiquitous and extensive underutilization of the labor supply through overt and disguised unemployment. The third is the presence of great inequalities in access to education and training and consequently to income and employment.

The conventional response to each of these conditions has been to reduce potential structural imbalance by acting on human resource endowments. Human resource policy has been concentrated on the expansion and redirection of expenditures for education and training in order to increase the skill supply and broaden access to the system. In this policy context, the role of manpower planning is limited to the estimation of potential inequalities in future manpower requirements and supplies and to their specification as allocative criteria for investments in educational and labor market institutions. Since the primary determinants of manpower requirements—the structure of economic activity and the techniques of production—are assumed to be given to the manpower planner, his role is essentially passive. Manpower policy is concerned with a limited allocation decision in the framework of a given growth policy.

This perception of policy and policy instruments is implied in rate-of-return analysis. It assumes that all manpower problems are structural in origin, that imbalance is marginal and that balance is readily achieved in the short term by factor substitution and by investment in factor mobility. Long-term balance is assured by the impact of individual career choice on educational supplies, given a free flow of labor market information and a competitive wage structure.

It is also reflected in simple manpower planning models where the structure of outputs is received as an unconditional forecast or as a product of the rate of capital formation, and when sectoral production functions are estimated through trend analysis or comparative data. In each case the policy instrument is not sufficient to the policy need. The magnitude of imbalance is too great to be resolved in the short term by manipulating labor supply conditions, and consequently the three objectives of manpower policy and indeed of economic development are in conflict. The techniques of production that will raise productivity and per capita output in this context are almost always labor saving. A high rate of technical change will generate little if any additional employment in the short term, in particular if the rate of growth of output is constrained by factor scarcities, market restriction or institutional factors. In this situation an appropriate growth strategy would require a structure of activity with emphasis on the growth of labor intensive sectors, the use of intermediate techniques in those sectors where the marginal productivity of capital is low, and a pattern of growth that will relax these constraints at a rate consistent with the rate of change in the capacity to change human resource endowments. In other terms it will specify the optimal short-term trade-off between unemployment and per capita output and the long-term conditions for eliminating or reducing the conflict between these objectives.

To elaborate such a strategy, planners must be able to specify, among other analytic elements, the set of production techniques that are available to the society, the criteria for the choice of technique and the means of implementing any given choice through policy interventions.

The planning methodology that has been most useful for strategic analysis is the disaggregate, iterative model usually described in the literature as a "manpower" model and associated with the OECD Mediterranean Regional Project. The general form of this model specifies a set of sectoral output targets for a planning period and estimates the differentiated labor inputs required to meet these production targets, given a specific pattern of change in sectoral production functions. It estimates the flow of human resources in the planning period as a function of demographic change, geographic and occupational mobility, changes in labor force participation and the outputs of existing systems of human resource development. Finally, it evaluates the consistency between anticipated manpower "requirements" and "supplies" as criteria for the development of manpower policies or growth strategies. This model is specified in iterative form rather than simultaneous form in order to permit a greater degree of disaggregation of the dependent variables and more explicit specifications of functional relationships.

For this discussion it is important to recognize that in its policy form, this model is a comprehensive planning model. The structure of economic activity, the choice of technique, and the rate and structure of resource development are all policy variables subject to manipulation and influence. In this sense, it is no longer appropriate to define the model as a "manpower" model since manpower policy is integral with general development policy and manpower planning is an integral part of general development planning.

TECHNOLOGICAL PLANNING

The specification of sectoral production functions over time as policy targets rather than as forecasts is the critical element of policy planning. The possible trade-offs between output and employment depend on the range of alternative techniques available to producing sectors. In turn, the effects of changes in the structure of output on aggregate employment and productivity depends on the pattern of technical change within sectors.

The technique for simulating technical change described below was developed in planning application in Bolivia, Ecuador, and Venezuela between 1965 and 1972. Although the specific form of the technique varies among countries as a function of differences in data availability, institutional factors, or resource constraints, the general construct is consistent over the range of this experience.

The construct assumes that in any economy the process of technical change involves what Salter (7) has described as "continuous disturbance and slow adjustment" in the form of a stream of new techniques and continuous but slow adjustment to these new options. Technical change is a continuous process of shifting to new production functions, but the process is never complete since the flow of new options exceeds the rate of adjustment. As a result, sector production is characterized by the simultaneous use of an assortment of techniques, and the average practice in the sector will be technically less efficient than the "best practice" technique available. In advanced countries, the stream of new techniques is a function of invention or innovation and thus incremental. Except in a period of very rapid innovation, following Schumpeter (8), the gap between the best practice and the average practice should not be great.

In the developing countries the flow of techniques is a product of the rate of diffusion of techniques developed in the advanced countries. It includes potentially the full historical inventory of advanced country technology. One would expect to find in use at any time a range of techniques from traditional artisan processes to highly sophisticated processes at the technical frontier. Since the rate of technological substitution is a function of new investment, in the putty-clay sense, the gap between the best-known practice and the average practice is likely to be great and, in the typical planning period, a large part of sector output will be produced by techniques that are currently in use.

The planning model assumes that it is possible to specify the set of alternative techniques in use in any sector and to estimate empirically a disaggregate production function for each technique. Given the current distribution of sector capacity or output, technical change is the process of shifting the relative weights of techniques (activities) in the sector set. The direction of change depends on the policy definition of the optimal or best practice technique. The rate of change is a function of the rate of disinvestment in existing, non-optimal techniques and of net investment in the optimal technique.

It is important to recognize that this model assumes that the technical coefficients of activity production functions are constant but that they are variable for the sector as a function of changes in the relative weights of activities. This assumption is similar to the distinction between "localized" and general technical progress suggested by Atkinson and Stiglitz (2). A shift in the sector production function is a result of the impact of technical progress on one production process with limited spillover effects on other processes. The planning model assumes that there are no spillover effects from the introduction of a new and superior technique. Given the fact that new techniques are usually imported, often by importing managerial and technical personnel, this assumption may not be unrealistic.

THE VENEZUELAN CASE

The use of this technique is illustrated here in application to the manufacturing sector of the Venezuelan economy, since it is the most recent experience and because it reflects greater technological diversity than the less-developed economies of Ecuador [Kelley et al. (5)] and Bolivia [Chirikos et al. (4)]. In Ecuador and in Venezuela the analysis was conceptually similar in all sectors, although obviously there are great differences in the relevant means for specifying activities and the feasibility of doing so.

In brief, the analysis uses a set of establishment data for 1970 in a cross-sectional analysis of the sector's technology. It clusters establishments in seven activity sets within two-digit subsectors on the basis of total establishment productivity and capital-intensity and estimates a production function for each of the seven activities in each of the two-digit sectors.

In simulating technical change, the model assumes that establishment scale and production coefficients are constant in real terms. Change in the sector production function is a function of change in the structure of activity capacity through depreciation of existing establishments and investment in new establishments. In the simulation trials described here, base period wage rates and the price of capital services were estimated empirically. Both factor and commodity prices are assumed to be constant in the planning period.

In the basic simulation model, the capacity of non-optimal activities is reduced over time as a function of activity-specific depreciation rates. The capacity of the optimal activity is increased as a function of gross investment in the activity at a level equal to the sum of sector depreciation and sector growth requirements. In subsequent trials, activity rates of depreciation are varied as a function of the ratios of the productivity of non-optimal to optimal activities. Since the maximum rate of depreciation allowed is the actual rate, the effect of this modification is to extend the time rate of convergence toward the optimal set of techniques.

In the initial trial, the most efficient activity is specified as optimal and the sector converges on this set of techniques. The efficiency criterion is the ratio of value added to total factor costs. In the second set, the activity with the highest productivity/employment trade-off value is specified as optimal. This value is the relationship between an employment gain and a reduction in factor productivity in moving from a more efficient to a less efficient activity. Convergence on this activity reflects the maximum employment growth attainable with the minimum opportunity cost in productivity.

The employment estimates derived from the growth simulation are disaggregated to occupations at the three-digit level of occupational classification by activity and subsequently aggregated to two-digit industries totals in matrix form. In long-term projections this detailed classification of occupations has little utility. They are maintained in detailed form in the model to permit aggregation with other sectors.

Finally, in this illustration, the rate of growth of the sector and the final composition of sector output were specified in the general development plan, and were accepted as given. However, they appear as independent variables in the model, and alternative growth rates for the sector and within the sector can be assumed.

As noted above, this illustration assumes that all prices remain constant over the planning period. This assumption in regard to commodity prices is consistent with the elasticity assumptions employed in projecting sector target outputs. The limitation of the assumptions concerning factor prices is tested by an analysis of future factor supply conditions after the specification of requirements by the simulation and after their aggregation with the manpower requirements of all other sectors.

In this application, the model uses a set of disaggregate establishment data in a cross-sectional analysis of the sector's technology. The data relate to 1970 and include detailed production data from 3,030 establishments and detailed occupational data from a sample of 966 firms. The production data provide for each firm the value of gross product (X), the total non-factor costs of production (M), total labor costs (LC), depreciation allowances (D), the value of fixed capital (KT^f) and the value of liquid assets including inventories (KT^w).

A measure of capital intensity or factor proportions (KT/LC) and a measure of total factor productivity are calculated as proxies for the technological characteristics of the firm. The productivity measure is the ratio of value added (VA) to total factor costs, where capital costs are the cost of capital services estimated by applying the market rate of interest (r) to the current value of fixed and variable assets plus depreciation allowances.

These two measures are the criteria for the ordering of establishments in sets. Since the relationship between productivity and capital intensity is clearly not linear, establishments were assigned on the basis of ordinal rankings on each variable to trifid sets. The characteristics of the sets are shown below:

	PT rank	KL rank
Activity set 1	Upper third	Upper third
Activity set 2	Upper third	Middle third
Activity set 3	Upper third	Lower third
Activity set 4	Middle third	Upper third
Activity set 5	Middle third	Middle third
Activity set 6	Middle third	Lower third
Activity set 7	Lower third	——

Activity sets 7, 8 and 9 have been compressed simply to reduce computational output and because they have little potential policy relevance in th disaggregate form. Further, activity sets were defined at the three-digit level of industrial classification to maintain the maximum, feasible degree c product homogeneity in the ranking process. They were then aggregated t two-digit industries to correspond to given output targets and are presume to be cross-sectionally representative of the commodity mix of the two-dig sector. Actually, variance in the relationship between the classificatio variables between three-digit sectors produces some bias in the commodity mix of the activity sets when aggregated to the two-digit industry level. The solution to this problem depends on the disaggregation of commodity output targets which was not feasible given the inadequacy of the data for estimating demand elasticities at that level of disaggregation.

PRODUCTION RELATIONSHIPS

Accepting these constraints, we estimated basic production relationships for each activity set (n) in each two-digit sector (m) as follows:

$$X\,mn = (LC\,mn, Dmn, KTmn, M\,mn)$$
$$m = 1, 2, \ldots 20$$
$$n - 1, 2, \ldots 7$$

In order to specify the optimal activity in each two-digit sector for any specified objective function, matrices of interactivity ratios for global productivity and fixed capital per worker are calculated and combined in a third matrix to estimate the relative trade-off of productivity for employment.

The first two of these matrices estimate the relative loss or gain in productivity or the relative change in factor proportions associated with a shift in production from one activity to another. The third matrix estimates the combined effects of changes in productivity and factor proportions on employment. If the simulation model is maximizing productivity, the distribution of output is shifted over time to the most productive activity as identified in the productivity matrix and at rates that are weighted by the relative productivities of the activities in the matrix.

Similarly, if the simulation is attempting to specify a technological position that will maximize employment without constraints, it would shift production toward the most labor-intensive activities. If, as is most realistic, the simulation is employed to estimate trade-off positions, the third matrix indicates the relative effect of an increase in labor intensity on total factor productivity. For example, activity set 3 in sector 25 is the most efficient set. It is also relatively labor-intensive and consequently is also optimal in terms of the trade-off between efficiency and employment growth.

In contrast, activity 2 represents the most efficient process in sector 20. Activity 3 is nearly as efficient and much more labor-intensive, which is to say that the elasticity of substitution of labor for capital is very high between these two activities. A 1 percent decline in productivity (or increase in total costs) is associated with a 9.5 percent increase in employment. No other process offers a larger employment gain with the same loss of efficiency and this activity is optimal in terms of a trade-off between conflicting objectives.

PROCESS DESCRIPTION

Conceptually, changes in the capital and labor requirements of subsectors through the planning period are estimated by changing the relative weights of activities in the aggregate sector production function and applying the production coefficients to the target output. Labor requirements are estimated in aggregate form and subsequently disaggregated by applying the weighted activity employment matrices to the aggregate employment estimate.

The model assumes the following fixed coefficient production functions for time period t $(t - 1, 2, \ldots)$, two-digit sector m $(m = 1, 2, \ldots, 20)$, and activity set n $(n = 1, 2, \ldots, 7)$:

$$X_{tmn} = \begin{cases} \min\left(\dfrac{LC_{tmn}}{b_{mn}^1}, \dfrac{KT_{tmn}^f}{b_{mn}^2}, \dfrac{KT_{tmn}^W}{b_{mn}^3}, \dfrac{M_{tmn}}{b_{mn}^4}\right) & \text{if } n = 1 \\[3ex] \min\left(\dfrac{LC_{tmn}}{b_{mn}^1}, \dfrac{KT_{tmn}^f}{b_{mn}^2}, \dfrac{KT_{tmn}^W}{b_{mn}^3}, \dfrac{M_{tmn}}{b_{mn}^4}\right) & \text{if } n = 2, 3, \ldots, 7 \end{cases}$$

b_{mn}^1, b_{mn}^2, b_{mn}^3, and b_{mn}^4 are fixed through time and are calculated using base period $(t = 1)$ values,

$$\text{e.g.,} \left(b_{mn}^1 = \frac{LC_{1mn}}{X_{1mn}}\right).$$

Let d_{mn} be the rate of depreciation of fixed capital in two-digit sector m and activity set n. Without loss of generality, let the optimal activity set be set 1 for each two-digit sector. Fixed capital is labeled $\overline{KT}_{tml}^f$ in the optimal activity set and KT_{tmn}^f $(n = 2, \ldots, 7)$ in the non-optimal activity sets. They are calculated as follows:

For non-optimal activity sets $(n = 2, 3, \ldots, 7)$

$$KT_{2mn}^f = KT_{1mn}^f - d_{mn} \cdot KT_{1mn}^f = (1 - d_{mn})KT_{1mn}^f$$
$$KT_{3mn}^f = KT_{2mn}^f - d_{mn} \cdot KT_{2mn}^f = (1 - d_{mn})KT_{1mn}^f - d_{mn}(1 - d_{mn})KT_{1mn}^f$$
$$= (1 - d_{mn})^2 KT_{1mn}$$

$$\cdot \qquad \cdot$$
$$\cdot \qquad \cdot$$
$$\cdot \qquad \cdot$$

$$KT_{tmn} = (1 - d_{mn})^{t-1} KT_{1mn}.$$

For the optimal activity set $(n = 1)$

$$KT_{1ml} = KT_{1ml}^f$$
$$KT_{2ml}^f = \overline{KT}_{1ml}^f - d_{ml} \cdot \overline{KT}_{1ml}^f = (1 - d_{ml}) \cdot \overline{KT}_{1ml}^f$$
$$\overline{KT}_{2ml}^f = KT_{2m}^f; + (\bar{X}_{2m} - X_{2m})b_{mn}^2$$

$$KT^f_{3ml} = \overline{KT}^f_{2ml} - d_{ml}\overline{KT}^f_{2ml} = (1 - d_{ml})\overline{KT}^f_{2ml}$$
$$\overline{KT}^f_{3ml} = KT_{3ml} + (X_{3m} - X_{3m})b^2_{mn}$$

.

.

.

$$KT^f_{tml} = \overline{KT}^f_{t-1ml} - d_{ml}KT^f_{t-1ml} = (1 - d_{ml})\overline{KT}^f_{t-1ml}$$
$$\overline{KT}^f_{tml} - KT^f_{tml} + (\bar{X}_{tm} - X_{tm})b^2mn.$$

Assume that fixed capital is the only constraining factor:

$$X_{tmn} = \begin{cases} \dfrac{KT^f_{tmn}}{b^2_{mn}} = \dfrac{(1 - d_{mn})^{t-1}KT^f_{1mn}}{b^2_{mn}} & \text{if } n = 2, 3, \ldots, 7 \\[4mm] \dfrac{\overline{KT}^f_{tmn}}{b^2_{mn}} & \text{if } n-1 \end{cases}$$

Let $\bar{X}_{tm}$ = target output in two-digit sector m in period t.
Assuming no reinvestment in the period t, the resulting output is

$$X_{tm} = \frac{(1 - d_{ml})\overline{KT}^f_{(t-1)ml}}{b^2_{mn}} + \sum_{n=2}^{7} X_{tmn}$$

$$= \hat{X}_{tml} + \sum_{n=2}^{7} X_{tmn}.$$

If $X_{tm} \geq \bar{X}_{tm}$, then no investment is needed in period t in two-digit sector m.
If $X_{tm} < \bar{X}_{tm}$, then $\bar{X}_{tm} - X_{tm}$ must be produced in the optimal activity.
KT^f_{tml} must be argumented by $(\bar{X}_{tm} - X_{tm})b^2_{mn}$ to yield $\overline{KT}^f_{tm}$:

$$\text{i.e.,} \left(\frac{KT^f_{tml}}{b^2_{ml}} + \sum_{n=2}^{7} \left(\frac{KT^f_{tmn}}{b^2_{mn}} \right) \right) =$$

$$= \left[\frac{KT^f_{tml}}{b^2_{ml}} + \frac{(\bar{X}_{tm} - X_{tm})b^2_{ml}}{b^2_{ml}7} \right] + \sum_{n=2}^{7} \left(\frac{KT^f_{tmn}}{b^2_{mn}} \right)$$

$$= X_{tm1} + (\bar{X}_{tm} - X_{tm}) + \sum_{n=2}^{7} X_{tmn}$$

$$= X_{tm} + \bar{X}_{tm} - X_{tm}$$

$$= \bar{X}_{tm.}$$

Thus in period t, each activity produces X_{tmn}. The optimal activity produces $X_{tml} = \hat{X}_{tml} + \bar{X}_{tml}$ where $\hat{X}_{tml}$ is produced if no investment takes place in period t and depreciation of the previous year's stock of fixed capital is taken into consideration and $\bar{X}_{tml}$ is produced as a result of the current year's investment in the optimal activity. This calculation for each period and two-digit sector yields a time schedule of output by activity set.

Assuming no redundancy in inputs, the above time schedule can be transformed into a time schedule of required inputs:

$$(LC_{tmn}, \overline{KT^f_{tmn}}, KT^w_{tmn}, M_{tmn}) \qquad \text{if } n = 1$$
$$(LC_{tmn}, KT^f_{tmn}, KT^w_{tmn}, M_{tmn}) \qquad \text{if } n = 2, 3, \ldots, 7$$

$$\text{where } LC_{tmn} = b^1_{mn} \cdot X_{ymn} = b^1_{mn} \cdot \frac{(1 - d_{mn})^{t-1} KT^f_{1mn}}{b^2_{mn}}$$

$$KT^f_{tmn} = b^2_{mn} \cdot X_{tmn} = (1 - d_{mn})^{t-1} KT^f_{1mn} \qquad \text{if } n = 2, 3, \ldots 7$$

$$KT^w_{tmn} = b^3_{mn} \cdot X_{ymn} = b^3_{mn} \cdot \frac{(1 - d_{mn})^{t-1} KT^f_{1mn}}{b^2_{mn}}$$

$$Mt_{mn} = b^4_{mn} \cdot X_{tmn} = b^4_{mn} \cdot \frac{(1 - d_{mn})^{t-1} KT^f_{1mn}}{b^2_{mn}}$$

$\overline{KT^f_{tmn}}$ are calculated as described above.

Now assume that five labor categories are related to output by

$$X_{tmn} = \min\left(\frac{L1_{tmn}}{a^1_{mn}}, \frac{L2_{tmn}}{a^2_{mn}}, \frac{L3_{tmn}}{a^3_{mn}}, \frac{L4_{tmn}}{a^4_{mn}}, \frac{L5_{tmn}}{a^5_{mn}}\right)$$

$$t = 1, 2, \ldots$$
$$m = 1, 2, \ldots, 20$$
$$n = 1, 2, \ldots, 7.$$

Assuming that the above relationship holds and that none of the five labor categories are redundant in any two-digit sector or in any of the seven activity sets within the sectors, the labor categories needed over time to maintain all the sectoral output targets are given below. Note the functional relationship permits no substitution. This time schedule of required inputs will be:

$$(L1_{tmn}, L2_{tmn}, L3_{tmn}, L4_{tmn}, L5_{tmn})$$
$$t = 1, 2, \ldots$$
$$m = 1, 2, \ldots, 20$$
$$n = 1, 2, \ldots, 7$$
$$\text{if } n = 2, 3, \ldots 7, \text{ then } L1_{tmn} = a^1_{mn} \cdot X_{tmn} = \frac{a^1_{mn}}{b^2_{mn}} \cdot (1 - d_{mn})^{t-1} KT^f_{1mn}$$

$$L2_{tmn} = a^2_{mn} \cdot X_{tmn} - \frac{a^2_{mn}}{b^2_{mn}} \cdot (1 - d_{mn})^{t-1} KT^f_{1mn}$$

$$L3_{tmn} = a^3_{mn} \cdot X_{tmn} = \frac{a^3_{mn}}{b^2_{mn}} \cdot (1 - d_{mn})^{t-1} KT^f_{1mn}$$

$$L4_{tmn} = a^4_{mn} \cdot X_{tmn} = \frac{a^4_{mn}}{b^2_{mn}} \cdot (1 - d_{mn})^{t-1} KT^f_{1mn}$$

$$L5_{tmn} - a^5_{mn} \cdot X_{ymn} - \frac{a^5_{mn}}{b^2_{mn}} \cdot (1 - d_{mn})^{t-1} KT^f_{1mn}$$

$$\text{if } n = 1, \text{ then } LJ_{tmn} = a^J_{mn} - X_{tmn} = a^J_{mn} \frac{\overline{KT^f_{tmn}}}{b^2_{mn}}; \quad J = 1, 2, 3, 4, 5.$$

To determine required sectoral labor categories in time t, aggregate the seven activity sets. Thus the sectoral required inputs will be

$$(L1_{tm}, L2_{tm}, L3_{tm}, L4_{tm}, L5_{tm})$$
$$t = 1, 2, \dots$$
$$m = 1, 2, \dots 20$$
$$\text{where } LJ_{tm} = \sum_{n=1}^{J} LJ_{tmn}, \quad J - 1, 2, 3, 4, 5.$$

To determine the required labor categories for the entire manufacturing sector, aggregate the 20 two-digit categories. The manufacturing sectors required inputs at time t will be

$$(L1_t, L2_t, L3_t, L4_t, L5_t)$$
$$t = 1, 2, \dots$$
$$\text{where } LJ_t = \sum_{m=1}^{20} LJ_{tm}, \quad J = 1, 2, 3, 4, 5.$$

These employment estimates describe only broad categories of labor. They are computed in the simulation analysis in aggregated form in order to reduce the computational time.

One procedure for disaggregation is to estimate the three-digit occupational distribution of employment in each labor category (i.e., L_1, L_2, etc.) in the matched firm set by activity and two-digit sector and apply these distributions to the computed value of the labor categories for each activity. If there are P distinct occupational skills in the sector, then:

$$LJ_{tmn} = (S1^J_{tmn}, S2^J_{tmn}, \dots SP^J_{tmn})$$
$$J = 1, 2, 3, 4, 5$$
$$m - 1, 2, \dots, 20$$
$$n - 1, 2, \dots, 7$$

$LJ_{tmn} = \sum\limits_{Q=1}^{P} SQ^J_{tmn}$, where LJ_{mn} and SQ^J_{mn} are the number of employees in each category, and

$$SQ^J_{tmn} = s^{QJ}_{1mn} \cdot LJ_{tmn} \text{ where } s^{QJ}_{1mn} = \frac{SQ_{1mn}}{LJ_{1mn}}, \qquad Q = 1, 2, \dots P.$$

Thus the skill requirements of the manufacturing sector in time t are as follows:

$$(S1_t, S2_t, \dots, SP_t)$$

$$\text{where } SQ = \sum\limits_{J=1}^{5} \sum\limits_{m=1}^{20} \sum\limits_{n=1}^{7} SQ^J_{tmn} \qquad \begin{array}{l} Q = 1, 2, \dots P \\ t \ -1, 2, \dots \end{array}$$

The procedure for calculating the terminal year manpower requirement vectors assumes that the industry output targets have been accurately projected, that the distribution of activity output within each two-digit sector has been correctly described by the simulation and that the activity-industry specific occupational skill mix will not change over time. If these assumptions hold then the terminal year activity-industry specific employment vectors are calculated by applying the activity-industry specific occupational percentage distributions based on the matched firm data to the projected activity-industry specific employment level calculated in the simulation. The occupational distribution for each two-digit sector is found by aggregating its seven activities and the overall manufacturing sector's occupational mix is determined by aggregating the 20 two-digit sectors. A mathematical description of this procedure is as follows:

L_{Tmn} = terminal year (T) employment by activity n
   ($n = 1, 3, \dots 7$) and two-digit sector m
   ($M = 1, 2, \dots 20$) as computed in the simulation. (Total: 140)   (1)

$$(a^{mn}) = \begin{bmatrix} a1^{mn} \\ a2^{mn} \\ \cdot \\ \cdot \\ \cdot \\ aP^{mn} \end{bmatrix}$$ = percentage distribution of employment by three-digit occupation category in the base year by activity n and two-digit sector m. $\sum\limits_{J=1}^{P} aJ^{mn} = 100.0$ This vector is based on the matched firm data (Total: 140)   (2)

$$\text{Multiply: } L_{Tmn} \cdot (a^{mn}) = \begin{bmatrix} L_{Tmn} \cdot a1^{mn} \\ L_{Tmn} \cdot a2^{mn} \\ \cdot \\ \cdot \\ \cdot \\ L_{Tmn} \cdot aP^{mn} \end{bmatrix} = \begin{bmatrix} L1^{mn}_T \\ L2^{mn}_T \\ \cdot \\ \cdot \\ \cdot \\ LP^{mn}_T \end{bmatrix} = \begin{bmatrix} L^{mn}_T \end{bmatrix}$$ (3)

$[L_T^{mn}]$ = terminal year employment distribution by three-digit occupational category in activity n and two-digit sector m (Total: 140).

$$\text{Aggregate the activities: } \sum_{n=1}^{7} [L_T^{mn}] = \begin{bmatrix} \sum_{n=1}^{7} L1_T^{mn} \\ \sum_{n=1}^{7} L2_T^{mn} \\ \cdot \\ \cdot \\ \cdot \\ \sum_{n=1}^{7} LP_T^{mn} \end{bmatrix} \begin{bmatrix} L1_T^{mn} \\ L2_T^{m} \\ \\ \\ \\ LP_T^{m} \end{bmatrix} = [L_T^m] \qquad (4)$$

$[L_T^m]$ – terminal year employment distribution by three-digit occupational category in two-digit sector m (Total: 20).

$$\text{Aggregate the two-digit sectors: } \sum_{m=1}^{20} [L_T^{m}] = \begin{bmatrix} \sum_{m=1}^{20} L1_T^{m} \\ \sum_{m=1}^{20} L2_T^{m} \\ \cdot \\ \cdot \\ \sum_{m=1}^{20} LP_T^{m} \end{bmatrix} \begin{bmatrix} L1_T \\ L2_T \\ \\ \\ LP_T \end{bmatrix} = = [L_T] \qquad (5)$$

$[L_T]$ = terminal year employment distribution by three-digit occupational category for the entire manufacturing sector (Total: 1).

THE APPLIED MODEL

The use of the model in analysis is illustrated below in application to the food processing sector (Sector 20). This sector contained 582 establishments with useable data. The most efficient set of establishments is Set 2 with value added 2.14 times its reported factor costs when current capital costs are estimated as 10 percent of the value of fixed assets and working capital plus depreciation. Activity 3 is nearly as efficient with a value added to cost ratio of 2.04. Further, its labor costs per unit of output are 36 percent greater than Activity 2 while its current capital costs are 40 percent less. Consequently it is an optimal technique in terms of a trade-off between employment and efficiency objectives.

    The target growth rate for the sector was given as an annual rate of increase in gross output of 7.9 percent. Gross output was estimated as 4.847 billion Bolivars in 1970 on the basis of establishment data. The target output for 1985 is 13.106 billion Bolivars in real terms, i.e., at 1970 prices. With these growth rates, simulation Trial 2 assumes a profit-maximizing objective and specifies Activity 2 as the optimal set of techniques. Trial 4 trades productivity for employment growth at the least cost rate. On this criterion Activity 3 is optimal. The values of the technical coefficients of the sector for 1970 and 1985 for both trials are given in Table 1 below. Under the assumptions of Trial 2, sector productivity would increase from 1.252 in 1970 to 2.076 in 1985. Employment would rise from 48,265 to 126,694, an increase of 162 percent or an annual rate of increase of 6.65 percent. Total capital requirements would increase at an annual rate of 5.8 percent.

    The pattern of technical change represented in Trial 4 would increase employment at an rate of 8.7 percent to 169,437 in the target year; an increase of 43,000 jobs over the more capital intensive process. At the same time, productivity would rise to a level of 2.003, only slightly lower than in Trial 2 and with a terminal year capital requirement 9 percent less.

    The difference in employment and investment outcomes of these two simulations are not relatively large in this sector because the most efficient activity is only moderately capital intensive and the sector as a whole is relatively labor intensive. Estimates of employment and productivity for each subsector are shown in summary form in Table 2. Each value is given for 1970 and for 1985 for two simulation conditions.

    In six of the twenty subsectors the most efficient set of techniques is also optimal in terms of employment and there is no difference in the growth patterns represented by the two simulation trials. For the total sector, the differences between alternative growth patterns are great. The more labor-intensive pattern would create about 340,000 more jobs by 1985 than the most efficient pattern. This is a difference of nearly 38 percent. The employment growth rate for Trial 2 would be about 9.5 percent while for Trial 4 it would be 11.9 percent.

    The labor-intensive growth pattern would require about three times as many professional and technical workers as were in the 1970 manufacturing sector labor force. The more capital intensive technique would require about four times the 1970 level and the ratio of professional and technical workers to total employment would be nearly twice the ratio for the labor intensive technique. It is doubtful, however, that the supply of professional workers could act as a constraint on this choice of technique. Since the annual growth rate in professional employment under the labor-intensive assumptions is less than 8 percent and clearly within acceptable bounds given the current capacity of institutions of higher learning.

    Neither of these growth paths would be constrained by investment require-

Table 1. Venezuelan Manufacturing Sector 20.

Sector	Gross Output	Labor Costs	Fixed Capital	Working Capital	Non Factor Costs	Employment	Productivity
Value[a]	X	(B_1)	(B_2)	(B_3)	(B_4)	(L)	(P)
1970	4,847,407	544,248	1,564,796	602,0?1	3,698,251	48,265	1.252
1985–T2[b]	15,190,706	1,428,601	3,245,434	1,806,018	10,569,576	126,694	2.076
1985–T4[c]	15,190,706	1,910,574	3,456,629	1,147,557	10,007,920	169,437	2.003
Coefficients[d]							
1970		.1123	.3228	.12?2	.7629		
1985–T2		.0940	.2136	.1187	.6958		
1985–T4		.1258	.2275	.0755	.6634		
Activity							
Coefficients							
1		.0695	.3759	.144?	.6911		
2		.0928	.2062	.1188	.6927		
3		.1271	.2212	.072?	.6577		
4		.0947	.3620	.1811	.7719		
5		.1491	.3428	.155?	.7160		
6		.1571	.3082	.0911	.7618		
7		.1240	.3810	.1125	.8931		

[a] Thousands of Bolivars at 1970 prices.
[b] Trial 2.
[c] Trial 4.
[d] Units per 1000 Bolivars of gross output.

Table 2. Venezuelan Manufacturing: 1970 and Simulated 1985 Productivity and Employment.

Sector	Productivity (1)			Employment (2)		
	1970	1985 Trial 2	1985 Trial 4	1970	1985 Trial 2	1985 Trial 4
20	1.252	2.076	2.003	48,265	126,694	169,437
21	2.399	3.500	3.008	10,201	27,518	33,470
22	2.493	2.687	1.708	1,628	5,279	16,949
23	1.047	1.903	1.712	23,902	88,019	170,834
24	1.255	2.264	1.895	23,682	59,283	77,299
25	1.054	1.989	1.989	4,919	14,759	14,759
26	1.128	1.927	1.927	10,636	28,912	28,912
27	1.616	4.531	4.531	8,436	28,832	28,832
28	1.189	2.736	1.492	8,162	22,193	48,787
29	.742	1.507	1.310	2,565	5,810	6,224
30	1.548	3.118	1.509	12,203	58,930	61,407
31	1.654	2.741	2.710	14,213	121,471	124,629
33	1.263	1.925	1.925	14,675	78,296	78,296
34	.802	2.446	1.459	10,775	38,500	54,966
35	1.190	2.347	2.086	10,976	67,959	82,692
36	1.264	1.967	1.937	8,598	66,826	142,623
37	1.251	2.857	2.857	4,374	21,816	21,816
38	.853	2.212	1.532	5,349	10,521	42,721
39	1.282	2.791	2.195	7,100	32,007	45,424
TOTAL				231,007	903,947	1,250,399

[1]Value added per unit of factor costs.
[2]Full-time equivalents = 2,000 man-hours per worker.

ments. The Trial 2 path would require a net increase in fixed assets at an annual rate of approximately 7.6 percent. The Trial 4 path would need an annual increase of less than 5 percent.

Differences in sector productivity in the two models are not as great as the differences in factor proportions might suggest. Productivity in Sector 20 varies by only 4 percent in the two simulations. In half of the twenty sectors the productivity of the labor-intensive technique is within 10 percent of the most efficient technique. In all cases, the profit rate of the activity is sufficiently high to induce investment at any normal market rate of return.

EFFECTS OF UNDERUTILIZATION

Further, one should note that investment requirements are overstated in the model because it assumes full use of existing capacity, an assumption that is not warranted. Unfortunately, utilization data were available only for those establishments in the "manpower" sample and the potential distortions involved in estimating utilization rates for individual firms in the universe appeared too great to justify an adjustment. The sample suggests however that underutilization is extensive and consequently capital coefficients have an upward bias while productivity estimates are biased downward.

Of the 966 firms with utilization data, nearly 24 percent are currently utilizing their plant and equipment less than 40 hours a week. Nearly 75 percent are operating less than 60 hours a week, and only 12 percent more than 120 hours a week. Of the firms that are operating 40 hours a week or less, nearly half indicated a desire to operate a greater number of hours, and most preferred an operating level that was at least twice their current rate. About 20 percent of those who are working between 43 and 82 hours a week would also prefer to work additional hours and the mean additional hours would be nearly twice the current rate. In contrast, only 11 percent are operating more than 124 hours a week and few of these (12 percent) prefer to work additional hours. In other words, about half of the firms that are operating at the equivalent of one 40-hour turn per week are doing so voluntarily, and the others are operating at that low level for other reasons.

About 60 percent of all of the reasons given for failure to operate at the desired rate of utilization were related to either the aggregate demand for the product or competition of other products. Only 2 percent indicated a constraint imposed by a lack of working capital and 16 percent indicated constraints imposed by other factor shortages. About 6 percent indicated that the scale of the enterprise was larger than justified by the market at the time the equipment was installed, and some 13 percent of all responses were related to other reasons. Clearly the current utilization rate is primarily a function of tradition and product demand rather than of factor constraints.

Although the current pattern of utilization may be a function of short-term conditions, given the cross-sectional nature of the data, more than 57 percent of all those operating at less than the desired rate indicated that they had been operating under those conditions all of the time since their machinery was installed. About 25 percent indicated that their plant had been underutilized more than half the time since its installation, and 20 percent were underutilized less than half of the period.

These rates are a partial function of the age of equipment. For example, of those firms indicating that their equipment had been installed after 1964, 43 percent indicated that they had been underutilized most of the time. In contrast, 93 percent of those whose equipment was installed between 1950 and 1959 indicated that they had been operating at less than desired rates most of the period.

The basic simulation model was applied to this set of firms to test the impact of a utilization adjustment on the technical coefficients. The process adjusts all variable costs and outputs by a factor which is the ratio of reported weekly hours of plant operation to 120. In Sectors 23, 33, and 34 many

many less efficient firms reported activity rates in excess of 120 hours and the effect of the adjustment was to reduce sector productivity. In all other sectors the adjusted productivity was from 10 to 30 percent greater than the unadjusted value. The productivity of the optimal activity was higher in all cases except sector 23 after adjustment and the differences were significant. In 11 out of 19 sectors, the activity that was most efficient before the adjustment was also optimal after adjustment. In eight sectors the adjustment made another activity more efficient and there is no consistent pattern of change.

AN ASSESSMENT

The extensive debate around terminological issues in the recent OECD conference on the choice of technology [OECD (6)] reflects the state of the art in incorporating technical change into growth theory. Nevertheless that conference did reflect a very strong consensus concerning the policy importance of conflicts between the growth and employment objectives of developing countries, and the consequent necessity of a strategy of technical choice. In the terminology of the conference, the technical condition for policy formation is the specification of the "appropriate" technology for a specific policy context and resource environment, and the elaboration of operational policy instruments.

The experience described in this paper in the use of a simulation model based on a highly disaggregated empirical analysis of sectoral production functions suggests an operational technique for the specification of an "appropriate" technology or pattern of technical change. It indicates, for example, that in each country in which the technique has been tested, a significant increase in output and employment was possible by an increase in the rate of utilization of existing capacity and that the appropriate policy instruments were those that would reduce cultural constraints and increase effective demand. It also suggests that in most sectors dramatic changes in productivity could be achieved by the extensive use of the "best practice" techniques in current use and that the shift to these techniques was largely independent of relative factor prices. Finally, it suggests that in most sectors there is sufficient variance in factor proportions among the set of best practice techniques that trade-offs based on the choice of technique are possible with minimum costs.

It is obvious, on the other hand, that in its present form the technique has several limitations. Many of these are functions of expediency or the paucity of historical data in developing countries. The assumption that the economy is closed to new techniques in the planning period is of the first order. The use of one-period cross-sectional data to estimate production coefficients is of the second order. Neither is generic to the model.

The most critical limitation, from a policy perspective, is in the specification of a production function in economic terms. The specification of a technique in terms of labor costs and asset values is useful in evaluating alternative techniques but choices are not readily translated into policy instruments or communicated to decision makers as choice criteria. For example, over 90 percent of the directors of establishments in the manpower survey said that they were not aware of any existing technique or process that was more efficient than the one they employed. Clearly, a primary policy instrument in this case is the diffusion of knowledge concerning alternatives. This requires the specification of the alternatives in "engineering" terms. The research design on which the model is based assumed a technological translation from a sample of establishments in relevant activities. Without it the operational value of the technique is limited. In this dimension, it reflects the state of the art in science policy. The development of a growth policy in which technical choice is a strategic policy variable requires a closing of a conceptual and methodological gap between technologists and technological users.

REFERENCES

1. Ahmad, B. and M. Blaug, eds. 1973. *The Practice of Manpower Forecasting.* San Francisco.
2. Atkinson, Anthony and Joseph E. Stiglitz. 1969. A New View of Technical Change. *The Economic Journal* September : 573–578.
3. Bowles, S. 1970. Aggregation of Labor Inputs in the Economics of Growth and Planning: Experiments with a Two-Level CES Function. *Journal of Political Economy* January : 68–81.
4. Chirikos, Thomas N., Clifton S. Kelley, G. C. Lamb, Donald P. Sanders and John R. Shea. 1971. *Human Resources in Bolivia: Problems, Planning and Policy.* Columbus: Center for Human Resource Research, The Ohio State University.
5. Kelley, S. Clifton, Stavros Apergis, Peter Barth and Thomas N. Chirikos, with Junta Nacional de Planificacion y Coordinacion. 1973. Human Resources in Ecuador: *Problems, Planning and Policy.* Columbus: Center for Human Resource Research, The Ohio State University.
6. OECD Development Center. 1974. *Choice and Adaptation of Technology in Developing Countries: An Overview of Major Policy Proceedings.* Paris.
7. Salter, W. E. G. 1966. *Productivity and Technical Change.* Cambridge University Press.
8. Schumpeter, Joseph. 1951. *The Theory of Economic Development.* Harvard University Press.

THE GROWTH OF
PROFESSIONAL OCCUPATIONS
IN U.S. MANUFACTURING:
1900–1973

Carmel Ullman Chiswick, UNIVERSITY OF
ILLINOIS AT CHICAGO CIRCLE

I. INTRODUCTION AND SUMMARY OF
FINDINGS

An important but little-understood aspect of the relationship between human capital and economic development is the shift in occupational structure in favor of white-collar occupations in general and professional-technical occupations in particular. Although historians and sociologists have perceived this shift as a dominant feature of modernization in the twentieth century [see, e.g., Parsons (16)], economists tend to regard such occupational changes as incidental to the rise in educational attainment. Even investiga-

Research in Human Capital and Development, Vol. 1, pp. 191–217.

tions of the degree of substitution between labor with different levels of schooling rarely consider the effect of changes in occupation in interpreting their results [see, e.g., Berndt and Christensen (2); Dougherty (8)].

Although all white-collar occupation groups have grown in importance since the turn of the century, the truly remarkable growth has been among the professional occupations and their clerical counterparts; these two groups accounted for only 7 percent of the active labor force in 1900 but had grown to 25 percent by 1960 and 32 percent by 1970. In the manufacturing sector, salaries (the form of remuneration typical for white-collar employees) have risen steadily from only 16 percent of the total wage bill at the turn of the century to 39 percent by the 1960s. Moreover, the numbers tell only part of the story since changes of this magnitude in the composition of the labor force have been accompanied by far-reaching changes in the socio-economic structure of the United States [Parsons (16)].

Some Hypotheses

The weight of these considerations suggests that high-level manpower should be incorporated into production analysis as a factor distinct from labor in the traditional sense, a type of human capital with productive attributes which are qualitatively different from the type of human capital embodied in conventional labor. This immediately suggests that the observed growth of professional occupations has been accompanied by factor-substituting changes in production techniques. The central hypothesis of this paper is that this factor substitution, induced by changes in relative factor proportions, can explain much of the growth of professional occupations in the U.S. manufacturing sector during the period 1900–1973. This hypothesis is consistent with recent findings that cross-country differences in the earnings of university-educated personnel relative to average earnings is inversely related to the proportion of the labor force with university education [Tinbergen (18)]. It is also consistent with the findings of growth-accounting studies that an index of the "education" embodied in the labor force can explain much "technical change" [see, for example, Denison (6); Nadiri (15); Psacharopoulous and Hirchliffe (17)]. Since any index of "education" for the labor force as a whole would be highly correlated with the relative importance of professional and technical occupations, a rise in this index would be associated with factor-substituting changes in production techniques.

The null hypothesis to be tested here is that both demand and supply for professionals relative to conventional labor have been stable functions of market prices throughout the period under consideration. This is consistent with the observed occupational shifts because the relevant price variables are different for the supply and demand functions; whereas the supply of professionals relative to nonprofessionals depends on the rate of return to an investment in professional skills, the demand depends on the relative price to employers of professional services. In order to discuss a market for professionals relative to conventional labor, it is necessary to convert either the supply function into relative-price units or the demand function into rate-of-return units so that they may be graphed on the same set of axes. Much of the literature on the role of human capital in the labor market treats supply as a stable function of the rate of return to an investment, implicitly converting demand into a function of this rate of return. Although this demand function has been shifting upward over time, it would be erroneous to infer secular shifts in relative demand for professionals expressed as a function of relative price. Becker (1) has used the notion of "neutral technical change" specifically to illustrate the case where the relative demand curve is not shifting; his is apparently the only discussion of this problem in the literature on labor markets.

An alternative hypothesis is that exogenous technical change has been biased in favor of professionals. To the author's knowledge, however, this has never been empirically confirmed, much less shown to be of a sufficient order of magnitude to explain the professionalization of the American labor force. Another hypothesized explanation of the growth of the professions is that American consumers have a high income elasticity of demand for services, so that a change in the composition of demand for labor has resulted directly from the growth in income over the last century. This is not a satisfactory explanation, however, since employment of professionals in goods-producing industries has been growing *pari passu* with that in the so-called service industries. Leaving aside the education sector, in 1960 one out of every three white-collar workers was employed in a "goods-producing" industry and 35 percent of persons in professional and technical occupations worked in manufacturing.

Summary of Findings

The model developed here considers the ratio of professional and technical employees to all other workers as the "quantity" variable and the ratio of the earnings of the former to the latter as the corresponding "price" variable for both demand and supply in the market for professional manpower. When the supply function is expressed in these units, the direct cost of higher education (tuition, fees, etc.) relative to the indirect cost (foregone earnings) is shown to be the relevant shift variable. This variable is fairly easy to measure and has been declining steadily throughout the period under consideration. The consequent shifts in the relative supply curve permit statistical identification of the relative demand curve and thus the testing of hypotheses about the behavior of demand during this period.

It will be shown that there is a significant negative slope to this relative demand curve and that the elasticity of substitution between professionals and nonprofessionals is on the order of 2.5.[1] It will also be shown that the data do not support any hypothesis that implies a secular shift in the relative demand curve in favor of professional manpower. The absence of such a shift implies that biased technical change could not have been responsible for increases in the demand for professionals. This stability in the relative demand curve also precludes statistical identification of the relative supply curve. However, the supply shift variable is the most important exogenous variable in the reduced form of this model; changes in the direct cost of higher education relative to its indirect cost can be used to predict changes in both the proportion and the relative earnings of salaried employees in manufacturing. The finding that the relative demand for professionals has not been shifting during the entire first three-quarters of the twentieth century implies that the increasing use of professional and technical skills in production cannot be attributed to biased income elasticities of demand, to the requirements of biased technical change, to the requirements of increasingly sophisticated forms of physical capital, or to the requirements of large-scale corporate enterprises. At the same time, the negative slope of the relative demand curve indicates that professional and technical manpower can be taken to be a separate resource, a factor of production in its own right that can be substituted for conventional labor and physical capital in production in response to a long-run decline in its relative price. The fairly high estimated elasticity of substitution between the two kinds of manpower validates the hypothesis that this kind of factor-substituting change in production techniques has been important.

Outline

In Section II the model of the market for professionals relative to non-professionals will be specified more rigorously along the lines outlined above. Although this model is developed in a general form, the specific equations to be estimated will also be presented and various tests for hypotheses about the labor market will be specified. In Section III, cross-section estimates of the parameters based on data for 1910 and 1920 will be presented and discussed. Since the basic hypothesis to be tested is that these parameters have remained constant throughout the period 1900–1973, Section IV compares the time-series estimates implied by this hypothesis with the actual data for this period. Section V includes a summary of results, with particular reference to their implications for the study of economic growth and development in the United States.

II. THE MODEL

This model considers human capital as a factor of production that is analogous, from the employer's point of view, to physical capital. As it has become conventional to think of physical capital as being measured in "efficiency" units, so human capital should be measured in "skill" units. The term "labor" is reserved in this paper for the concept "number of people." To consider "raw" or "pure" labor as a factor of production distinct from human capital would be the same as to consider the number of machines as a factor of production distinct from physical capital. The approach followed here therefore treats the number of workers as a component of human capital. The number of workers in nonprofessional and professional occupations are denoted L_1 and L_2, respectively; the amounts of the two kinds of human capital embodied in each group of workers are denoted H_1 and H_2, respectively.[2] The average skill level of each group, h_1 and h_2, respectively, is defined so that

$$H_1 = h_1 L_1 \quad \text{and} \quad H_2 = h_2 L_2. \tag{1}$$

There are two labor markets, one for each kind of worker. Since H_1 and H_2 represent the resources available for use in production, they are the relevant "quantity" variables in the two markets for labor services. The market price for each skill unit will be denoted r_1 and r_2, respectively, for the two kinds of human capital. The total wage bill for a group of workers is the same thing as the total factor payment for human capital embodied in those workers,

$$r_1 H_1 \equiv w_1 L_1 \quad \text{and} \quad r_2 H_2 \equiv w_2 L_2$$

where w_1 and w_2 denote the average earnings of each group of workers. Taking the ratio of these two expressions, substituting equations (1) into the result and manipulating terms yields the following relationship between the relative earnings of professionals and the relative price of the human factor of production embodied in them:

$$\frac{w_2}{w_1} = \frac{h_2}{h_1} \cdot \frac{r_2}{r_1}. \tag{2}$$

In effect, the average wage of a group of workers is the market value of the average "amount" of the appropriate type of human capital embodied in those workers.

The Demand Function

The derived demand for high-level manpower relative to conventional manpower is most easily obtained from a three-factor production function:

$V = F(H_1, H_2, K)$ where V = aggregate value-added
                                and K = physical capital (expressed in efficiency
                                units).   (3)

The ratio of marginal products of any two factors of production should equal the ratio of their market prices in an economy with competitive markets and profit-maximizing firms. Assuming these conditions implies that

$$r_2/r_1 = \frac{MPH_2}{MPH_1} = G(H_1, H_2 ; K) \qquad (4)$$

where the function G is derived directly from the function F in equation (3). This is the derived demand for factors, for it expresses the amounts for the two kinds of human capital that employers wish to hire as a function of their relative prices. The elasticity of substitution between these two factors of production is by definition:

$$\sigma^* \equiv \frac{-d(\log H_2/H_1)}{d(\log r_2/r_1)}. \qquad (5)$$

The problem posed by the hypothesis to be tested is to describe not the relative demand for factors of production but rather the demand for persons in professional occupations relative to the rest of the labor force. Substituting equation (4) and then (1) into (2) transforms the demand function into units relevant for the labor market:

$$w_2/w_1 = D(L_1, L_2 ; h_1, h_2, K) \qquad (6)$$

where the function D is derived directly from the function G.

The elasticity of substitution between the two human factors of production, H_1 and H_2, is conceptually distinct from the elasticity of relative demand for professionals, L_2/L_1. The latter is the elasticity of the demand curve of equation (6) and is defined as:

$$\sigma \equiv \frac{-d(\log L_2/L_1)}{d(\log w_2/w_1)}, \qquad (7)$$

the percentage change in the relative number of professionals demanded induced by a percentage change, ceteris paribus, in their relative price. By substituting equations (1) and (2) into equation (5) and manipulating terms, the elasticity of substitution between the two types of human capital may be expressed as:

$$\sigma^* = \frac{-[d(\log L_2/L_1) + d(\log h_2/h_1)]}{d(\log w_2/w_1) - d(\log h_2/h_1)}.$$

The two elasticities σ and σ^* will be identical in the case where $d(\log h_2/h_1) =$

0; in the case of changes over time, this condition is the special case in which h_1 and h_2 are growing at the same rate. Thus it is important to note that even though the elasticity of substitution between factors of production cannot be estimated directly, as long as the difference in the rates of growth of h_1 and h_2 is small it is possible to use the estimated elasticity of relative demand as an approximation of the elasticity of substitution.

Note that there is no variable in equation (6) for the effect of industry mix on the derived demand for professionals relative to other workers. Industry mix is treated as endogenous to the system, being a function of relative wages and relative factor supplies among other things; changes in industrial composition constitute an important mechanism whereby changes in relative factor supplies affect relative marginal products and hence relative wages. This mechanism is embodied in the aggregate production function itself, especially in the parameter σ^*, and does not enter the demand equation as an independent variable.

To give further concreteness to this discussion, consider the Dhrymes-Kurz generalization of the CES production function:

$$V = [\beta_1 H_1^{-\rho_1} + \beta_2 H_2^{-\rho_2} + \beta_3 K^{-\rho_3}]^{-1/\rho}. \tag{3a}$$

Taking first partial derivatives with respect to each factor of production gives:

$$MPH_1 = \left(\frac{\beta_1 \rho_1}{\rho}\right) V^{(1+\rho)} H_1^{-(1+\rho_1)}$$

$$MPH_2 = \left(\frac{\beta_2 \rho_2}{\rho}\right) V^{(1+\rho)} H_2^{-(1+\rho_2)}$$

$$MPK = \left(\frac{\beta_3 \rho_3}{\rho}\right) V^{(1+\rho)} K^{-(1+\rho_3)}.$$

From this is easily derived the specific form for the function G, the demand for H_2 relative to H_1, associated with this particular production function:

$$r_2/r_1 = \frac{MPH_2}{MPH_1} = \left(\frac{\beta_2 \rho_2}{\beta_1 \rho_1}\right) H_1^{(1+\rho_1)} H_2^{-(1+\rho_2)}. \tag{4a}$$

Substituting (4a) and then (1) into equation (2) and collecting terms results in the relative demand function:

$$w_2/w_1 = \left(\frac{\beta_2 \rho_2}{\beta_1 \rho_1}\right) L_1^{(1+\rho_1)} L_2^{-(1+\rho_2)} h_1^{\rho_1} h_2^{-\rho_2}. \tag{6a}$$

Shifts in the relative demand for professionals may be analyzed by differentiating equation (6a) with respect to the relevant variables. Changes in average skill levels, the human analogue to capital accumulation (or depreciation), may shift the relative demand curve by changing h_1 and h_2:[3]

$$d(\log w_2/w_1) = \rho_1 d(\log h_1) - \rho_2 d(\log h_2). \qquad (8)$$

The demand curve will shift rightward if, and only if, $d(\log w_2/w_1)$ is positive; that is, if and only if

$$\frac{d(\log h_2)}{d(\log h_1)} > \frac{\rho_1}{\rho_2} \text{ for } \rho_2 < 0 \text{ and } d(\log h_1) > 0.$$

In the constant-elasticity-of-substitution case where $\rho_1 = \rho_2$ skill-acquisition causes the relative demand curve to shift in favor of professionals if, and only if, the average skill level of the professional labor force is growing at a faster rate than the average skill level of conventional labor. Similarly, factor-augmenting technical change (which is formally the equivalent of an increase in skill levels) can be said to shift the composition of demand in favor of professional occupations if, and only if, it "augments" h_2 at a faster rate than h_1.

The Supply Function

The supply of persons qualified for professional and technical occupations relative to other members of the labor force has depended primarily on the output of institutions for higher education and on immigration. The other source of high-level manpower, mid-career promotions from nonprofessional to professional positions, was not sufficiently important during the period of this study to have contributed significantly to the observed increase in the proportion of the labor force in professional occupations.

Assuming that college places were available to anyone who wanted higher education, the output of colleges and universities will be directly related to the demand for higher education in a straightforward way. This demand may be thought of as having two components: the demand for an investment in future earning power and the demand for higher education as an item of consumption. In order to introduce as few new variables as possible into the analysis, it is assumed that (1) the expected annual increase in earnings due to college is approximated by the average difference in earnings between professionals and nonprofessionals, $w_2 - w_1$, (2) the opportunity cost of a year of higher education is the average annual earnings of a nonprofessional, w_1, and (3) the length of the working life is very long.

The total annual cost of higher education is the sum of the direct costs, T, and the indirect cost. The consumption demand, denoted $(L_2/L)_c$, is a negative function of this total cost and a positive function of family income, Y:

$$(L_2/L)_c = C(T + w_1; Y) \qquad (9)$$

$$\text{where } \frac{\partial C}{\partial (T + w_1)} < 0 \text{ and } \frac{\partial C}{\partial Y} > 0.$$

The investment demand, denoted $(L_2/L)_I$, is also inversely related to cost through the rate of return. Let the benefit-cost ratio R' be an approximation of the rate of return for the aggregate supply function:

$$R' \equiv \frac{w_2 - w_1}{N \cdot (w_1 + T)} \tag{10}$$

where N = number of years of higher education.

The investment demand for higher education is a positive function of R'; it is also a positive function of income, Y, insofar as families with higher incomes find it easier (cheaper) to finance such an investment. Finally, note that R' may be expressed as a positive function of the relative earnings of colleges graduates since dividing both numerator and denominator in equation (10) by w_1 gives the expression:

$$R' = \frac{(w_2/w_1) - 1}{N \cdot T'} \quad \text{where } T' = 1 + (T/w_1).$$

In summary, the investment demand for higher education may be expressed as:

$$(L_2/L)_I = I(w_2/w_1 ; T', Y) \tag{11}$$

$$\text{where } \frac{\partial I}{\partial (w_2/w_1)} > 0, \frac{\partial I}{\partial T'} < 0 \text{ and } \frac{\partial I}{\partial Y} > 0.$$

Equations (9) and (11) may thus be added together and manipulated to express the total demand for higher education relative to the supply of other workers, $(L_2/L_1)_{C+I}$, as a positive function of relative average earnings, w_2/w_1, and average family income Y, and a negative function of the total cost of higher education relative to its opportunity cost, T'.

The relative supply of high level manpower due to differential migration is also a positive function of w_2/w_1 and Y. That is, given the average income in the place of destination, relative immigration of high level manpower will be higher the higher their earnings relative to other workers. Similarly, given the average income in the place of origin, relative emigration of high-level manpower will be smaller the higher their relative earnings. The relative supply of high-level manpower due to migration may thus be expressed:

$$(L_2/L)_M = M(w_2/w_1 ; Y) \text{ where } \frac{\partial M}{\partial (w_2/w_1)} > 0 \text{ and } \frac{\partial M}{\partial Y} > 0. \tag{12}$$

This may be combined with the relationship for the supply due to higher education to arrive at the total supply of high-level manpower relative to the rest of the labor force:

$$L_2/L_1 = S(w_2/w_1 ; T', Y) \tag{13}$$

$$\text{where } \frac{\partial S}{\partial T'} < 0 \text{ and } \frac{\partial S}{\partial Y} > 0.$$

Since the investment and migration components of supply are positively related to relative earnings and the consumption component is independent of relative earnings, this supply curve should, *ceteris paribus*, have a non-negative slope. If L_2 constitutes a small fraction of the labor force, however, a decline in relative earnings associated with an increase in w_1 could have a positive income effect on the supply of high-level manpower if w_1 and Y are closely related to each other. This would generally be true regardless of the behavior of w_2; it is particularly important if w_1 is a reasonable approximation of family income as it pertains to the demand for higher education. (This would be the case if, for example, within the relevant price range all professionals and persons with large property incomes would be willing to send their children to college, for then it would be the average earnings of nonprofessionals that would be relevant for explaining changes at the margin in the demand for higher education.) The slope of the supply curve is therefore of indeterminate sign although if it should be negative it is necessary, for stability in the market, that the elasticity of supply not exceed in magnitude the elasticity of demand.

The Estimating Equations

The equations chosen with which to estimate this model are:

DEMAND:

$$\log(w_2/w_1) = b_0 + b_1 \log L_1 + b_2 \log L_2 + b_3 \log K + b_4 \log h_1 + b_5 \log h_2 \tag{14}$$

SUPPLY:

$$\log(L_2/L_1) = a_0 + a_1 \log w_1 + a_2 \log w_2 + a_3 \log T' + a_4 \log Y. \tag{15}$$

Equation (14) was chosen so as to enhance comparability with some of the most commonly used production functions.[4] By comparing equation (14) with the logarithm of equation (6a), it is apparent that the coefficient b_1 may be interpreted as $(1 + \rho_1)$ and b_2 as $- (1 + \rho_2)$. The elasticity of substitution between the two kinds of labor lies within the range established by $1/b_1$ and $- 1/b_2$ and should exceed unity. The general approach to the treatment of human capital as a factor of production in this model may be tested by means of the following null hypotheses:

$$b_1 > 0 \text{ and } b_2 < 0 \qquad (16)$$

$$b_3 = 0. \qquad (17)$$

Equation (16) represents the null hypothesis that professional manpower constitutes a factor of production in its own right; formally, it says that the elasticity of substitution between the two kinds of labor is finite. Equation (17) describes the separability of the production function with respect to physical capital; in order for the accumulation of physical capital to bias the demand for labor in favor of professional occupations it is necessary for b_3 to be positive. If in addition to both of these conditions,

$$b_4 = b_1 - 1 \quad \text{and} \quad b_5 = b_2 + 1, \qquad (18)$$

then the observed demand for labor is consistent with an underlying production function of the type described in equation (3a); equation (14) would merely be the logarithmic form of equation (6a).

The form of equation (15) was chosen so as to be compatible with (14) for purposes of estimation. The elasticity of supply lies within the range established by $-a_1$ and a_2. The "price" elasticity of demand for higher education is a_3 and the "income" elasticity is a_4; the former should be negative and the latter, non-negative.

Technical problems of estimation are greatly reduced under the assumption of constant elasticities for both supply and demand:

$$-a_1 = a_2 \qquad (19)$$

$$b_1 = -b_2 \qquad (20)$$

Under the assumptions described in equations (17), (19) and (20), a reduced-form equation for the system is:

$$\log(w_2/w_1) = c_1 \log T' + c_2 \log Y + c_3 \log h_1 + c_4 \log h_2 + c_0 \qquad (21)$$

where, setting $c_5 = 1/(1 - a_2 b_2)$,
$$c_1 = c_5(b_2 a_3)$$
$$c_2 = c_5(b_2 a_4)$$
$$c_3 = c_5 b_4$$
$$c_4 = c_5 b_5$$
and $c_0 = c_5(b_0 + b_2 a_0)$.

The five coefficients in equation (21) may be estimated directly using ordinary least-squares techniques.

This system is underidentified by three parameters, but if the underlying production function may be expressed as Dhrymes-Kurz, equations (18) are valid and the system is underidentified by only one parameter. Equations

(17), (18) and (20) imply that b_2 is the only independent parameter in the demand equation. Since $\hat{\sigma} = -1/b_2$, this permits the parameters of the supply equation to be solved as a function of the reduced-form coefficients and the elasticity of substitution between professionals and other workers:

$$a_2 = \left[\frac{1}{c_3}(1-\sigma)\right] - \sigma$$

$$a_3 = -\frac{c_1}{c_3}(1-\sigma) \tag{22}$$

$$a_4 = -\frac{c_2}{c_3}(1-\sigma)$$

where a_2 is the elasticity of relative supply, a_3 is the "price" elasticity of demand for higher education, and a_4 is the income elasticity of demand for higher education.

Estimation of the supply parameters in equation (22) is possible only for the case $d(\log h_1) \neq d(\log h_2)$; if the rates of human capital deepening are the same for professional and other types of labor there is no shift in the demand curve and the supply function can not be identified. In this case, however, $\sigma = -1/b_2$ can be estimated directly from equation (14) without simultaneous-equation bias. Since there is no reason a priori to make any assumptions about the rate of change in h_2/h_1, the null hypothesis will be that both types of human capital have been increasing in quality at the same rate. The alternative hypothesis will also be tested by estimating equation (21) and solving for the supply parameters with alternative estimates of σ. The two hypotheses may then be evaluated by comparing their relative merits as an explanation of the growth of professional occupations in U.S. manufacturing.

III. THE PARAMETER ESTIMATES

The parameters of the model may be estimated by multiple regression analysis of data from mutually independent labor markets all of which face the same technology (in the sense of knowledge about possible techniques of production). The development of national networks of transport and communications during the last decades of the nineteenth century suggests that technology was in fact fairly homogeneous throughout the United States by 1900. By the early part of the twentieth century interstate trade and factor movements had already contributed significantly to the "nationalization" of markets (in the sense of relatively homogeneous factor prices throughout the country) for nonhuman capital and, to a somewhat lesser degree, for professional-level human capital. Nevertheless, unskilled labor probably still faced a market corresponding to a single industrial or metropolitan area;

the fact that substantial migration streams continued throughout subsequent decades suggests that by 1920 the "nationalization" of this factor market was far from complete. Even though industrial areas may not have coincided with state boundaries, cross-state data were used to estimate the model's parameters because this is the only basis on which data are available for all of the variables in the model.[5]

Two separate estimates of the parameters were made based on data for 1910 and 1920, respectively. These were the earliest dates for which appropriate data could be found for the relative numbers of professionals in the labor force and their relative earnings. As will be evident from the discussion below, many of the assumptions made in order to measure the "quality" variables h_1 and h_2 are more appropriate for these decades than they would be for more recent years. Thus there has been no attempt in this paper to repeat the cross-state parameter estimates using more current data. It should be remarked, however, that Johnson (13) and Welch (20) present cross-state estimates for 1960 of equations similar to these but with completely different "quality" variables and find empirical results remarkably close to those reported here.

The Null Hypothesis: Unidentified Supply

(a) *Measurement of Variables* Earnings of persons were not reported in censuses prior to 1940. The average number of persons employed by firms, however, along with the total payments made by firms to their employees, were reported for certain sectors. Dividing the latter figure by the former gives an estimate for the average annual earnings of a group of workers in the sector. Only firms in the manufacturing sector reported information separately for wage-earners and salaried employees and, within the latter category, separately for "clerks and other subordinate salaried employees" and "salaried officers of corporations, superintendents and managers".[6] Since changes in the composition of labor in manufacturing establishments reflected changes occurring in the economy as a whole, and since factor prices should be the same for every sector drawing on the same factor market, data for manufacturing establishments were used to indicate interstate differences in the variables L_1, L_2, w_1 and w_2. By assuming that the price of capital, r_k, was the same throughout the country, book value of capital reported by manufacturing establishments could be used to indicate interstate differences in K. At the same time, all states in which the manufacturing sector produced less than $50 million in value-added during the census year were dropped from the sample.[7]

Educational attainment is sometimes used as an indicator of human capital "levels" in studies using recent data, but even if this information were available for the early decades of this century it is not clear that it would be appropriate for a population as heterogeneous as that of the United States during this period. A better indicator of the characteristics of American adults might be the extent of their commitment to quality education for their children. Parents with high levels of human capital are more likely to have enhanced their children's ability in school by providing a favorable home environment and they may also have been more optimistic about the economic benefits of schooling; if so, their children are more likely to have had higher ability in school and lower time preferences than others with the same opportunity costs and family incomes. Alternatively since many school districts were still fairly small, autonomous, and self-supporting, the financial commitment that a community was willing to make to quality education might be taken as an indicator of the amount of human capital embodied in its members. The presumption in either case is that parents, directly or indirectly, exercised considerable influence over a child's decision to remain enrolled through high school. A higher commitment to high school education, *ceteris paribus*, would thus reflect a higher average labor quality embodied in members of the nonprofessional labor force. Two different variables were defined to serve as proxies for interstate differences in the quality of conventional labor: the school attendance rate for children aged 14–15 (since by age 14 schooling was no longer compulsory in any state), denoted R, and the expenditure on public schools per pupil enrolled, denoted Q_1.[8] Both of these variables refer to statewide averages. There is no presumption as to which, if either, of these variables is the better indicator of h_1.

Information on educational attainment of persons in professional and technical occupations is not available for many occupations and states during the period of this study. It is assumed, however, that there was a rough correspondence within each state between professional standards in the community at large and intellectual standards in its universities. The presumption is that many professionals maintained an interest in the performance of local institutions of higher education, had close intellectual and social ties with other members of their own profession, and in some cases experienced a certain mobility in and out of academic employment. High earnings of professionals would generate increases in the quality of universities only if these earnings are associated with high professional quality, since otherwise the economic incentives would argue for expanding the number of places rather than improving quality. There are many indicators of college quality which might be chosen as a proxy for h_2; since they are generally highly correlated with each other the best criteria for choosing one is the reliability of data. The variable chosen for this purpose, denoted Q_2, was the teacher-student ratio for all universities, colleges, and schools of technology located within the state.[9]

(b) *Testing of Hypotheses* Each variable of the demand function is measured as a statewide average over a one-year period roughly coextensive with the years 1910 and 1920. The OLS estimates of equation (14) are presented as equation (A) in Table 1 for each of these years. The coefficients of L_1 and L_2 both have the expected signs and are of a magnitude greater than zero but less than unity at the 5 percent level of significance. In contrast, the coefficient of K is not statistically significant for either year. As a null hypothesis, therefore, nonseparability of the production function with respect to physical capital is rejected, and with it the hypothesis that the derived demand for professionals relative to conventional workers depends on the accumulation of physical capital. As an additional test of the validity of this result, all three relative factor price equations were estimated under the assumption of functional separability; these are equations (B), (C), and (D) in Table 1. The fact that the coefficient of K generally behaves as expected in equations (C) and (D) indicates that the zero coefficient of K in the original equation is not attributable to poor measurement of that variable. The fact that the estimated coefficients of L_1 and L_2 and their standard errors are essentially the same in equations (A) and (B) indicates that the insignificance of the coefficient of K in equation (A) is not attributable to multicollinearity among the variables. The conclusion, therefore, is that interstate differences in the accumulation of physical capital cannot be considered an important cause of the differences in relative earnings of the two groups of workers. It is thus unlikely that the accumulation of physical capital could have affected the relative demand for labor enough to have been responsible for the observed increase in professional and technical occupations.

The coefficient of the school enrollment rate is always significant in these equations and always has the predicted sign. Interpreting this coefficient as an estimate of b_4 and the coefficient of L_1 as an estimate of b_1, the null hypothesis that $b_4 = (b_1 - 1)$ cannot be rejected.[10] This result is all the more striking in that the variables L_1 and R have been measured using completely different sources of data. On the strength of this result, the notion of an underlying production function of the Dhrymes-Kurz type can hardly be rejected even though the coefficients of Q_1 and Q_2 are not always significant. Q_1 always has the predicted sign and is highly significant in the equations for the price of conventional labor relative to that of physical capital; the fact that it is not always significant in the relative-earnings equations suggests that it captures an important aspect of human capital which for some reason is not relevant to its substitutability with high-level manpower. Q_2 is significant in only one equation, perhaps because it is a poor proxy for the variable h_2, although it should be noted that it always has the predicted sign.

Estimates of the elasticity of substitution, $1/b_1$ and $-1/b_2$, range from 2.0 to 2.5 in equations (B). The null hypothesis that $b_1 = -b_2$ can be rejected for the 1910 equation but not for the 1920 equation at the 5 percent level of significance. (The t-statistics for this test are 4.23 and 1.60, respectively.)

Table 1. Estimated Demand for Labor

1920

Nonseparable Production Function:

(A) $\log (w_2/w_1) = .35 \log L_1 - .44 \log L_2 + .11 \log K - .56 \log R - .01 \log Q_1 + .18 \log Q_2 - 1.51$ $(\bar{R}^2 = .62)$
$\quad\quad\quad\quad\quad\;\; (.09)^* \quad\quad (.09)^* \quad\quad (.09) \quad\quad (.20)^* \quad\quad (.03) \quad\quad\quad (.07)^* \quad\quad (.46)^*$

Separable Production Function:

(B) $\log (w_2/w_1) = .42 \log L_1 - .39 \log L_2 - .56 \log R + .00 \log Q_1 + .18 \log Q_2 - 1.25$ $(\bar{R}^2 = .61)$
$\quad\quad\quad\quad\quad\;\; (.08)^* \quad\quad (.08)^* \quad\quad (.20)^* \quad\quad (.03) \quad\quad\quad (.07)^* \quad\quad (.42)^*$

(C) $\log w_2 = -.31 \log L_2 + .38 \log K + .15 \log Q_2 + 5.53$ $(\bar{R}^2 = .50)$
$\quad\quad\quad\quad\; (.08)^* \quad\quad (.09)^* \quad\quad (.08) \quad\quad\quad (.55)^*$

(D) $\log w_1 = -.08 \log L_1 + .10 \log K + .41 \log R + .15 \log Q_1 + 6.34$ $(\bar{R}^2 = .63)$
$\quad\quad\quad\quad\; (.08) \quad\quad\;\; (.08) \quad\quad (.19)^* \quad\quad (.03)^* \quad\quad (.15)^*$

1910

Nonseparable Production Function:

(A) $\log (w_2/w_1) = .58 \log L_1 - .32 \log L_2 - .16 \log K - .42 \log R - .06 \log Q_1 + .03 \log Q_2 - .22$ $(\bar{R}^2 = .81)$
$\quad\quad\quad\quad\quad\;\; (.09)^* \quad\quad (.10)^* \quad\quad (.14) \quad\quad\;\; (.16)^* \quad\quad (.05) \quad\quad\quad (.07) \quad\quad (.35)$

Separable Production Function:

(B) $\log(w_2/w_1) = .51 \log L_1 - .42 \log L_2 - .40 \log R - .10 \log Q_1 - .00 \log Q_2 - .44$ $(\bar{R}^2 = .80)$
$\quad\quad\quad\quad\quad (.07)^* \quad\quad (.07)^* \quad\quad (.16)^* \quad\quad (.04)^* \quad\quad\quad (.07) \quad\quad (.29)$

(C) $\log w_2 = -.40 \log L_2 + .50 \log K + .06 \log Q_2 + 4.93$ $(\bar{R}^2 = .74)$
$\quad\quad\quad\quad\; (.10)^* \quad\quad (.09)^* \quad\quad (.07) \quad\quad\quad (.37)$

(D) $\log w_1 = -.46 \log L_1 + .43 \log K + .32 \log R + .20 \log Q_1 + 5.48$ $(\bar{R}^2 = .89)$
$\quad\quad\quad\quad\; (.08)^* \quad\quad (.08)^* \quad\quad (.11)^* \quad\quad (.03)^* \quad\quad (.10)^*$

Symbols are defined in the text. To summarize briefly:
L_1 = employment of wage-earners and clerks in manufacturing
L_2 = employment of other salary-earners in manufacturing
K = book value of capital (plant and equipment) as reported by owners of manufacturing establishments
R = school attendance rates of children aged 14–15
Q_1 = expenditure per student enrolled in public schools
Q_2 = number of teachers (excluding those in secondary departments) per student in colleges and universities
*Numbers in parentheses are standard errors of the coefficients.
An asterisk indicates that the estimated coefficient is significantly different from zero at the 5% significance level.

In the latter year, both b_1 and $-b_2$ are approximately .4. This estimate is also well within a 90 percent confidence interval constructed around either b_1 or $-b_2$ in the 1910 equation. The "best" estimate of the elasticity of substitution between the two kinds of human capital will therefore be taken to be 2.5 for the remainder of the analysis in this paper.[11]

It is clear from the results in Table 1 that the theoretical approach used to integrate human capital into the production function is consistent with the behavior of the factor markets during the period of this study. The conditions developed in equations (16), (17) and (18) cannot be rejected for either 1910 or 1920. The data for 1920 are also consistent with equation (20), a constant elasticity of substitution, permitting use of the reduced-form equation to estimate the parameters of the supply function.

The Alternative Hypothesis: Identified Supply

(*a*) *Measurement of Variables* Measurement of variables pertaining to the labor force has already been described. The average income of consumers, Y, was measured as personal income per capita in the state.[12] The direct cost of higher education, T (from which $T' = (1 + T/w_1)$ can be computed), was taken to be the cost of tuition and fees at the least expensive university or college in the state.[13] This institution was usually a state university or land-grant college and it also had by far the largest number of students enrolled. In fifteen states, mostly those along the Atlantic coast, these institutions charged tuitions of about $100–$150; the rest were tuition-free for residents of the state.

(*b*) *Testing of Hypotheses* The estimated reduced-form equation was as follows:

$$\log(w_2/w_1) = 1.64 \log T' + .20 \log Y - .87 \log R$$
$$(.50)^* \qquad (.11) \qquad (.22)^*$$
$$- .09 \log Q_1 + .05 \log Q_2 - .35 \qquad (\bar{R}^2 = .51).$$
$$(.07) \qquad (.09) \qquad (.52)$$

(An asterisk (*) following the standard error of the coefficient indicates significance at the 5 percent level.) Referring to the notation of equation (21), $c_1 = 1.6$ and $c_3 = -.9$. Equations (22) permit a solution for the parameters of relative supply as a function of the elasticity of substitution between the two kinds of manpower. If this elasticity is 2.5, the elasticity of the relative supply curve is $-.83$ and the "price" elasticity of demand for higher education is -2.74; if the elasticity of substitution is permitted to vary from 2.3 to 2.7, the corresponding ranges for the estimates of a_2 and a_3 are $-.85$ to $-.81$ and -2.37 to -3.10, respectively. The coefficient of Y is not significantly different from zero at the 5 percent level. This is consistent with the negative slope of the relative supply curve which, as indicated earlier, would be expected if w_1 is a better measure than Y of the relevant income variable. For the remainder of this paper it will be assumed that $a_4 = 0$ and the variable Y will be dropped from the analysis.

It should be emphasized that observed shifts in the relative supply of professionals in manufacturing depend on the exogenous variables and their coefficients in the supply equation, a_3 and a_4. The negative slope of the supply curve is presented in this paper as an empirical finding which is not well established; although estimates of the supply equation using two-stage least-squares techniques also yield negative slopes, the generally unsatisfactory results suggest that the supply curve is in fact not well identified.[14] Nevertheless the findings are consistent with a stable equilibrium since the elasticity of relative supply ($-.83$) is smaller in absolute value than the elasticity of the relative demand curve (2.5).

IV. THE GROWTH OF PROFESSIONAL OCCUPATIONS

The model developed and estimated in the preceding sections of this paper can be used to explain secular increases in the proportion of the U.S. labor force in professional and technical occupations. The labor market equations are:

Demand: $(w_2/w_1) = (L_2/L_1)^{-.4}(h_2/h_1)^{.6}$

Supply: $(L_2/L_1) = (w_2/w_1)^{-.8}(T')^{-2.7}$ (23)

where the coefficients are those derived in the preceding section of this paper on the basis of cross-state data for 1920. These two equations will be hypothesized stable over the entire period 1900–1973 and their ability to explain secular changes in relative prices and quantities of the two types of labor will be evaluated. The null hypothesis that the rate of human capital "deepening" has been approximately the same for both groups of workers (so that h_2/h_1 would have been constant) implies that secular increases in L_2/L_1 have been largely the result of changes in the costs associated with acquiring the necessary training.

Measurement of Variables

Data for the average numbers of production and nonproduction workers and the total wage bill for each of these two categories are available from the U.S. Census of Manufacturers for approximately five year intervals since 1899.[15] It should be noted that starting with 1939 the data do not include employees engaged in distribution or construction activities. The data do not distinguish between clerks and other salaried employees except

Table 2. The Cost of Higher Education.

Year	Consumer Price Index[a]	Cost of Attending College (*1967 dollars*)		Direct Relative to Indirect (%)
		Direct[b]	Indirect[c]	
	(1967 = 100)	(T)	(w_1)	($100(T/w_1)$)
1929	51.3		2536	57.6
1930–31	50.0	1460		
1939	41.6		2769	71.4
1940–41	42.0	1976		
1954	80.5		4478	33.0
1954–55	80.5	1478		
1962–63	90.6	1634		29.5
1963	91.7		5535	
1966–67	97.2	1687		28.9
1967	100.0		5833	
1971–72	121.3	1558		25.0
1972	125.3		6224	

[a]Consumer price Index for Urban Wage Earners and Clerical Workers, Bureau of Labor Statistics, as reported in *Economic Report of the President 1974*, p. 300.
[b]Estimated Total Cost per Student Attending College (Public), Department of Health, Education and Welfare, as reported in *Statistical Abstract of the U.S. 1968*, Table 191.
[c]Average Earnings of Production Workers in Manufacturing Establishments, U.S. Census of Manufactures as reported in *Historical Statistics of the U.S.*, Series P1–8.

for a few years so both of these groups are included in L_2. This means that L_2/L_1 is overestimated and w_2/w_1 is underestimated. Although including a large amount of H_1 in the measured factor H_2 would introduce an upward bias into any estimate of the elasticity of substitution, it is not clear that the predictive value of equation (23) would be affected.

Estimates of the direct cost of attending college for a year were available for only six dates during this period. Although the cost of attending college has been growing rapidly, the increase is not especially large when compared with the increased costs of other goods and services. Table 2 presents the figures for the direct cost of college per student after they have been deflated by a consumer price index. The noteworthy feature of this series is how little it appears to have risen over time. The relatively high direct cost of college in 1940 is probably explained by the relative stability of college tuition during the Great Depression when most consumer prices were declining. This should be interpreted as a marked deviation from the long-term trend of which the effect on long-term supply behavior would be minimal as long as people expected it to be temporary. The average earnings of a conventional worker are also presented in Table 2 after deflation by the same index. It is clear from this table that opportunity costs have been growing much more rapidly than the direct costs of higher education. The price variable T′, which expresses total costs relative to the indirect cost, has clearly been declining steadily over time although the changes since 1954 have been fairly small.

Testing of Hypotheses

If the null hypothesis is correct, it should be possible to predict relative earnings as a function of the relative numbers of persons in salaried occupations using only the relative demand equation. In Figure 1 time-series data for these two variables have been plotted. The curve corresponding to demand in equation (23) has been drawn for the case where $h_2/h_1 \equiv 1$ to provide a frame of reference. In general, the observed values of the variables tend toward this reference curve; there is no tendency of movement away from it and for many years the points are quite close to the curve.

Data on the variables of the model covering the period 1899–1971 are presented in the first three columns of Table 3. The reduced-form estimates of the relative earnings of nonproduction workers as a function of T′ and

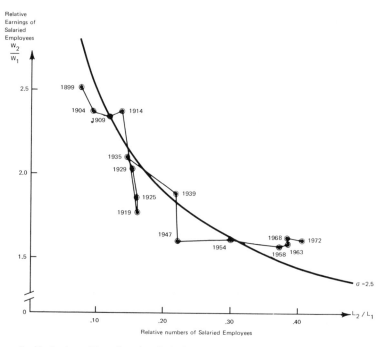

Figure. 1. Relative Earnings of Salaried Employees in Manufacturing Industries, 1899–1972.

Table 3. Earnings of Nonproduction Relative to Production Workers, U.S. Manufacturing Industries 1899–1972

Year	Relative earnings[a] (w_2/w_1)	Relative numbers[a] (L_2/L_1)	Relative cost of college[b] (T')	Estimated relative earnings[c] Reduced Form	Demand Curve $\sigma = 2.5$	$\sigma = 2.7$	Percentage Error of Estimate[d] Reduced Form	Demand Curve $\sigma = 2.5$	$\sigma = 2.7$
1899	2.512	.077	—	—	2.79	2.58	—	11	−3
1904	2.372	.095	—	—	2.57	2.39	—	8	1
1909	2.320	.120	—	—	2.34	2.19	—	0	−6
1914	2.363	.138	—	—	2.21	2.08	—	−6	−12
1919	1.764	.162	—	—	2.07	1.96	—	17	11
1925	1.853	.161	—	—	2.08	1.97	—	12	6
1929	2.028	.154	1.576	2.11	2.11	2.00	4	4	−1
1935	2.097	.147	—	—	2.16	2.03	—	3	−3
1939	1.873	.220	1.714	2.42	1.83	1.75	29	−2	−7
1947	1.595	.223	—	—	1.82	1.74	—	14	9
1954	1.585	.301	1.330	1.60	1.52	1.56	1	2	−2
1958	1.552	.374	—	—	1.48	1.44	—	−5	7
1963	1.578	.386	1.295	1.53	1.46	1.42	−3	−7	−10
1967	1.623	.385	1.289	1.52	1.47	1.42	−6	−9	−12
1972	1.600	.407	1.250	1.44	1.43	1.40	−10	−11	−12

[a]Source: U.S. Census of Manufactures. (See Text.)
[b]Source: Table 2.
[c]Estimated relative earnings are computed as $(T')^{1.64}$ for the reduced form and as $(L_2/L_1)^{-1/\sigma}$ for the demand-curve estimates.
[d]Percentage error of estimate is the difference between estimated and actual values of relative earnings as a percent of the actual value.

Table 4. Nonproduction Relative to Production Workers
U.S. Manufactures, 1929–1972.

Year	Relative numbers[a]	Cost of college[a]	Estimated relative numbers[b]			Percentage error of estimates[c]		
	(L_2/L_1)	(T')	$\sigma = 2.7$	$\sigma = 2.5$	$\sigma = 2.3$	$\sigma = 2.7$	$\sigma = 2.5$	$\sigma = 2.3$
1929	.154	1.576	.133	.155	.180	− 14	1	17
1939	.220	1.714	.092	.110	.131	− 58	− 50	− 40
1954	.301	1.330	.283	.311	.341	− 6	3	13
1963	.386	1.295	.317	.347	.377	− 18	− 10	− 2
1967	.385	1.289	.325	.353	.384	− 16	− 8	0
1972	.407	1.250	.372	.400	.431	− 9	− 2	6

[a]Source: See Table 3.
[b]Estimated relative numbers are computed as $(T')^{-\sigma(1.64)}$.
[c]Percentage error of estimate is the difference between estimated and actual values of relative earnings as a percent of the actual value.

estimates of relative earnings based on the demand curve (with $\sigma = 2.5$ and $h_2/h_1 \equiv 1$) are given in columns three and four, respectively. Estimates based on a demand curve with $\sigma = 2.7$ are presented in column six to permit an assessment of the sensitivity of the results to the elasticity of substitution. The percentage errors are remarkably small for all of these estimates, and it is evident that there are no substantive differences in the predictions between these two values of σ.

The reduced-form estimates of the relative numbers of nonproduction workers as a function of T' are presented in Table 4. Apart from 1940, the year in which the real direct cost of college deviated markedly from its long-term trend, the percentage errors of these estimates are also fairly small, especially for the best estimate of the elasticity of substitution ($\sigma = 2.5$) between the two kinds of manpower. There is no obvious trend in the direction of the error, indicating the absence of long-term shifts in relative demand. The evidence thus supports the hypothesis that both of the functions in equation (23) have indeed been stable over the entire period. Changes in the relative proportion and the equilibrium relative price of high level manpower can be predicted on the basis of shifts in the relative supply curve caused by changes in the variable T'. Much of the observed increase in professional and technical occupations in the U.S. can thus be explained by factor substitution induced by increases in the supply of college-educated manpower.

V. CONCLUSIONS

The model developed here treats persons in high level professional and technical occupations as having production characteristics which are qualitatively different from those of other workers. The elasticity of substitution between these and other workers is estimated from cross-section data to be about 2.5, and the estimated elasticities of substitution between each of these two groups of workers and physical capital are of approximately the same order of magnitude. This suggests that American entrepreneurs were quite innovative when it came to devising ways of substituting factors of production for each other in response to changing relative factor prices, for an elasticity of substitution of 2.5 is fairly high and movement along the relative demand curve in response to shifts in the relative supply curve has been quite rapid.

The evidence does not support the hypothesis that technical change has affected the information embodied in the parameters of the production function itself. This may be inferred from the success of the estimated demand function in predicting long-term trends: the derived demand for high level manpower relative to conventional labor appears to have been quite stable throughout the entire period from 1900 to 1973. The evidence also does not support the hypothesis that the relative demand function for high level manpower during this period has been affected by the accumulation of physical capital. This may be inferred from the finding that the underlying aggregate production function is separable with respect to physical capital and the two kinds of manpower. Since the model as it is presented here does not distinguish between capital accumulation and factor-augmenting technical change, this finding implies that if capital-augmenting technical change was actually occurring it must necessarily have been "neutral" with respect to the two kinds of manpower. It follows that technical change could have affected the proportion of the labor force in professional and technical occupations only indirectly by generating rightward shifts in the relative supply curve.

The approach used here for analyzing the derived demand for labor should be valid for any study of long-run economic change. The major elements of this approach are (1) the identification of high-level manpower as a factor of production distinct from conventional labor, (2) the treatment of both kinds of human capital as factors which are analogous to physical capital in the production function, and (3) the distinction between human capital *per se* and the people in whom it is embodied. Each of these features is important for an analysis of economic development and growth within a context of changing factor proportions, and the findings presented here confirm that they can be integrated into an aggregate analysis so as to study many important aspects of the American development experience.

Although the success of this model in interpreting the American experience is relevant to the analysis of economic development in general, the model cannot be automatically transferred to other countries without modification. The crucial role played by shifts in the relative supply curve depends on two assumptions about professional and technical training: first, that access to this training was rationed primarily through the market mechanism and second, that the student and his family bore a substantial amount of the cost of this training. In countries where nonprice rationing of places in institutions of higher education is more important or where the costs of higher education are not borne by the student and his family, the shift variable for the supply function used here would not be operative. In such a case, the effect of capital accumulation and technical change on the composition of the labor force would necessarily be somewhat different from what was found to have been the case for the United States.

The author is grateful to Barry R. Chiswick and Cynthia Taft Morris for helpful comments.

FOOTNOTES

1. Similar results have been obtained in a number of recent empirical studies using cross-country data for workers with different levels of education [Carnoy and Thias (4); Psacharopoulos and Hirchliffe (17); Watanabe (19); and Bowles (3)]. Of these studies, Bowles's conclusions are most often cited in the literature even though they are less convincing than those of the later works. Since he did not control for the quality of the nonprofessional labor force his estimated elasticity of substitution between professionals and conventional workers has an upward bias; whereas the other studies find estimated elasticities of approximately the same order of magnitude as those found here, his estimates are larger. Nevertheless they are still significantly less than infinity. Since a high but finite elasticity of substitution means that the composition of demand for labor is quite sensitive to changes in relative price, it is clearly important to distinguish between different kinds of labor whenever the primary interest is with occupational structure. It is therefore difficult to accept Bowles's conclusion for which he is widely cited—that his finding justifies considering labor as a single factor of production.

2. The indices of the stock of human capital used in these relationships are conceptually the equivalent of the indices of "quality corrected" labor that are used in the aggregate analyses of Griliches (9, 10, 11) and Denison (6, 7).

3. In order for an increase in h_1 or h_2, *ceteris paribus*, to result in an increase in the average earnings of the corresponding group of workers, ρ_1 and ρ_2 must each be negative. However the usual inverse relationship between quantity and price in the relative demand function requires that both $(1 + \rho_1)$ and $(1 + \rho_2)$ be non-negative. These conditions imply $0 > \rho_i > -1$ for all i and hence in the constant elasticity of substitution case $\sigma^* = 1/(1 + \rho) > 1$. For further elaboration of this point and a discussion of the empirical evidence that this has in fact been the case for the U.S., see Chiswick (5).

4. The position of (w_2/w_1) as a dependent variable in the estimating equation is not intended to violate the usual role of "price" as the independent variable in a demand function. Equation (14) may be thought of as the reduced form for a system in which supply is exogenously determined and hence price is the only dependent variable. An important advantage of this formulation is that it permits separate estimates of b_1 and b_2 so that the hypothesis $b_1 = -b_2$ may be tested.

5. States with small land area should probably be combined with their neighbors

since they could hardly be considered "independent" markets. In most cases, however, such states have more than one large neighbor; for example, it is difficult to combine Delaware with Maryland since its largest industrial area is near Pennsylvania as well. In the case of Rhode Island, which can be combined with Massachusetts, this procedure was tried. There was no effect on the results of the analysis even though Rhode Island is an extreme point in the sample.

6. The separate reporting of these categories is essential to our purpose since the variable L_2 should include only professionals and high level managerial personnel and not clerical, sales or other "subordinate" white-collar employees. These latter groups belong with wage-earners in L_1; since they constitute a large proportion of all salary-earners the distinction is important. The practice of reporting clerical and other "subordinate" salaried employees as a separate classification, however, was only begun with the manufacturing census of 1909 and was discontinued as of the census of 1929. 1909 and 1919 are therefore the only census years for which there is appropriate data.

7. Data for these variables are published in the *Abstract of the 14th Census* (pp. 1256–9) and *Manufactures 1909, Volume IX of the 13th Census of the U.S., Reports for the States* (Table II, "Detail Statement" in the report for each state.) By 1919 the only states with small manufacturing sectors were North Dakota, South Dakota, Montana, Idaho, Wyoming, Utah, Nevada, Arizona and New Mexico. States in which that sector was still small in 1909 but not in 1919 were Oregon, Colorado, Nebraska, Oklahoma, Arkansas, Mississippi, South Carolina, Florida, Vermont and Delaware.

8. Data for R are from the *Abstract of the 14th Census*, p. 410. The *Statistical Abstract of the U.S. 1931* (p. 116) gives expenditures on public schools per capita of the population ages 5–17 and *Biennial Survey of Education 1920–22* (Vol. II, p. 39) gives "percent of school population 5 to 17 years, inclusive, enrolled in public schools." Q_1 is computed as a ratio of the former to the latter series.

9. U.S. Office of Education, *Report of the Commissioner, 1910–11, p. 893–4*, and *Biennial Survey of Education, 1918–20*, p. 8 and p. 21. Students and teachers associated with preparatory programs were excluded from the data. For a discussion of some indicators of professional quality of institutions of higher education, see Lazarsfeld and Thielens (14).

10. This interpretation of b_4 can be made as long as R is proportional to h_1. The t-statistic for testing this hypothesis is $-.096$ and $-.553$ for equation (B), 1920 and 1910, respectively.

11. Similar values for the elasticity of substitution between high-level manpower and all other workers have been estimated on the basis of cross-state data for 1960. Welch (20) uses data for agriculture to obtain a "best" estimate of 2.5. Johnson (13) uses data for manufacturing to obtain a range of 1.3 to 3.1 for the estimated elasticity of substitution. (Johnson's lower estimate of 1.3 is obtained by using "quantity" rather than "price" as the dependent variable in the estimating equation; the procedure that he follows, however, does not permit the testing of hypotheses about the elasticity of substitution.) These estimates are generally lower than those obtained in the cross-country analyses referred to in a previous footnote, although as Johnson demonstrates this is probably due mainly to the omission of "quality" variables in the estimating equations.

12. Data on per capita personal income by state are presented as Series C-11 through C-58 in Appendix 3 of *Long-Term Economic Growth, 1960–1965* (U.S. Department of Commerce).

13. U.S. Office of Education, *Biennial Survey of Education 1918–1920* pp. 384 ff. Tuition and fees for Arts and Sciences, where appropriate, for residents of the state. Institutions which were either very small or clearly a theological seminary were not considered.

14. A positively sloped supply curve may be inferred from the same reduced-form parameters by arguing that the quality variable (h_2/h_1) should enter negatively into the supply function, due perhaps to the effects of migration or interstate resource flows. If so, the coefficients of the reduced-form equation would have to be reinterpreted. The "true" slope of the relative supply curve in this case would be: $a_2{}^* = a_2 + (a_5/c_3)$ where a_5 is the (negative) coefficient of log (h_2/h_1) in the modified supply equation and a_2 is the slope of the relative supply curve as defined above. Since the estimated value of c_3 is negative, negative values of a_2 would be consistent with a positively sloped supply curve as long as $-a_5 > a_2 c_3 = .75$.

15. These data are reported in *Historical Statistics of the United States* (Series P1-P12) for the years 1899–1939. Since 1947, however, this source excludes from the data all employees of central administrative offices and auxiliary units; the latter would include specialized service and repair units for multi-plant enterprises as well as any unit devoted to research and development. Beginning with 1954, data which does not exclude these workers are reported in the *Statistical Abstract of the United States* (1972: Table 1172 and 1975: Table 1266). Adjustment to the 1947 figures were obtained by extrapolation from the data for 1937 and 1954–1972: L_2 and w_2 were adjusted upward by 12 percent and 1.6 percent, respectively, implying that the average earnings of this omitted group was about 15 percent higher than the earnings of other workers in L_2.

REFERENCES

1. Becker, Gary S. (1964) *Human Capital*, New York: National Bureau of Economic Research.
2. Berndt, E. R., and L. R. Christensen. (June 1974) "Testing for the Existence of a Consistent Aggregate Index of Labor Inputs," *American Economic Review*.
3. Bowles, Samuel. (January-February 1970) "Aggregation of Labor Inputs in the Economics of Growth and Planning: Experiments with a Two-Level CES Function," *Journal of Political Economy*.
4. Carnoy, M., and H. Thias. (April 1972) "Educational Planning with Flexible Wages: A Kenyan Example," *Economic Development and Cultural Change*.
5. Chiswick, Carmel U. (July 1976) "Does the Elasticity of Substitution Exceed Unity?" IBRD mimeo.
6. Denison, E. F. (1962) *The Sources of Economic Growth in the U.S. and the Alternatives Before Us*, New York: Committee for Economic Development.
7. ———. (1967) *Why Growth Rates Differ*, Washington: D.C. The Brookings Institution.
8. Dougherty, C. R. S. (November-December 1972) "Estimates of Labor Aggregation Functions," *Journal of Political Economy*.
9. Griliches, Zvi. (May 1963) "Estimates of the Aggregate Agricultural Production Function from Cross-sectional Data," *Journal of Farm Economics*.
10. ——— (1967) "Production Functions in Manufacturing: Some Preliminary Results," in M. Brown, ed., *The Theory and Empirical Analysis of Production*, New York: National Bureau of Economic Research.
11. ———. (1970) "Notes on the Role of Education in Production Functions and Growth Accounting," in L. Hansen, ed., *Education, Income, and Human Capital*, New York: National Bureau of Economic Research.
12. Hansen, W. Lee, ed. (1970) *Education, Income, and Human Capital*, New York: National Bureau of Economic Research.
13. Johnson, George E. (October 1970) "The Demand for Labor by Educational Category," *Southern Economic Journal*.

14. Lazarsfeld, Paul Felix, and Wagner Thielens, Jr. (1958) *The Academic Mind: Social Scientists in a Time of Crisis*, Glencoe, Ill.: The Free Press.
15. Nadiri, M. I. (December 1970) "Some Approaches to the Theory and Measurement of Total Factor Productivity: A Survey," *Journal of Economic Literature*.
16. Parsons, Talcott. (1968) "Professions," in *International Encyclopedia of the Social Sciences*, Vol. 12.
17. Psacharopoulos, G., and A. Hirchliffe. (July-August 1972) "Further Evidence on the Elasticity of Substitution Among Different Types of Educated Labor," *Journal of Political Economy*.
18. Tinbergen, J. (1975) *Income Distribution: Analysis and Policy*, Amsterdam: North Holland.
19. Watanabe, T. (October 1972) "Improvements of Labor Quality and Economic Growth-Japan's Postwar Experience," *Economic Development and Cultural Change*.
20. Welch, F. (January-February 1970) "Education in Production," *Journal of Political Economy*.

SUMMARY AND DISCUSSION

Alan L. Sorkin, UNIVERSITY OF MARYLAND

The primary purpose of the paper by Morgan and Duncan is to determine, for a national sample of several hundred men and women, the effect of college quality on hourly earnings. Quality is measured by the ACT scores of entering college freshmen, expenditures per pupil, and a subjective ranking of the college's prestige. The findings indicate that regarding women none of the quality variables are associated with earnings while for men, only the freshman ACT scores are significant (after earnings are adjusted for a number of background characteristics). One interpretation of the results suggested by the authors is that students from higher-quality schools obtain greater earnings because they learn more from their classmates and because the standards set by the latter are higher.

Research in Human Capital and Development, Vol. 1, pp. 219–224.
ISBN: 0–89232–019–2

It should be noted that the two objectively measurable quality variables, freshman ACT scores and educational expenditures per pupil, represent in different ways quantities of educational *inputs*. These inputs provide little direct information about the quality of the *outputs* of the educational system. It is analogous to evaluating the quality of medical care rendered in a hospital by examining the qualifications of the attending physicians. Such an examination would not tell us anything about the *process* of hospital care or the *outcome* of certain medical procedures. It is possible that a stronger association between quality of education and subsequent earnings would be indicated if better measures of the output of the educational system were devised. Ideally such measures should reflect what students learn in college rather than relying on estimates of aptitudes or potentials such as ACT scores.

In a study done by this writer it was found that aptitude examination results were strongly associated with tuition charges [Sorkin (11)]. Since the "best" schools have the highest direct costs, it is possible that the rate of return to investment in higher education does not differ greatly among graduates and dropouts of colleges of varying quality. This is an important area for future research.

Moreover, it is known that blacks generally score lower on standardized aptitude examinations than whites. Would this imply that in the absence of discrimination graduates of predominantly black colleges would earn less than graduates of other colleges? No light is shed on this or related questions because the sample of persons surveyed by Duncan and Morgan is not stratified by race.

The paper by Kristen Tornes will be perceived by many as a radical critique of existing educational and economic policies in developing countries. Much of the discussion is ideological and the "evidence" seems to be interpreted in such a way as to be consonant with the ideology.

The two main theses of the paper are that developing countries' economies are subservient to and exploited by developed economies, and that the educational institutions and policies developed in the former are designed to maintain and perhaps even strengthen this dependency relationship.

Tornes distinguishes between an *explicit educational policy* which is promulgated in official plans and programs and an *implicit educational policy* which refers to the set of actions that are actually undertaken. It is argued that implicit educational policies (actually) work against the realization of explicitly stated goals such as equality of educational opportunity. Because verbal emphasis is given by public authorities to this concept, individuals allegedly perceive their failure to complete a certain level of schooling as a personal failure.

The divergence between explicit and implicit educational policy is "tested" using the country of Venezuela as a case study. It is argued that Venezuela is an economy characterized by "dependent capitalism." After the country's economy began to stagnate, it became necessary to limit access to educational institutions. This was done, according to Tornes, in order to minimize educated unemployment while simultaneously preserving the belief that lack of education among the populace was the reason for low living standards.

However, my interpretation of Tables 2 and 3 is not consistent with the argument presented above. Enrollment rates are rising rapidly at all educational levels. The share of educational expenditures in the total budget is rising—while it is increasing at a slower rate than previously, it is still increasing. The fact that from 1969 to 1971 there was a decreasing proportion of funds spent on capital investments in education proves little. One needs to consider a longer period of time in order to establish a definite trend.

From the evidence presented in the paper, it appears to this writer that Venezuela is making a reasonable effort to expand and improve its educational system. Moreover, since it is one of the major oil-producing countries of the world, it is more likely that the industrialized societies may come to be more dependent on Venezuela than the reverse situation.

Alamgir's paper differs from the others because it reviews the literature instead of undertaking a new contribution to knowledge. However, he does focus on some previous attempts to undertake manpower and educational planning in Bangladesh and offers a valuable appraisal of previous work. His literature review covers the following main areas: (1) the development of the concept of human capital and its use in rate of return analysis and growth studies; (2) manpower and educational development; and (3) manpower and educational planning in developing countries.

Perhaps the most important point made in the paper is that a development plan which includes the educational sector must be based on a clear understanding of three separate production processes: the production of goods and services; the production of skills; and the production of educational output. While researchers often assume a one-to-one correspondence between educational output and skill production, in fact, in most countries there is considerable educational dispersion among workers in a particular skill or occupational category.

Both Tornes and Alamgir point to the high dropout rate among students of elementary school age in Venezuela and in a number of developing countries. The implication is that structural and other weaknesses in the educational system are primarily responsible for the high rate of wastage. However, there is an alternative partial explanation. It is argued that malnutrition may be responsible for much of this problem. There is evidence that malnutrition limits mental and physical development [Cabak and Najdonvic (4); Naeye *et al.* (9); Ashworth (1), and Craviato (6)]. According to Berg (3), p. 11, "this child is less aware of his world than are his well-nourished counterparts. He is mentally and physically fatigued and thus has difficulty being attentive in class. Frequently he seems detached from the life around him."

Moreover, there is evidence that the malnourished youngster falls further behind because of nutritionally related illnesses. Thus in four Latin American countries, illness caused children to miss more than 50 days of school a year [Correa (5)]. In this context, Selowsky (10) found that a program in Chile which provided 20 liters of milk per year to children during their first two years of life would yield a rate of return of 19 percent or more. The benefits were primarily measured in terms of increased incomes which would accrue to the milk recipients because their mental ability would be greater than would have occurred in the absence of the milk supplement. This result compares favorably with the rate of return to primary education in Chile obtained by Harberger and Selowsky (7) and Sorkin (12).

The paper by Kelley begins with an indictment of the usefulness of the concept of the rate of return on human investment. This concept is criticized because it has little policy relevance with respect to planning and development. Moreover, he argues that the restrictive assumptions of labor market theory in general have limited its role to allocation decisions of a peripheral nature.

Because developing economies are characterized by large scale unemployment and underemployment, it is important, according to the author, to develop an appropriate growth strategy which emphasizes labor intensive techniques of production in the short run.

The author rigorously develops a comprehensive planning model which specifies sectoral output targets and estimates the differentiated labor inputs necessary to reach these targets given a pattern of change in sectoral production functions. This model is applied to the manufacturing sector of Venezuela. Although technical change is simulated, important variables such as base period wage rates and the price of capital services are obtained from empirical estimates.

The simulation model is illustrated with respect to the food processing industry. It is shown that labor-intensive techniques would reduce total output by an inconsequential amount compared to the most "efficient" technique, but the former would create an additional 43,000 jobs in this sector. When applied to manufacturing as a whole, the more labor-intensive technique would create about 340,000 additional jobs than the most efficient pattern.

Although this approach is an improvement over simpler, less comprehensive planning models, it has its limitations. First, Venezuela is a country in the intermediate stage of development; it is not a developing country. Because of the rigorous data requirements for this model, it is unlikely that such information would be available in most poor nations. Moreover, as Kelley observes, most entrepreneurs are unaware of alternatives to the production techniques they are presently using. Thus producer ignorance may prevent the adoption of more labor-intensive methods of production.

It would appear that international assistance agencies could play an important role in encouraging the adoption of labor intensive production techniques by establishing and funding a number of centers for the development of appropriate technology. The main object of these centers should be to develop and commercialize inexpensive products that could be produced locally to meet important needs [Khan (8)]. These products should make an optimum use of available labor, raw material, and capital inputs in the developing countries.

In Chiswick's paper, a model is rigorously developed, hypotheses are carefully formulated and tested, and important conclusions are reached. The author is seeking to explain the rapid growth in the proportion of professional workers in the U.S. manufacturing sector during the past three-quarters of a century. A related question which Chiswick considers is whether exogenous technical change has been neutral or biased in favor of professionals. This important issue, first mentioned by Becker (2), has been neglected in the literature.

After developing supply and demand equations for professional manpower, it is determined that these functions have been relatively stable for the period 1900–1973. The absence of a shift in the demand curve implies that biased technical change was not responsible for the rapid growth of professionals in manufacturing. However, the supply shift variable is most important; changes in the direct cost of higher education relative to foregone earnings can be used to predict changes in both the proportion and the relative earnings of salaried workers in manufacturing.

Chiswick also indicates that in terms of the production function in manufacturing, professional and technical manpower can be considered a separate resource that can be substituted for conventional labor or physical capital. She finds that the elasticity of substitution between professional and nonprofessional workers is approximately 2.5.

Some readers may be troubled by the finding that the slope of the supply curve is negative. The author's explanation that the supply curve is not well identified may be interpreted as an incomplete and unsatisfactory explanation. However, the findings are consistent with a stable equilibrium since the elasticity of relative demand exceeds the elasticity of relative supply.

This paper represents an important contribution to the literature on growth, development, and technical change. This writer hopes that it gets the attention it deserves.

REFERENCES

1. Ashworth, Ann. (1969) "Growth Rates in Children Recovering from Protein-Calorie Malnutrition," *British Journal of Nutrition* 23:835.
2. Becker, Gary. (1964) *Human Capital*, New York: National Bureau of Economic Research, pp. 53–54.
3. Berg, Alan. (1973) *The Nutrition Factor: Its Role in National Development*, Washington, D.C.: The Brookings Institution, p. 11.
4. Cabak, Vera, and R. Najdonvic. (1965) "Effects of Undernutrition in Early Life on Physical and Mental Development," *Archives of Disease in Childhood* 40:532–534.
5. Correa, Hector. (1969) "Nutrition, Health and Education," Mimeographed, New Orleans: Tulane University.
6. Craviato, Joaquin. (1966) "Malnutrition and Behavioral Development in the Preschool Child," in *Preschool Child Malnutrition, Primary Deterrent to Human Progress*, Washington, D.C.: National Academy of Sciences, National Research Council, pp. 74–84.
7. Harberger, Arnold C., and Marcelo Selowsky. (1966) "Key Factors in the Economic Growth of Chile," mimeo.
8. Khan, Amir U. (1974) "Appropriate Technologies: Do We Transfer, Adopt or Develop?" In *Employment in Developing Nations: Report of a Ford Foundation Study*, ed. Edgar O. Edwards, New York: Columbia University Press, p. 230.
9. Naeye, R. L.; M. M. Diener; W. S. Dillinger; and W. A. Blanc. (1969) "Effects on Prenatal Nutrition," *Science* 166:1026.
10. Selowsky, M. (1971) "An Attempt to Estimate Rates of Return to Investment in Infant Nutrition Programs," paper presented at the International Conference on Nutrition, National Development and Planning, Massachusetts Institute of Technology, p. 24.
11. Sorkin, Alan. (1968) "Some Factors Associated with Tuition in Public and Private Colleges and Universities," *College and University* 44:77–87.
12. ———. (1974) "Education and Income in Chile," *Journal of Economic Studies* 1:53.

PART III
DISTRIBUTION AND EQUITY

EQUITY, SOCIAL STRIVING, AND RURAL FERTILITY

Ismail Sirageldin and John Kantner, JOHNS
HOPKINS UNIVERSITY, BALTIMORE

What are the advantages which we propose by the great purpose of
human life which we call bettering our conditions? To be observed,
to be attended to, to be taken notice of with sympathy, complacency,
and approbation, are all the advantages which we can propose to
derive from them. It is the vanity, not the ease or the pleasure, which
interests us. But vanity is always founded upon the belief of our
being the object of attention and approbation [Adam Smith (59)].

Research in Human Capital and Development, Vol. 1, pp. 227–252.
Copyright © 1979 by JAI Press, Inc.
All rights of reproduction in any form reserved.
ISBN: 0–89232–019–2

I. GENERAL PERSPECTIVE

The broad notion of an antithesis between a social order based on ascription (as opposed to achievement) and declining fertility is one of the oldest to be found in social theory. An individual's ambition to improve his relative position in society is perceived as the mechanism through which the desire for procreation is weakened, especially during periods of economic development, and progress. Even according to Malthus (40), that most dismal of social philosophers, those with an opportunity to improve their life situations do so by reducing their family obligations and thus improve their chances of success. Relating individual ambitions to fertility is particularly associated with the name of Arsene Dumont (13) who, in 1890, declared that "while an ambitious man can be served by a good marriage, either because of the wealth or the contacts it brings him, his own children, particularly if they are numerous, almost inevitably slow him down."[1] He formulated the principle of "social capillarity," which held that as water rises by capillary action if the tubules are sufficiently fine, so an individual can improve his social standing/status by having fewer children, success being inverse to the number of children.

Social capillarity, now more commonly referred to as social mobility, implies the existence of a set of opportunities or life chances, and mobility itself is involved both as cause and effect of such opportunities [Duncan, Featherman, and Duncan (14)]. In one form or another equitable distribution of opportunities and rewards, linked to the process of social mobility and the relative valuation of achieved rewards, underlies most of the current ideas regarding the root causes of variations in fertility.[2] The distribution of income and wealth which some believe influences fertility is a reflection of the rules by which social and economic rewards are bestowed, the opportunities for obtaining them, and the extent to which such opportunities are realized. The variation in valuation of children, another popular paradigm for explaining fertility differences, involves a comparative judgment of the advantages and disadvantages of children in some quantity relative to parental strategies for getting ahead or maintaining status for themselves and for their children. That most patent of fertility determinants, education, either in its sociological or economic aspects is one of the main instrumentalities for changing life chances: by redefining what is worth achieving in life and by changing the odds on the possibility of achievement. The connection between mortality and fertility quite literally involves differential or changing life chances, whether the linkage be biological or psychological. Opportunities for women to take up new roles is also a special case of the general idea of social advancement, since women do not enter the labor force to avoid pregnancy but to improve their own and their family's life chances. The same can be said for most other determinants of fertility:

change of residence which is essentially an attempt at economic escalation, psychic bombardment by the mass media, and the temptations of new consumer goods generate new schedules of wants competitive with the desire for a large number of children which are to be achieved by striving to change one's relative social position.[3] That is, human behavior in general and fertility behavior in particular can be influenced through changes in the extent to which relative opportunities or life chances are altered and people are motivated toward new patterns of achievement. The social engineering that is proposed to create new opportunities and facilitate their achievement is generally justified (and judged) in terms of the enhancement of social equity.[4]

Thus we are dealing with a basic, if somewhat shopworn, paradigm: the way to fertility reduction is by so changing opportunities as to increase social striving which in turn will induce family limitation. It may also upgrade the general level of social equity, but this result is not guaranteed. If this idea in its explicit form has suffered some neglect in recent years, it may be in part because of the acceptance by conventional development theorists of an antithesis between equity and development and, more prosaically, because fertility reduction as a national goal has never been accorded sufficient importance to challenge development strategy. Moreover, one might fairly ask whether this broad formulation associated with the writings of Dumont is not too lacking in specification to be of much use with respect to the goal of fertility reduction. How does one stimulate greater social striving? If social striving could be engendered, how certain are its effects on fertility? What are the consequences for fertility of class mobility versus individual mobility, of upward versus downward movement? Does the abstract idea of changing the probabilities of status change add any policy insight not now incorporated in specific attempts to alter opportunities favoring income equalization, enhancement of educational opportunity, emancipation of women, the stimulation of demand for consumer goods and other such achievements? Even though we don't know much about the mechanics of these specific approaches to fertility reduction, might we not be well advised at this stage to give them our full attention without probing deeper into what Pen (48) has called "the fundamentals underlying the distribution of the productive contributions?" We shall argue that the general notion of social striving for new opportunity, if properly formulated, can assist in the enunciation of population policy. But first we need to define some terms basic to this discussion, namely, equity, equality of opportunity, social striving, and social stratification.

Equity, according to the *Oxford English Dictionary* (46, p. 262), refers to "the quality of being equal or fair, fairness, impartiality, or even handed dealing." In English jurisprudence, "equity refers to a system of laws existing side by side with the common and statute law (together called law in a narrow sense) and superseding these when they conflict with it. The original notion was that of sense, a decision 'in equity' being understood to be given in accordance with natural justice, in a case for which the law did not provide adequate remedy, or in which its operation would have been unfair" [*Oxford English Dictionary* (46)]. The concept of equality is a closely related notion. It refers to the condition of being equal in some quantity, such as income, wealth, level of living, leisure, prestige, recognition, power, authority, skill, information, civil liberties, welfare, life chances, or more generally, the rewards and status distinctions conferred by a society on its members [Duncan (14)].

We define equity as a set of rules or criteria by which the equality of the distribution of a set of rewards or status distinctions can be evaluated in a population. The idea commonly comes into play in connection with the development of social policies, e.g., how to give equal treatment to presumed equals (horizontal equity); how to adjust relative positions of unequals (vertical equity), or more fundamentally, how to assign social weights to various rewards and status distinctions. The optimum degree of equality is a complex and relativistic question which must be defined by a social welfare function for each particular society. It may be, as Kenneth Boulding (8) asserts, that the pursuit of equality will be the greatest challenge confronting the political and social thought of the human race in the next 500 years. Broadly speaking, while societies vary in their rules regarding equity and in the degree of equality they achieve, the notion of perfect equality appears to be incompatible with the structural requirements of a large and continuing social system. So long as there is a division of labor, there will be differentiation in power except in generally short-lived utopian situations.

Equality of opportunity is one of a number of possible equity criteria, there being no unique criterion of equity even within the same social system [Pen (48)]. Equality of opportunity can mean equal access to educational facilities, allocation of jobs on the basis of competitive performance rather than by ascription, equal rights to public facilities, absence of restrictions on residence, and so forth. Certain social domains such as the family, while ideally equitable in the treatment accorded to its members, do practice discrimination against some whose characteristics bar them from membership. Analytically, opportunity can be defined and measured in probabilistic terms by comparing the observed and expected distribution of individuals, families, or population groups relative to a set of rewards or status scales. For individuals the concept of opportunity reflects their perception of the available and acceptable means for satisfying their aspirations. Opportunities may increase for all individuals as a result of the existence of a positive overall rate of social and economic growth (e.g., more jobs, schools, and income for all), but the equality of its distribution will depend on the differentials in individual rates of attainment (or failure). In ecological parlance, an opportunity is a niche. To examine the relationship between a changing structure of opportunities (implying a division of labor) and some item of behavior, say fertility, both the change in the absolute and relative positions of individuals must be considered.

Social striving is a purely kinetic term. Successful social striving leads to upward social mobility, which is recognized by individual (or group) movement from one social state to another. Social mobility is determined by the available opportunities within the community and by the individual's motivation to compete for such opportunities. The more candidates for an opportunity, the brisker the competition and, other things equal, the greater the tendency toward further differentiation, i.e., creation of new opportunities. Growth and development thus entail an expansion of opportunities but these may not be equally available to all individuals. Attainment of opportunities is a function of the system of stratification. Thus, for a given individual or group, the attainment of opportunities is enhanced either by expansion of the social structure or by successful challenges to the system of stratification, or as often is the case, by both concurrently. The motivation of individuals to seek out opportunities depends upon their perception of what lines of action are open to them (the openness of the status system), their assessment of the advantages to be gained, and their individual and social equipage in terms of personality, talent, skill, and social backing.

The concept of social stratification is not uniquely defined in the literature. Aside from its multidimensionality, there is no general agreement among social scientists regarding its basic elements. Some students of social stratification define the term as the horizontal integration of various rank systems and are mainly interested in examining income classes, occupations, or educational attainment as indicators of social status.[5] Fallers (18) suggests discarding the whole concept of social stratification in favor of the concept of inequality. This is an instance of an ancient debate among social theorists who favor structural constructs (stages, periods, classes, personality types, etc.) over process.

Social mobility is measured in terms of change in occupation, education, or social status as indicated by change in income either within the individual's own life cycle (i.e., intragenerational) or between generations. Geographic mobility, while conceptually distinct, is an important aspect of the process of social mobility. While social mobility is only a partial rendering of the larger concept of social striving, it is more readily recognized, measured, and modeled, and hence has been a favored object of study by social scientists. It also has been the proxy variable (not always explicitly recognized as such) for the more generic idea of social striving, the process by which an individual level status is preserved or enhanced in accordance with prevailing equity standards. It is natural to inquire what effects such a basic social transformation might have on the behavior, outlook, and indeed the health of those involved. Let us examine the evidence as regards the connection between social mobility as cause and fertility as effect.

II. SOCIAL MOBILITY AND FERTILITY: THE GENERAL HYPOTHESIS

Societies differ markedly in the extent to which their systems of stratification are rigid rather than open. Cross-national comparisons of levels of social mobility have been confined to developed countries and, while differences can be observed that are associated with differences in technology, education, and rural-urban composition [Fox and Miller (21); Cutright (11)], Western countries appear to be characterized by basically similar patterns of mobility. In the pioneering work on this subject, Lipset and Bendix (39), traced this similarity to that of the occupational structures of Western societies which in turn is taken to be a response to a common technology. If this interpretation is valid, it would suggest that the degree of social mobility in developing countries would differ to the extent that their technologies and occupational structures are different. Most probably the degree of social mobility is of lesser magnitude in developing than in developed countries which must recruit personnel for a highly specialized and dynamic occupational structure [Ramsøy (51)]. Nevertheless, the impact of occupational structure on social mobility, referred to as "net mobility" by Ramsøy, is likely to be great also in most developing societies because of large, unidirectional shifts out of agriculture. The extent of social mobility thus depends on the complexity of the division of labor: the more specialization the more opportunities, although this principle is obviously modified by the level of economic activity and various social constraints.

Social mobility is a complex phenomenon. Tumin (61) identifies six dimensions: direction (up or down); time (lifetime or generational); context or rank system involved (e.g., occupational or educational); mechanism (e.g., ascription, achievement or maturation); unit (e.g., individuals, families, groups, social strata or whole societies); and the perceptual aspect (viz. objective versus subjective). Furthermore, the literature on social mobility distinguishes approaches emphasizing individuals and approaches focused on larger units such as the community. In individualistically centered theory, social mobility refers to the changes in an individual's or family's relative social status and is usually studied by means of career histories, data on intergenerational occupational change, and various indicators of achievement within the life cycle. In community or societally centered theory, social mobility usually refers to the replacement and displacement of persons in functional categories [Lasswell and Benbrook (34)]. The former approach is concerned with the circulation of individuals within a structure, and analysis is complicated by structural change; the latter approach is concerned with structural change and assumes that recruitment into new occupations will follow, either through a concomitant degree of circulation, migration, or labor substitution.

Finally, there are important political issues related to the study of social mobility. There is the delicate balance between the continuation of established authority and the concessions it must make in order to contain discontent due to change [Ridker (53)]. The question is how to satisfy popular aspirations and rising expectations — in short, how to enhance opportunity, without igniting revolution.[6] Strong regimes can pursue policies of denial with regard to the gratifications of popular aspirations. It is a difficult policy, short of absolutist control, for a government that cannot base the legitimacy of the policy on a well grounded and accepted ideology. If a policy involving deferred gratification is enthusiastically adopted by those whose lives it involves directly, then their aspirations are achieved even though the achievement is deferred, vicarious, and a matter of faith. A further political complexity associated with policies that directly raise equity considerations has to do with reconciling the requirements for productivity and economic growth with equality of opportunity. As in the case of blacks in the United States, Malays in Malaysia, and other populations that suffer disadvantages in a completely free application of the criterion of equal opportunity based on merit, other criteria of equity may be adopted. This may be done to redress ancient wrongs, to guarantee the hegemony of an economically weak majority, or to some other end. Policies which affect the structure of opportunities and the terms of achievement cannot avoid these political dilemmas.

With these provisos in mind, let us now examine whether the available empirical evidence supports what for convenience can be called the "social mobility hypothesis," that is, the proposition that social mobility is negatively related to family size and positively related to fertility regulation.

Blau and Duncan (6) distinguish between the strong versus the weak form of this general hypothesis. The strong form asserts that social mobility by itself explains differentials in fertility as related to socio-economic status, social class, or some similar type of variable. The weak form, on the other hand, asserts that social mobility, either in its subjective or in its objective dimensions, is positively related to fertility planning and negatively related to the size of the planned family.

The empirical record of the "social mobility hypothesis" is not impressive in those developed countries where it has been investigated. A reasoned case for its validity in Victorian England has been made by Banks (3). That era faced the nouveau bourgeoisie with increased costs of the various types of status display required to validate membership in the middle class. It is also alleged to have brought an intensified competition for social advancement due to the Great Depression of 1873. These were the factors presumably which led to later marriage and to curtailed marital fertility in order to maintain status or, if possible, to "get ahead." In general, however, the findings from research elsewhere on the "social mobility hypothesis" are mixed. The only instances where the hypothesis appears to be fairly robust involve social mobility in combination with rural-urban migration. And even in such cases, the result for the generation involved in the move may be a partial reduction in fertility—a compromise between rural and urban levels. It is impossible in this situation to disentangle the effects of a change in status from all other aspects of what amounts to a fundamental change in the way of life. A comprehensive review of findings on the relation between social mobility and fertility notes a lack of conclusiveness and consistency [United Nations (62)].

At the same time there are pieces of evidence which are consistent with the hypothesis. For example, a study by Berent (5) based on a sample survey in England and Wales in 1949 indicated that upward intergenerational mobility was associated with lower fertility, while downward mobility was associated with higher fertility. Similar findings have been reported from some other European countries [United Nations (62)]. The study by Girard [United Nations (63)] showed that high status students at lycees and law schools came from larger families than did those belonging to more modest social classes, the inference being that a smaller family of orientation promotes upward social mobility.

For the United States, research findings are contradictory. For example, analysis of data from the Indianapolis Study showed that couples who experienced intergenerational upward mobility originated from smaller families than those who did not [Kantner and Kiser (31)]. On the other hand, intragenerational mobility among Indianapolis couples failed to show any effect on fertility [Riemer and Kiser (55)]. Other researchers found either weak or inconsistent interrelations between social mobility and fertility [Goldberg (26); Westoff et al. (66)]. Blau and Duncan (6) and Featherman (19) are not encouraging regarding the tenability of even a weak form of the mobility hypothesis. It seems then that Matras (41), p. 414, is entitled to his conclusion that "no convincing support has most accrued to the hypothesis that low-fertility couples are more likely to be mobile or to the hypothesis that mobile couples are more likely to control and depress family size." However, it might be noted that the fertility side of the hypothesis has most often been handled in a demographically primitive fashion. Generally cross-sectional data have been used and a mobility classification (inter- or intragenerational) has been set against either a measure of cumulative fertility or a measure of contraceptive behavior. The sequential dimensions of these processes, either alone or in relation to each other, are ignored. Thus it is possible that appropriate longitudinal designs with sensitive measures of the timing of fertility and fertility-related behavior could rehabilitate the scientific reputation of the hypothesis.[7]

In its original form the hypothesis is deficient, in that it is moot regarding the expected consequences for fertility of downward mobility or of individual immobility in association with structural shifts which alter status and the sense of relative deprivation but leave the individual, in some sense, where he was. Nor is it clear what the appropriate referents are for one involved in social mobility. While the usual procedure has been to consider either moves within a generation or between generations, at least one study has demonstrated that a consideration of pathways across three generations yields different predictions [Allingham (2)]. In reality the assessment of one's status position is probably not done merely by reference to the position of parents or grandparents or of one's own starting point, but *also* in relation to the achievements of one's age peers whose human capital endowments are similar [D. Freedman (22)]. Understandably one may be tempted to abandon the entire formulation as theoretically inadequate as well as empirically inconsistent.

Part of the difficulty is clearly a lack of adequate theoretical specification. When it is effective in reducing fertility, social mobility apparently operates by affecting negatively the assessment of the advantages of children. This presumably operates through psychological mechanisms that have not been critically spelled out. According to Westoff (65), social mobility is one manifestation of total personality organization—a "success-orientation." The implication is that given such an orientation, a "maintained rationality of behavior," will lead to decisions in which the utility of children relative to status enhancement is called in question. This is perfectly in keeping with the older formulations, differing essentially in its articulation of psychological notions. R. Freedman (23), p. 60, on the other hand, has noted that there may be no differential effect on fertility for those who are mobile and those who are not if, as in the American case, mobility becomes "so predictable and routine as to minimize its social and monetary costs and where the goal of mobility is a life style which includes a moderate number of children. The fertility level of the whole society may be affected by a dominant high valuation of mobility, even if mobility differences within the society do not lead to internal fertility differentials. In a society with high mobility, even the nonmobile may limit family size simply to maintain their place in the social order." Freedman's formulation suggests that the effect of mobility on fertility cannot be specified apart from its social context. In addition to the high mobility society in which the "success-orientation" described by Westoff may extend to the nonmobile who lighten their dependency burden so as not to fall behind in the competition for status, Freedman suggests the possibility of a relatively low mobility society in which even those who are mobile do not feel the need to reduce fertility since status achievements are easily consolidated and relatively unchallenged. Thus "social capillarity" becomes a relative matter having greater consequences for fertility in some settings than in others. The possibility also emerges from this view of the matter that there may be threshold levels of social mobility below and above which the fertility of mobile and nonmobile couples is indistinguishable but between which upward mobility may have a negative effect on fertility.

III. SOCIAL MOBILITY, OPPORTUNITY AND FERTILITY: A RECONCEPTUALIZATION

Our brief survey of the "social mobility hypothesis" has brought to the surface some of its conceptual and empirical deficiencies. Its validity appears to be dependent not only on variations in individuals' basic personality dispositions regarding risk-taking and the length of plan horizons, but also on social context which includes, among other things, the average level of mobility. Thus the interrelation of mobility and fertility involves both the *social* (ecological) *context* and a repertoire of patterned *individual* responses to it.

It is the social context that defines and channels individual behavior through at least two mechanisms, namely, the "existing" technology and its implied pattern of social contracts. The pattern of social contracts implies more than labor market relations. It includes the existing social system of individual and group rewards and deprivations. People are what they are and do what they do in response to the anticipated evaluation of their behavior by others. Adam Smith's theory of Moral Sentiments was based on this insight into human action which later social scientists attempted to revive and refine: in economics, notably Veblen (63) in his *Theory of the Leisure Class*, and in sociology entire schools of scholars trace their theoretic ancestry back to George Mead and Charles Cooley.

Recently there has been a revival of incorporating community variables in the study of fertility behavior in order to understand how reproductive behavior is affected by personal characteristics and the social context. However, knowledge about the structure of such relationships is inadequate.[8] There is even a lack of substantive hypotheses relating community structure to fertility patterns and thus, *a fortiori*, to policy designed to affect fertility.

Another development in the study of fertility is the modern theory of household behavior as applied to fertility decisions. The theory in its general form provides no useful insight into these relationships since it does no better than to consign such influences to a box labeled "tastes" which are given exogenously.[9] Such theory fails to account explicitly for the interactions between individual behavior and the prevailing sentiments of the groups to which the individual belongs or refers himself.[10] Very recently, however, some attempts have been made to incorporate into the economic theory of household behavior some of the social determinants of tastes, expecially of social interactions [Becker (4)] and social status groups [Easterlin (16); Leibenstein (36)] that previously were taken as given.

Starting from the familiar individual utility function

$$U_i = U_i(Z_1, \ldots, Z_m), \tag{1}$$

where U_i is the utility function of the ith person, and $Z_1, \ldots, Z_m$ are the basic wants or commodities, Becker (4) defined the individual production functions that determine how much of these commodities can be produced to include the characteristics of other persons that affect his output of commodities:

$$Z_j = f_j^i(X_j, t_j, E^i, R_j^1, \ldots R_j^r), \tag{2}$$

where X_j are quantities of different market goods and services; t_j are quantities of the person's own time; E^i stands for his education, experience, and "environmental" variables; and the R_j represent the characteristics of other persons affecting his output of commodities. Becker's point of departure from the conventional analysis is to assume that the individual can change R_j by his own efforts. Accordingly, his expenditures with respect to R_j are determined partly by his social environmental and partly by his efforts to change that environment; his "social income" will equal the sum of his money income and the value to him of his social environment. Given the usual marginal conditions, it is shown that for an individual "the greater the contribution of his social environment to his social income, the more his welfare is determined by the attitudes and behavior of others rather than by his own income" [Becker (4), p. 1070]. For the empirical estimation of the relative importance of the social environment in an individual's social income, it seems important to understand household behavior, especially with reference to the evaluation of income and price effects. For example, the smaller the effect of a change in an individual's own income on his utility-output, the more important is his social environment.

Leibenstein (38) examined the effect of change in social status on fertility decisions. He distinguishes between status and nonstatus expenditures as income changes. Status expenditures are viewed as long-run commitments that are related to a given life style or status group. He argues that the inter-status elasticity is greater than the intrastatus elasticity implying that a movement from one status to another involves an increase in the proportion spent on status goods. The relatively rich within a status will experience the same average utilities and costs within their status and accordingly will be able to afford and desire relatively more children—that is, birth rates are positively associated with income within status but not between statuses. But for status increases and for increases in income, there are factors that work in opposite directions in terms of their impact on the desire for different

Table 1. Direction Taken by Fertility Decisions
Relative to Changes in Income and Social Status.

	Change in Social Status		
Change in Income	Increase	No Change	Decrease
Increase	?	+	?
No Change	−	0	?
Decrease	−	−	?

Note: + = increase in fertility; − = decline in fertility;
0 = no change in fertility; ? = effect unknown.

parity children thus making·it difficult to assess the net results.[11] These possibilities are illustrated in Table 1. An increase in income with no change in status may have a pure income effect resulting in a higher demand for children, especially if there is no increase or only a minimal increase in status expenditures. Those who experience a relative decline in income without change in status may decide to reduce their fertility in order to stay in their social class. These and other possible outcomes are largely uncertain since they depend on the balance between social costs and benefits resulting from both the change in income and in social status.

However, behavior is not based on realized outcomes alone but also on expectations and aspirations. It is possible, for example, to increase the general level of aspirations through a marginal increase in opportunities, say for a socially deprived group, but by an amount just enough to ignite individual motivation for mobility and achievement sufficient to conflict with large family size. But the process could be self-defeating. If aspirations were raised too high relative to realizable achievement, the result could be either unrest or a cumulative dampening effect on achievement motivation resulting in a reliance on high fertility as a surer source of personal satisfaction.

In our view a convergence among social scientists is emerging towards a unifying frame for the study of fertility, although using different terminology. An important area of agreement is that market prices and costs constitute only part of the category of social prices and costs (or rewards and sanctions) with which individuals have to contend. This is so because individual motivation and taste are to a considerable degree a function of social position, that is, of both ascription and achievement. And, as we have noted, achievement is circumscribed by the system of social stratification. As we shall see, the system of social stratification and its implied social contracts is closely related to the level of technology. However, despite the recognized importance of social influence on human behavior, the taxonomy of social groups remains one of the most unsatisfactory domains of knowledge in the social sciences.

Are there some general propositions generated from this review and discussion that relate opportunities and social mobility to fertility behavior in such a way as to suggest population policy recommendations? In attempting to answer this question, it may be useful to summarize our discussion in a set of propositions, some of which have been implicit, some explicit in the foregoing:

1. Social mobility is negatively related to family size and positively related to fertility regulation only under specific social conditions and for certain type of individuals.
2. For a given state of technology, social conditions become relevant in terms of their ability to generate opportunities for advancement that provide choices and pose contradictions between new and old values, thus opening new avenues for individual decisions.
3. Psychological or personality traits that are success oriented lead to decisions in which the utility of children relative to status enhancement becomes subject to rational calculation.
4. Individual decisions are largely influenced by "social income" which includes what individuals achieve through their own efforts as well as what is ascribed to them because of their relative status in their own communities.
5. The extent to which individuals perceive a sense of control over their status depends partly on the rigidity of the system of social stratification and partly on their ability to escape the limitations of local opportunity structures, as for example, through migration.
6. The average level of social mobility may influence the effect of mobility on fertility behavior. If the system of stratification allows social mobility only within a narrow range and for a fraction of its members, then children may not act as a serious constraint on advancement since for those who are mobile, status achievement is easily consolidated and relatively unchallenged.

These propositions indicate some general relationships between fertility and opportunities for advancement, and the system of stratification that sets relative private and social costs for individuals who may take advantage of such opportunities. A schematic representation of these relationships with respect to fertility in a rural community is presented in Figure 1. An isolated community with a rigidly ascribed system of stratification would be reasonably well described by reference to the center row of five boxes in the diagram. As the community becomes less isolated, it becomes subject to various policies of intervention. At first these may be highly one-sided, bent on exacting tribute and other levies and, often as part of the same process, on winning converts to centrally espoused dogma. In later phases the connections become denser, more complex and, in theory at least, less exploitative as

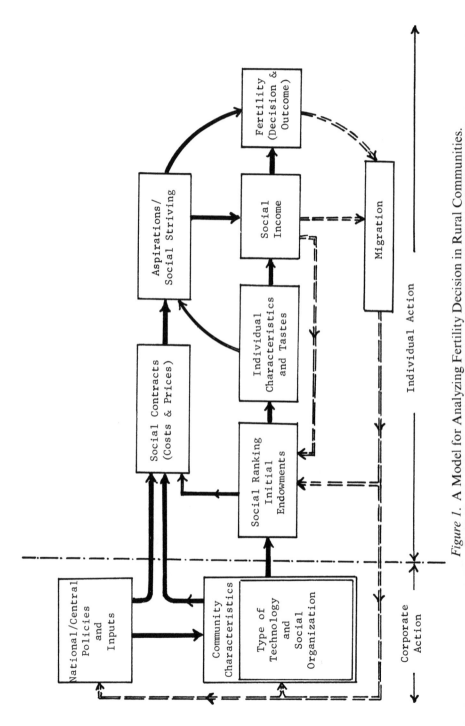

Figure 1. A Model for Analyzing Fertility Decision in Rural Communities.

the local community obtains institutional means to assert its counterclaims against the larger system.

The community as illustrated here is an ecological entity with time and place coordinates which, through its various instrumentalities, is engaged in the basic business of sustenance. Its component parts are corporate groups engaged in the production of goods and services as well as common interest groups and associations which promote and protect the rights of their members, e.g., religious groups, ethnic associations, factions, labor unions, and so on. For purposes of this discussion we do not include as an element of community structure the family and family support systems such as the lineage or caste. While these institutions are obviously basic parts of the social system, and in agrarian societies have especially prominent production, service, and protective functions, we prefer, because of our interest in stratification and social mobility, to treat them separately as the capsulated version of the individual.[12]

Community structure along with community characteristics, e.g., population size and composition, accessibility to markets and the flow of commerce, soil fertility, security from natural and man-made dangers, the availability of energy and the prevailing technology, determine the socio-economic roles of individual members of the population, the social stratification system and, in general, the "taste" structure.

The fertility of couples reflects differences in social status in two ways: directly as a function of differences in level and standard of living, and indirectly as the result of the weighing of social prices and costs. Examples of the direct connection between social status and fertility would include the barrenness of an upper status spinster for whom a suitable marriage could not be arranged or the higher marital fertility of upper status women in a community where status differences were associated with significant differences in nutrition [Cohen (10)]. The indirect linkage of status to fertility operates by way of the assessment, in terms of a broad range of criteria, of the advantages (prices) and disadvantages (costs) of alternative reproductive pathways. For example, an increase in the standard of living through increased opportunities for advancement—given education—will allow the purchase of more goods (including children) if such an increase is not outweighed by status expenditures or expenditures required in the pursuit of these very opportunities. That is why, in the highly simplified presentation of Figure 1, opportunities are implied in social contracts along with prices and costs. Change in opportunities in one area of human endeavor, e.g., enrolling in adult education or training, will affect the relative prices of other activities, e.g., an elaborate wedding or funeral.

There are three feedback loops that relate fertility performance back to the system. One of these relates to the reproductive performance of individual couples and follows the same path as the dotted lines which represent signals relative to aggregate fertility behavior. Outmigration modifies the demographic impact signals and may thus have an effect on policy at either the local or central level. For example, low fertility combined with high outmigration were major reasons for erecting the Berlin Wall. Going back in time, Friedlander (25) has argued that in contrast to the early fall in Swedish rural fertility where rural-urban migration was retarded, the large volume of outmigration from rural England considerably postponed the buildup of pressure for fertility regulation until the latter part of the nineteenth century.

Under premodern conditions, so long as fertility and mortality were more or less in equilibrium, no policy initiatives were called for. The demographic balance was customarily struck safely below the environmental carrying capacity under the prevailing modes of production with reserve replacement potential available to make up for periodic surges in mortality. The exogenous introduction of improved death control has changed the nature of the demographic impact signals. These register weakly, if at all, at community levels but may be picked up at the national level where they may give rise to policy.

Change in the opportunity structure of the community with consequent effect on the status system by way of a change in the amount and kind of social mobility alters the parameters of choice, that is, social prices and costs. As we noted earlier, such changes may or may not affect fertility in the manner specified by Dumont (13) and Banks (3). It will depend on the existing level of social mobility and the influence of the system of stratification on individual expectations and aspirations. From the point of view of a population policy that would be aligned with locally run community development efforts, the object would be to understand how the process of population growth influences the existing system of social rewards and sanctions, how it influences the integrity of the existing social contracts among the various social groups, and how much of the resulting costs are being borne outside the community. There are no ready answers to these questions, and this paper is largely exploratory. To give a sense of realism to these concepts and questions, we examine some specific situations.

The problem of population pressure is most apparent in rural sectors of developing societies. It is here also that efforts to create new opportunities have the highest priority. Let us now elucidate the nature of the local rural community and the way our discussion to this point fits in that context.

In the traditional peasant community the boundaries of the local community are virtually coterminous with the effective social universe. Migration in and out of the community may occur; earnings of absent members may be repatriated; the larger social system may engage the community in trade, alter its environment, or exact tribute but the peasant community tends to remain highly parochial and inward-looking. Life gets its meaning from local happenings; one's sense of worth and achievement, vanity in Smith's terms, are read in the reactions of fellow villagers. In her description of a traditional peasant community in the Oaxacan Valley of Mexico, Lees (35) observes that

> until ten or fifteen years ago the accumulation of material wealth received little emphasis. Prestige and respect could be obtained only by fulfilling community obligations. Among the most important of these was the personal sponsorship of a fiesta in celebration of one of the saints whose image was kept in the village church … the sponsor was expected to borrow goods and money from his friends and neighbors. Such loans would be repaid at a later date, perhaps when the lenders sponsored their own fiestas. [There was] a continual flow of small surpluses within communities and the frequent borrowing and lending helped to mitigate the risk of crop failure in this uncertain environment …. This traditional system depended on the isolation and relative autonomy of the local communities from the national government and economic institutions. Historically left to themselves, rural communities in an unpredictably varying environment devised social systems that spread the costs of community government and the risks of poverty. The result of this isolation and self-sufficiency was minimal participation in national and world markets, minimal aid on the part of the national government in developing agriculture, low production levels and a low standard of living for Oaxacan farmers.

With the end of village isolation, local institutions lose much of their adaptive function. Cash cropping erodes the economic base of the extended family, and increased production rather than ceremonial sponsorship is considered "as a means of raising their standard of living and, hence, their social status according to values outside the local community" [Lees (35)]. Again, according to Lees,

> once farmers begin to base their prestige on material achievements, they intensify their use of local resources …. While traditional farmers decreased their acreage in good years because they could satisfy their needs with limited effort, the goal of today's farmers is … to maximize their profits. In the effort to fulfill these new goals, farmers avoid—and then abandon—the former ideals of community and religious obligation.

Thus the goals that people pursue are a function of the type of community in which they live, a basic feature of which is the system of stratification. As Epstein's studies (17) in South India have shown, certain kinds of external interventions, e.g., irrigation, may "confirm" the structure of village organization leaving its system of stratification intact. This can happen if the economic roles and exchange relationship (e.g., annual payments by landlords to their untouchable clients) retain their functional importance even though the level of production may change significantly. If, on the other hand, economic roles change, possibly through closer implication in a regional division of labor, the basis of local exchange changes and the system of stratification undergoes radical modification as new economic roles are sought out. In either case, as Epstein notes, there is economic development in the sense of increased output, but in only the latter instance is there a significant degree of economic, one could say social, change.

It seems clear then that to speak of social mobility and its effects, or indeed of the effects of any change in individual circumstances, one has to do so with regard to community structure. A corollary is that policies which lead to change in the economic base of community organization may reinforce that structure or may undermine it. Such consequences are seldom perceived or intended by the makers of policy.

IV. SOME POLICY ISSUES

The recent emphasis on developing national policies that consider the population problem in the larger context of development strategy thus emphasizing the complementarity between population growth, equity and economic development, is exemplified by Mahbub ul Haq (27) who argues that governments need to worry more about the content than the growth of GNP. Rich (52) and Kocher (32) argue further that greater equity will induce motivation for smaller families.

> Policies that bring health, education, and meaningful jobs to lower income groups can at the same time contribute toward reducing population growth and accelerating economic growth, and can thus provide a solid base on which to build future development policies. These *policies*, when combined with large-scale, well-executed family planning programs, should make it possible to stabilize a developing country's population much more rapidly than reliance on either approach alone" [Rich (52), pp. 55–56].

This line of argument became a salient position at the World Population Conference in 1974. Social justice and equity are explicit policy goals in many current development plans, although they are not usually made explicit in specific programs [Sirageldin (58)]. Indeed, some countries specify these as basic human rights for their citizens. For example, the Constitution of the People's Republic of Bangladesh states that "conditions are to be created to emancipate the toiling masses from all forces of exploitation ... all citizens are to be assured equal opportunity so that an equalitarian society can be established" [Hossain and Sirageldin (29)]. But how is this to be done? What are the intermediate steps that are needed to achieve these broad social goals and to what extent are they compatible with the goal of stabilizing population growth? These are difficult questions for any planned change in the opportunity structure and thus in the underlying stratification system. It implies an equity judgment that can be evaluated only in a social welfare context. What may be acceptable to China, for example, may not work in the Indian or Iranian context.

At the bottom of the Rich-Kocher prescription is a presumed linkage between equity and motivation for smaller families. Equality of opportunity, a leading equity criterion, implies equal access to education, jobs, credit, public facilities, and so on. While neither Rich nor Kocher spells out the mechanism whereby enhanced equity promotes fertility limitation, it may be assumed to rest on their assumptions about the organization of village life, the structure of the local community. Although there are a few outstanding exceptions, peasant societies generally are organized along feudal lines wherein the mass of the peasantry are dispossessed, held in semi-bondage across generations. Class lines are virtually impenetrable and the family, the elementary particle of class organization, serves in traditional village society as the guarantor of perpetual low estate. The family, as a conservator and transmitter of values, reinforces the traditional order even though that order seen from the outside may appear to be exploitative and to deny aspiration for social betterment. In such societies, to have sons not only contributes hands to the family enterprise but marks the father as a man of substance whose children, in effect, are his collateral. A man with responsibilities is expected to act responsibly in meeting his contractual obligations. Such a system can be undermined in various ways although the forces of conservatism are strong. Change is threatening to the only order the peasant family knows, and there is thus a tendency, even as conditions of life decline, to minimize losses by reasserting traditional values and insisting on traditional behavior. Greater equality of opportunity which could come through social collapse or through external intervention in the form of "development" programs challenges the basis of the social contracts which are the root system of village life. Whether this kind of change should have predictable effects on family size is not at all clear. The experience of the Moslem population of Soviet Central Asia, for example, suggests that a change in village organization toward a less feudalistic organization need not be antithetical to the large-family system.

A second strategy for fertility reduction which involves alteration in local community organization has been outlined by McNicoll (42). According to him, in rural sectors of densely populated countries with relatively low levels of industrialization, a major reduction in fertility can be achieved through a unified community development program, provided that *appropriate inducement* is given to the *social control of fertility*. If such a program is otherwise successful, it is likely that *social pressures* regulating births will appear naturally. In the more common and intractable case, where high fertility is itself inhibiting success, it is argued here that policies should be designed to establish or reinforce community autonomy and solidarity, and provide *incentives* at the community level that reward economic performance and demographic restraint. The shift in emphasis called for in government population programs is from regarding individuals as clients to regarding *communities* as *clients* [italics added].

The general notion that local communities should play an important role in influencing (and designing) the system of rewards that induce both rural development and changes in fertility behavior appears sound. The concept is not new, but the underlying rationale is novel. The object of policy from this point of view is to internalize the costs of reproduction at a group or community level since there is abundant evidence that at the individual level benefits are generally *perceived* as outweighing costs. Moreover, since the local community finds ways of spreading or avoiding the full costs of its demographic output (through outmigration and external aid principally), policies that might register these costs more completely and bring them to bear on the local community have the potential of enlisting extrafamilial pressures against excessive reproductive output. There are, however, a number of problems to such a scheme. At a minimum the connection between high fertility and various community costs must be specified and sentiments favoring lower fertility must be effectively mobilized by the community leadership if the strategy is to work.

Some of the problems associated with this approach relate to the fact that basic social inputs may not be equally distributed among communities, but national governments nevertheless may be committed to promoting greater equity in their rural development schemes. Moreover there is no reason for newly created opportunities to be in harmony with the objective of internalizing the costs and benefits locally. In fact it is easy to think of schemes that, while resulting in local improvements, stimulate the export of local problems. The Green Revolution is one such example. Whether there are policy prescriptions that are not prohibitively expensive and in which costs and benefits could be effectively internalized is not immediately clear. McNicoll (42) makes the strong argument that we should seek our insights from historical periods prior to the "demographic transition." He examines the case of Japan in the Tokugawa era and China in the 1950s and 1960s with suggestions of practical measures to internalize community costs and benefits. But specific policies will differ depending on local conditions. In places where individual hardship is borne by kin groups that cut across communities, internalization within geographic areas becomes problematic.

An important question that should be examined in the context of any such scheme that perceives a "social control of fertility" is where the demand for a given level of fertility originates. If, for a given rural technology and social order, landlords have a preference for families with many children when entering into tenural contracts, the policy question becomes more complex, especially if employment opportunities are also related to social stratifications.

Finally, the loss in potential economic growth resulting from restricting intercommunity mobility could be a serious matter. One possible measure, although not easy to manage, that may reduce the negative economic effects of restricting migration from the community as a means of making the cost of demographic growth more visible, is to increase the cost of migration, for example, by imposing exit taxes on migrants to be paid partly by the migrants, and partly by their community, or by giving all the citizens of the community (who were born there) a claim in its resources—similar to the Swiss law which requires that all citizens have a sponsoring village to support them in old age. Despite its difficulties, the attempt to internalize at a local level the costs and benefits of fertility appears to us a promising approach. However, as with the prescriptions relative to equity in income distribution, more detailed analysis of community organization is required. What are the various types of externalities resulting from high fertility; on what groups do they fall most heavily; how is the proper accounting and bearing of costs translated into antinatal motivation; and what are the implications for achieving a greater share of life satisfaction?

V. FINAL THOUGHTS

Will more research on fertility behavior give us more insight and guidance for policy recommendations or do we already know as much about fertility as we will ever know or need to know on a practical level? While some informed students of the field have answered this question in the affirmative, we cannot agree, especially if our perception of the needed research is of the problem-solving rather than the puzzle-solving variety.

One of the main hypotheses that we have been dealing with is that the effect of community development on fertility will depend on the types of opportunity such development creates and on the nature of the system of stratification which regulates access to such opportunities. Studies of these interrelations should uncover the main types of externalities arising from high rates of natural increase and relate them to individual characteristics and behavior. At the present time there is a lack of systematic analysis of the connections between the induced process of rural community development and expected change in fertility. A country specific review of the objectives of various community development experiments using the basic general frame discussed in this paper would be a profitable point of departure in the search for greater insight into the broad but basic question of how individual life chances are linked to fertility and how the local community can be enlisted in devising new adaptive responses to the problems posed, at least at the macro-level, by rapid population growth. What we have tried to offer is some perspective on the nature and complexity of the problem and to point up the gaps in current prescriptions.

The authors would like to acknowledge helpful comments and suggestions by Ronald Ridker, Paul Demeny and David Goldberg. Also we would like to thank Farida Shah for her helpfulness as Research Assistant. An initial version of this paper was presented at the Conference on Population Policy from a Socio-Economic Perspective sponsored by Resources for the Future, Washington, D.C., 1975.

FOOTNOTES

1. For a more detailed discussion, see Peterson (49).
2. For a recent review of the art relative to the more manipulative determinants of fertility, see Ridker (53).
3. Everyone could run faster to stay in the same place but, in general, an escalation of tastes leads to increased striving with differential attainment.
4. For example, Rich (52) and Kocher (32) have argued that emphasis should be given to questions of equity in social planning on the grounds that greater equity and social mobility will induce motivation for smaller families. However, they offer no rigorous criteria of equity nor do they indicate how the process is supposed to work. See, for example, Kocher (32), pp. 56–57, where he argues that "if increased agricultural product ... is widely diffused so that rural incomes are rising in a fairly egalitarian manner, then a set of processes will be activated that will lead to improved living conditions and a more modern life style in most of the population ... leading to an increased desire for smaller family sizes." It is not clear under what conditions the increase in agricultural output can or should be widely diffused and how this is related to an egalitarian rural income distribution, or what those processes are which lead to a more modern "life style" or how they reduce family size.
5. For a review and a discussion of social stratification concepts, see Lasswell (33) and Lasswell and Benbrook (34).
6. Many policy options, if adopted and implemented, would contain the potential for revolutionary change. In the present discussion the underlying model assumes the assent and cooperation of prevailing authority with the tacit recognition that, if that authority cannot work its will, nothing will come of the policy.
7. See the work of Berent (5).
8. See Heer and Turner (28), Srikantan (60), and R. Freedman (24) for additional discussion and references.
9. For a recent exposition of the theory, see Michael and Becker (43). There are of

course problems with this approach as noted by Easterlin (16), Ryder (56), Namboodiri (44), Nerlove (45), Leibenstein (37), and others. For example, the problem of interdependent utility within the family (and the definition of the family itself) and the problem of joint inputs and outputs have raised serious theoretical and methodological questions that are yet to be answered.

10. This is not to say that interaction between individuals has been completely ignored by economists. But, according to Becker (4), p. 1065, Pigou (50), Fisher (20), and Panteleoni (47) included attributes of others in utility functions (but did nothing with them). In recent literature, "demonstration" and "relative income" effects on savings and consumption (e.g., Brady and Friedman (9), Duesenbery (12), or Johnson (30) "bandwagon" and "snob" influences on ordinary consumption theory (Leibenstein (36), and the economics of philanthropic contributions [Vickery (64), Schwartz (57), Alchian and Allen (1), pp. 135–142, and Boulding (7)] have been discussed. But these efforts have not been unified and, more significantly, have not captured the dominance attributed to social interactions by nineteenth century economists."

11. Leibenstein's analysis is more detailed than our brief summary indicates. The model is summarized in five basic functions:

$$U_{ij} = f_{ij}(y_j, s_j, y^*) \tag{1}$$
$$U_{ij}^c = F_{ij}(y_j, n_j, y^*) \tag{2}$$
$$y_j = fy(y^*) \tag{3}$$
$$s_j = f_s(y^*) \tag{4}$$
$$y^* \text{ is given exogenously} \tag{5}$$

where

y_j = household income
s_j − status level
y^* = per capita income of the economy
U_{ij} = utility of the ith child the jth household
U_{ij}^c = utility cost

12. Individuals are of interest to us in a dyadic association as reproducing couples who either by themselves or in more extensive associations constitute families. Stratification is external to the family, that is, families are homogeneous with respect to social status even though there may be great differences in the esteem with which various members of the family are held, e.g., the childless or widowed wife.

13. Outmigration may itself stimulate policy initiative relative to fertility, for example, when excessive rates of city growth renew calls for more effective birth control for rural areas.

REFERENCES

1. Alchian, A. A., and W. R. Allen. (1967) *University Economics*, 2nd edition, Belmont, Cal.: Wadsworth.
2. Allingham, J. D. (1967) "Class Regression: An Aspect of the Social Stratification Process," *American Sociological Review* 32(3).
3. Banks, J. A. (1959) *Prosperity and Parenthood: A Study of Family Planning Among the Victorian Middle Classes*, London: Routledge and Kegan Paul.

4. Becker, G. S. (1974) "A Theory of Social Interaction," *Journal of Political Economy* 82(6).
5. Berent, J. (1952) "Fertility and Social Mobility," *Population Studies* 5.
6. Blau, P. M., and O. D. Duncan. (1967) *The American Occupational Structure*, New York: Wiley and Sons.
7. Boulding, K. E. (1973) *The Economy of Love and Fear*, Belmont, Cal.: Wadsworth.
8. ———. (1975) "Pursuit of Equality," in *Personal Distribution of Income and Wealth*, Vol. 79, ed. James D. Smith, New York: National Bureau of Economic Research.
9. Brady, D., and R. D. Friedman. (1947) "Saving and Income Distribution," in *Studies in Income and Wealth*, Conference on Research on Income and Wealth, Vol. 10, New York: National Bureau of Economic Research.
10. Cohen, A. (1970) "The Politics of Marriage in Changing Middle Eastern Stratification Systems," in *Essays in Comparative Social Stratification*, eds. L. Plotnicov and A. Tuden, Pittsburgh, Pa.: University of Pittsburgh Press.
11. Cutright, P. (1968) "Occupational Inheritance: A Cross National Analysis," *American Journal of Sociology* 73(4).
12. Duesenbury, J. S. (1949) *Income, Savings and the Theory of Consumer Behavior*, Cambridge, Mass.: Harvard University Press.
13. Dumont, A. (1890) *Dépopulation et Civilisation*, Paris: Lecrosnier et Babé.
14. Duncan, O. D. (1968) "Inheritance of Poverty or Inheritance of Race?" in *On Understanding Poverty: Perspectives from the Social Sciences*, ed. Daniel P. Moynihan, New York: Basic Books.
15. ———; D. L. Featherman; and B. Duncan. (1972) *Socioeconomic Background and Achievement*, New York: Seminar Press.
16. Easterlin, R. (1969) "Toward a Socioeconomic Theory of Fertility," in *Fertility and Family Planning: A World View*, eds. S. J. Behrman *et al.*, Ann Arbor, Mich.: University of Michigan Press, pp. 127–157.
17. Epstein, T. S. (1962) *Economic Development and Social Change in South India*, Manchester, Eng.: University of Manchester Press.
18. Fallers, Lloyd A. (1973) *Inequality: Social Stratification Reconsidered*, Chicago: The University of Chicago Press.
19. Featherman, D. L. (1970) "Marital Fertility and the Process of Socio-economic Achievement: An Examination of the Mobility Hypothesis," in *The Later Years of Childbearing*, eds. L. L. Bumpass and C. F. Westoff, Princeton, N. J.: Princeton University Press.
20. Fisher, I. (1926) *Mathematical Investigations in the Theory of Value and Price*, New Haven: Yale University Press.
21. Fox, T. C., and S. M. Miller. (1966) "Intra-Country Variations: Occupational Stratification and Mobility," in *Class, Status and Power*, eds. Bendix and Lipset, New York: Free Press.
22. Freedman, D. (1963) "The Relation of Economic Status to Fertility," *American Economic Review* 53.
23. Freedman, R. (1961–1962) "The Sociology of Human Fertility," *Current Sociology*, No. 2.
24. ———. (1974) *Community-Level Data in Fertility Surveys*, Occasional Paper No. 8, London: The World Fertility Survey.
25. Friedlander, D. O. V. (1969) "Demographic Responses and Population Change," *Demography* 6(4).
26. Goldberg, D. (1959) "The Fertility of Two-Generation Urbanites," *Population Studies* 12.
27. Haq, Mahbub ul. (1971) "Employment in the 1970s: A New Perspective," *International Development Review* 13(4).

28. Heer, D. and E. S. Turner. (1965) "Areal Differences in Latin American Fertility," *Population Studies* 18.
29. Hossain, M., and I. Sirageldin. (1974) "Population Research in Bangladesh and the Role of PSC/BIDS," Bangladesh Institute of Development Studies.
30. Johnson, H. (1952) "The Effects of Income-Redistribution on Aggregate Consumption with Interdependence of Consumers' Preferences," *Economica*.
31. Kantner, J. F., and C. V. Kiser. (1954) "The Interrelationships of Fertility Planning and Intergenerational Social Mobility," *Milbank Memorial Fund Quarterly* 32(1).
32. Kocher, J. E. (1973) *Rural Development, Income Distribution and Fertility Decline*, New York: Population Council.
33. Lasswell, T. E. (1969) "Social Stratification: 1964–1968," *The Annals of the American Academy of Political and Social Science* 384.
34. ————, and Sandra L. Benbrook. (1974) "Social Stratification: 1969–1973, *The Annals of the American Academy of Political and Social Science* 414 : 105–137.
35. Lees, S. H. (1974) "Oaxaca's Spiraling Race for Water," *Natural History*.
36. Leibenstein, H. (1950) "Bandwagon, Snob, Veblen Effects in the Theory of Consumer Demand," *Quarterly Journal of Economics* 64.
37. ————. (1974) "An Interpretation of the Economic Theory of Fertility," *Journal of Economic Literature* XII.
38. ————. (1975) "The Economic Theory of Fertility Decline," *Quarterly Journal of Economics*, No. 1.
39. Lipset, S. M., and R. Bendix. (1959) *Social Mobility in Industrial Society*, Berkeley: University of California Press.
40. Malthus, T. R. (1872) *An essay on the principle of population*; or, a view of its past and present effects on human happiness with an inquiry into our prospects respecting the future removal or mitigation of the evils which it occasions, 7th edition, London.
41. Matras, J. (1973) *Population and Societies*, Englewood Cliffs, N.J.: Prentice-Hall.
42. McNicoll, J. (1974) "Community-Level Population Policy: An Exploration," New York: Population Council mimeo.
43. Michael, R. T., and G. S. Becker. (1973) "On the New Theory of Consumer Behavior," *Swedish Journal of Economics* 75(4).
44. Namboodiri, N. K. (1972) "Some Observations on the Economic Framework for Fertility Analysis," *Population Studies* 26.
45. Nerlove, M. (1974) "Household and Economy: Toward a New Theory of Population and Economic Growth," *Journal of Political Economy* 82(2), Part II.
46. *Oxford English Dictionary*. (1971) Eds. J. A. Murray *et al.*
47. Panteleoni, M. (1898) *Pure Economics*, Clifton, N.J.: Augustus M. Kelley.
48. Pen, Jan. (1971) *Income Distribution: Facts, Theories and Policies*, New York: Praeger.
49. Peterson, W. (1969) *Population*, 2nd edition, New York: Macmillan.
50. Pigou, A. C. (1903) "Some Remarks on Utility," *Economics*, No. 13.
51. Ramsøy, N. R. (1966) "Changes in Rates and Forms of Mobility," in *Social Structure and Mobility in Economic Development*, eds. N. J. Smelser and S. M. Lipset, Chicago: Aldine.
52. Rich, W. (1973) *Smaller Families through Social and Economic Progress*, Overseas Development Council Monograph No. 7.
53. Ridker, R. (1962) "Discontent and Economic Growth," *Economic Development and Cultural Change* 11(1).
54. ————.,ed. (1976) *Population and Development: The Search for Selective Intervention*, Baltimore: The Johns Hopkins University Press.
55. Riemer, R., and C. V. Kiser. (1954) "Economic Tension and Social Mobility in Rela-

tion to Fertility Planning and Size of Planned Family," *Milbank Memorial Fund Quarterly* 32.

56. Ryder, N. (1973) "Comment," *Journal of Political Economy* 81.

57. Schwartz, R. (1970) "Personal Philanthropic Contributions," *Journal of Political Economy* 78 (6).

58. Sirageldin, I. (1975) "The Demographic Aspects of Income Distribution," in *Population in Economic Planning*, ed. W. Robinson, New York: The Population Council.

59. Smith, Adam. (1880) "The Theory of Moral Sentiments," in *Essays, Philosophical and Literary*, London.

60. Srikantan, K. S. (1967) "Effects of Neighborhood and Individual Factors on Family Planning in Taichung," doctoral dissertation in sociology, Ann Arbor: University of Michigan.

61. Tumin, M. M. (1967) *Social Stratification, the Forms and Functions of Inequality.* Englewood Cliffs, N.J.: Prentice-Hall.

62. United Nations. (1973) *The Determinants and Consequences of Population Trends*, Vol. 1, New York: United Nations.

63. Veblen, T. (1934) *The Theory of the Leisure Class*, New York: Modern Library.

64. Vickery, W. S. (1962) "One Economist's View of Philanthropy," in *Philanthropy and Public Policy*, ed. F. Dickenson, New York: National Bureau of Economic Research.

65. Westoff, C. (1953) "The Changing Focus of Differential Fertility Research: The Social Mobility Hypothesis," *Milbank Memorial Fund Quarterly* 31.

66. ———; R. G. Potter, Jr.; P. C. Sagi; and E. G. Mishler. (1961) *Family Growth in Metropolitan America.* Princeton, N.J.: Princeton University Press.

AUTHOR INDEX

Research in Human Capital and Development

A Research Annual

Guest Editor: **M. Ali Kahn, Department of Political Economy
The Johns Hopkins University.**

Volume 2.	**Fall 1980**	**Cloth**	**Ca. 325 pages**	**Institutions: $ 28.50**
ISBN 0-89232-098-2				**Individuals: $ 14.50**

CONTENTS: **Measures of Poverty and their Policy Implications,** K. Hamada and N. Takayama, University of Tokyo. **Intergenerational Transfers and Distribution of Earnings,** G. Loury, Northwestern University. **Investment in Human Capital and Two-Sector Growth Models,** R. K. Findlay and C. Rodriguez, Columbia University. **The Effects on Income Maintenance on School Performance and Educational Attainment,** C. R. Mallar and R. A. Maynard, Mathematica. **An Analysis of Education, Employment and Income Distribution Using an Economic Demographic Model of the Phillippines,** G. Rogers, International Labour Organization. **Work and Consumption in the Twenty-First Century: Some Paradoxes of Late Twentieth Century Trends,** N. Keyfitz, Harvard University. **Relative Price Distortions and Inflation: An Application to the Case of Argentina,** K. Chu and A. Feltenstein, International Monetary Fund. **Theoretical Notes on Lactation and Fertility Behavior,** W. Butz, The Rand Corporation. **Index.**

Supplument 1 to Reseaich In Human Capital and Development

Manpower Planning in the Oil Countries

Editor: **Naiem A. Sherbiny, International Bank for Reconstruction
and Development, Washington, D.C.**

	Fall 1980	**Cloth**	**Ca. 350 pages**	**Institutions: $ 31.50**
ISBN 0-89232-129-6				**Individuals: $ 16.00**

Editor's Introduction, I. Sirageldin. Introduction, Jan Tinbergen.

CONTENTS: **The Issues,** Naiem A. Sherbiny, International Bank for Reconstruction and Development, Washington, D.C. **Structural Changes in Output and Employment in the Arab Countries,** Maurice Girgis, Indiana University, Ball State University and Kuwait Institute for Scientific Research. **Modeling and Methodology of Manpower Planning in the Arab Countries,** Ismail Serageldin, The World Bank. **An Econometric/Input-Output Approach for Projecting Sectoral Manpower Requirements: The Case of Kuwait,** M. Shokri Marzouk, Kuwait Institute for Scientific Research. **A Macroeconomic Simulation Model of High Level Manpower Requirements in Iraq,** Atif Kubursi, McMaster University and George T. Abed, International Monetary Fund,Washington, D.C. **Sectoral Employment Projections with Minimum Data Base: The Case of Saudi Arabia,** Naiem A. Sherbiny, International Bank for Reconstruction and Development, Washington, D.C. **Vocational and Technical Education and Development Needs in the Arab World,** Atif Kubursi, McMaster University. **The Complementarity of Labor and Capital Flows in the Arab World: Issues in Policy Planning,** Naiem A. Sherbiny, International Bank for Reconstruction and Development, Washington, D.C. **Index.**

A 10 percent discount will be granted on all institutional standing orders placed directly with the publisher. Standing orders will be filled automatically upon publication and will continue until cancelled. Please indicate with which volume Standing Order is to begin.

JAI PRESS INC., P.O. Box 1678, 165 West Putnam Avenue, Greenwich, Connecticut 06830.

Telephone: 203-661-7602   Cable Address: JAIPUBL

OTHER SERIES OF INTEREST FROM JAI PRESS INC.

Consulting Editor for Economics: Paul Uselding, University of Illinois

ADVANCES IN ACCOUNTING
Series Editor: George H. Sorter, New York University

ADVANCES IN APPLIED MICRO-ECONOMICS
Series Editor: V. Kerry Smith, Resources for the Future, Washington, D. C.

ADVANCES IN ECONOMETRICS
Series Editors: R. L. Basmann, Texas A & M University, and George F. Rhodes,
Jr., Colorado State University

ADVANCES IN ECONOMIC THEORY
Series Editor: David Levhari, The Hebrew University

ADVANCES IN THE ECONOMICS OF ENERGY AND RESOURCES
Series Editor: Robert S. Pindyck, Sloan School of Management, Massachusetts
Institute of Technology

APPLICATIONS OF MANAGEMENT SCIENCE
Series Editor: Randall L. Schultz, Krannert Graduate School of Management,
Purdue University

RESEARCH IN AGRICULTURAL ECONOMICS
Series Editor: Earl O. Heady, The Center for Agricultural and Rural
Development, Iowa State University

RESEARCH IN CORPORATE SOCIAL PERFORMANCE AND POLICY
Series Editor: Lee E. Preston, School of Management and Center for Policy
Studies, State University of New York — Buffalo

RESEARCH IN ECONOMIC ANTHROPOLOGY
Series Editor: George Dalton, Northwestern University

RESEARCH IN ECONOMIC HISTORY
Series Editor: Paul Uselding, University of Illinois

RESEARCH IN EXPERIMENTAL ECONOMICS
Series Editor: Vernon L. Smith, College of Business and Public Administration,
University of Arizona

RESEARCH IN FINANCE
Series Editor: Haim Levy, School of Business, The Hebrew University

RESEARCH IN HEALTH ECONOMICS
Series Editor: Richard M. Scheffler, George Washington University

RESEARCH IN HUMAN CAPITAL AND DEVELOPMENT
Series Editor: Ismail Sirageldin, The Johns Hopkins University

RESEARCH IN INTERNATIONAL BUSINESS AND FINANCE
Series Editor: Robert G. Hawkins, Graduate School of Business Administration,
New York University

RESEARCH IN LABOR ECONOMICS
Series Editor: Ronald G. Ehrenberg, School of Industrial and Labor Relations,
Cornell University

RESEARCH IN LAW AND ECONOMICS
Series Editor: Richard O. Zerbe, Jr., SMT Program, University of Washington

RESEARCH IN MARKETING
Series Editor: Jagdish N. Sheth, University of Illinois

RESEARCH IN ORGANIZATIONAL BEHAVIOR
Series Editors: Barry M. Staw, Graduate School of Management, Northwestern University, and L. L. Cummings, Graduate School of Business, University of Wisconsin

RESEARCH IN PHILOSOPHY AND TECHNOLOGY
Series Editor: Paul T. Durbin, Center for Science and Culture, University of Delaware

RESEARCH IN POLITICAL ECONOMY
Series Editor: Paul Zarembka, State University of New York—Buffalo

RESEARCH IN POPULATION ECONOMICS
Series Editors: Julian L. Simoin, University of Illinois, and Julie DaVanzo, The Rand Corporation

RESEARCH IN PUBLIC POLICY AND MANAGEMENT
Series Editor: Colin Blaydon, Institute of Policy Studies and Public Affairs, Duke University

RESEARCH IN URBAN ECONOMICS
Series Editor: J. Vernon Henderson, Brown University

*ALL VOLUMES IN THESE ANNUAL SERIES ARE AVAILABLE AT
INSTITUTIONAL AND INDIVIDUAL SUBSCRIPTION RATES.
PLEASE ASK FOR DETAILED BROCHURE ON EACH SERIES.*

A 10 percent discount will be granted on all institutional standing orders placed directly with the publisher. Standing orders will be filled automatically upon publication and will continue until cancelled. Please indicate with which volume Standing Order is to begin.

 **JAI PRESS INC.**
P.O. Box 1678
165 West Putnam Avenue
Greenwich, Connecticut 06830

(203) 661-7602   Cable Address: JAIPUBL

Supplement 1 to Research in Labor Economics

Evaluating Manpower Training Programs

(Revisions of papers originally presented at the Conference on Evaluating Manpower Training Programs, Princeton University, May 1976)

Editor: **Farrell Bloch, Princeton University.**

June 1979   Cloth   375 pages   Institutions: $ 29.50
ISBN 0-89232-046-X   Individuals: $ 15.00

CONTENTS: Series Editor's Introduction. Editor's Introduction. **A Decision Theoretic Approach to the Evaluation of Training Programs,** *Frank P. Stafford, U.S. Department of Labor and University of Michigan.* **A Sensitivity Analysis to Determine Sample Sizes for Performing Impact Evaluation of the CETA Programs,** *Hugh M. Pitcher, U.S. Department of Labor: (Discussant: John Conlisk, University of California - San Diego).* **Estimating the Effect of Training Programs on Earnings with Longitudinal Data,** *Orley Ashenfelter, Princeton University.* **Earnings and Employment Dynamics of Manpower Trainees: An Explanatory Econometric Analysis,** *Thomas F. Cooley, Tufts University and National Bureau of Economic Research, Timothy W. McGuire and Edward C. Prescott, Carnegie-Mellon University: (Discussant: Ronald G. Ehrenberg, Cornell University).* **The Economic Benefits from Four Government Training Programs,** *Nicholas M. Kiefer, Princeton University.* **Estimates of the Benefits of Training for Four Manpower Training Programs,** *Gordon P. Goodfellow, U.S. Department of Health, Education and Welfare: (Discussant: Daniel S. Hamermesh, Michigan State University).* **The Labor Market Displacement Effect in the Analysis of the Net Impact of Manpower Training Programs,** *George E. Johnson, University of Michigan: (Discussant: Robert E. Hall, Massachusetts Institute of Technology).* **Potential Use of Markov Process Models to Determine Program Impact,** *Hyman B. Kaitz, Westat, Inc: (Discussant: Michael L. Wachter, University of Pennsylvania).* **Theoretical Issues in the Estimation of Production Functions in Manpower Programs,** *Burt S. Barnow, U.S. Department of Labor.* **Information Issues in Department of Labor Program Evaluation,** *Ernst W. Stromsdorfer, U.S. Department of Labor: (Discussants: Michael E. Borus, Michigan State University and Robert S. Gay, Brooklyn College).*

A 10 percent discount will be granted on all institutional standing orders placed directly with the publisher. Standing orders will be filled automatically upon publication and will continue until cancelled. Please indicate which volume Standing Order is to begin with.

JAI JAI PRESS INC., P.O. Box 1678, 165 West Putnam Avenue, Greenwich, Connecticut 06830.

Telephone: 203-661-7602   Cable Address: JAIPUBL

Research in Labor Economics

A Research Annual

Series Editor: **Ronald G. Ehrenberg, School of Industrial and Labor Relations, Cornell University.**

Volume 1. **Published 1977** **Cloth** **384 pages** **Institutions: $ 27.50**
ISBN 0-89232-017-6 **Individuals: $ 14.00**

REVIEWS: "...This volume, the first in a projected annual series, resembles a journal both in the diversity of subjects covered and the presence of advertisements at the back of the issue, but resembles a collection of essays in that the pieces are longer than the usual journal articles....If the editor can continue to find papers as high in quality as those published in this volume, the need for a publication like RLE will have demonstrated itself."— *Industrial and Labor Relations Review*

"Overall, the book should be very useful. The collection of papers presented in the volume is good and presents potentially new directions for future research in labor market phenomena." — *Southern Economic Journal*

CONTENTS: **Human Capital: A Survey of Empirical Research,** *Sherwin Rosen, University of Rochester.* **The Incentive Effects of the U.S. Unemployment Insurance Tax,** *Frank Brechling, Northwestern University.* **A Life Cycle Approach to Migration: Analysis of the Perspicacious Peregrinator,** *Solomon W. Polachek and Francis W. Horvath, University of North Carolina.* **Manpower Requirements and Substitution Analysis of Labor Skills: A Synthesis,** *Richard B. Freeman, Harvard University.* **Models of Labor Market Turnover: A Theoretical and Empirical Survey,** *Donald O. Parsons, Ohio State University.* **Work Effort, On-the-Job Screening and Alternative Methods of Remuneration,** *John H. Pencavel, Stanford University.* **A Simulation Model of the Demographic Composition of Employment, Unemployment and Labor Force Participation,** *Ralph E. Smith, The Urban Institute.* **Extensions of a Structural Model of the Demographic Labor Market,** *Richard S. Toikka, William J. Scanlon and Charles C. Holt, The Urban Institute.* **The Institutionalist Analysis of Wage Inflation: A Critical Appraisal,** *John Burton, Kingston Polytechnical and John Addison, Aberdeen University.*

Volume 2. **Published 1978** **Cloth** **381 pages** **Institutions: $ 27.50**
ISBN 0-89232-097-4 **Individuals: $ 14.00**

CONTENTS: **Introduction,** *Ronald Ehrenberg, Cornell University.* **The United Mine Workers and the Demand for Coal: An Econometric Analysis of Union Behavior,** *Henry S. Farber, Massachusetts Institute of Technology.* **Quelling for Union Jobs and the Social Returns to Schooling,** *John Bishop, University of Wisconsin.* **Labor Supply Under Uncertainty,** *Kenneth Burdett, University of Wisconsin and Dale T. Mortensen, Northwestern University.* **Governmentally Imposed Standards: Some Normative Aspects,** *Russell F. Settle, University of Delaware and Burton Weisbrod, University of Wisconsin.* **Cyclical Earnings Changes of Low Wage Workers,** *Wayne Vroman, National Bureau of Economic Research, Washington, D.C.* **Earnings, Transfers, and Poverty Reduction,** *Peter T. Gottschalk, Mount Holyoke College.* **The Influence of Fertility on Labor Supply of Married Women: Simultaneous Equation Estimates,** *T. Paul Schultz, Yale University.* **The Labor Market Adjustments of Trade Displaced Workers: The Evidence from the Trade Adjustment Assistance Program,** *George R. Newmann, University of Chicago.*

Research in Health Economics

A Research Annual

Series Editor: **Richard M. Scheffler, Department of Economics George Washington University.**

Volume 1. **April 1979** **Cloth** **375 pages** **Institutions: $ 28.50**
ISBN 0-89232-042-7 **Individuals: $ 14.50**

CONTENTS: **Introduction,** *Richard M. Scheffler.* **Planning a National Health Manpower Policy: A Critique and A Strategy,** *Kenneth R. Smith, Northwestern University, Uwe E. Reinhardt, Princeton University and Ralph L. Andreano, University of Wisconsin.* **The Productivity of New Health Practitioners: Physicians Assistants and Mendex,** *Richard M. Scheffler, George Washington University.* **New Developments In the Market for Rural Health Care,** *Karen Davis, Brookings' Institute and Ray Marshall, University of Texas - Austin.* **A Disaggregated Model of Medical Speciality Choice,** *Jack Hadley, The Urban Institute.* **Retention of Medical School Graduates: A Case Study of Michigan,** *Gail Wilensky, National Center for Health Services Research, Department of Health, Education and Welfare.* **A Model of Physician Location and Pricing Behavior,** *Roger Feldman, University of North Carolina - Chapel Hill.* **A Model of Professional Nurse Wage Setting in Hospitals,** *Frank Sloan, Vanderbilt University and Richard A. Elnicki, University of Florida.* **Nurse Market Policy Simulations Using an Econometric Model,** *Robert Deane, Applied Management Sciences Inc., Washington, D.C. and Donald Yett, University of Southern California.* **Health Status Maximization and Manpower Allocation,** *Joseph Lipscomb, Duke University, Lawrence E. Berg, Virginia L. London and Paul A. Nutting, Office of Research and Development, Tucson.* **Bibliography.**

Volume 2. **Spring 1980** **Cloth** **375 pages** **Institutions: $ 28.50**
ISBN 0-89232-100-8 **Individuals: $ 14.50**

CONTENTS: **Demand for Dental Care,** *Teh-Wei Hu, Pennsylvania State University.* **Physician Reimbursement,** *Martha Blaxall and John Gabel, Health Care Financing Administration.* **H.E.W. Demand for Medical Care in a Rural Area,** *Larry Miners, State University of New York, Stony Brook.* **Economic Incentives in Health Maintenance Organizations,** *David Wipple, U.S. Navy Post Graduate School.* **A Theoretical and Empirical Investigation into Hospital Output Measures,** *Mark Hornbrook and John Rafferty, Division of Intramural Research, National Center for Health Services Research.* **H.E.W. Economics of Community Pharmacies,** *Lou Rossiter, Division of Intramural Research, National Center for Health Services Research.* **H.E.W. Current Issues in the Economics of Dentistry,** *John Cushman, University of California - Davis and Richard M. Scheffler, George Washington University.* **The American Hospital Industry Since 1900: A Short History,** *William D. White, University of Illinois - Chicago Circle.* **Health Manpower Credit Subsidies,** *Richard C. McKibbin, Wichita State University.* **Permanently Disabling Injuries: A General Model to Florida Work Injuries,** *Wayne Vroman, The Urban Institute.* **Determinants of Work Loss Days by Illness,** *Lynn Parringer, The Urban Institute.* **The Distribution of Health Services and the Effect on Health Status,** *Charles Stewart, George Washington University.* **Bibliography.**

A 10 percent discount will be granted on all institutional standing orders placed directly with the publisher. Standing orders will be filled automatically upon publication and will continue until cancelled. Please indicate with which volume Standing Order is to begin.

JAI JAI PRESS INC., P.O. Box 1678, 165 West Putnam Avenue, Greenwich, Connecticut 06830.

Telephone: 203-661-7602 Cable Address: JAIPUBL

Research In Organizational Behavior

An Annual Series of Analytical Essays and Critical Reviews

Series Editor: **Barry M. Staw, Graduate School of Management
Northwestern University.**

Volume 1.   Published 1979 Cloth   478 pages   Institutions: $ 32.50
ISBN 0-89232-045-1   Individuals: $ 16.50

CONTENTS: **Editorial Statement,** Barry M. Staw, Northwestern University. **Beyond Open System Models of Organization,** Louis R. Pondy, University of Illinois and Ian I. Mitroff, University of Pittsburgh. **Cognitive Processes in Organizations,** Karl E. Weick, Cornell University. **Organizational Learning: Implications for Organizational Design,** Robert Duncan and Andrew Weiss, Northwestern University. **Organizational Design and Adult Learning,** Douglas T. Hall and Cynthia V. Fukami, Northwestern University. **Organizational Structure, Attitudes and Behaviors,** Chris J. Berger, Purdue University and L. L. Cummings, University of Wisconsin - Madison. **Toward a Theory of Organizational Socialization,** John Van Maanen and Edgar H. Schein, Massachusetts Institute of Technology. **Participation in Decision-Making: One More Look,** Edwin A. Locke and David M. Schweiger, University of Maryland. **Leadership: Some Empirical Generalizations and New Research Directions,** Robert J. House and Mary L. Baetz, University of Toronto. **Performance Appraisal Effectiveness: Its Assessment and Determinants,** Jeffery S. Kane, Western Electric Company and Edward E. Lawler, III, University of Michigan. **Bibliography. Index.**

Series Editors: **Barry M. Staw, Graduate School of Management,
Northwestern University, and Larry L. Cummings,
Graduate School of Business, University of
Wisconsin.**

Volume 2.   Fall 1979   Cloth   450 pages   Institutions: $ 32.50
ISBN 0-89232-099-0   Individuals: $ 16.50

CONTENTS: **Construct Validity in Organizational Behavior,** Donald P. Schwab, University of Wisconsin. **Rationality and Justification in Organizational Life,** Barry M. Staw, Northwestern University. **Time and Work: Towards an Integrative Perspective,** Ralph Katz, Massachusetts Institute of Technology. **Collective Bargaining and Organizational Behavior Research,** Thomas A. Kochan, Cornell University. **Behavioral Research on Unions and Union Management Systems,** Jeanne Brett, Northern University. **Institutionalization of Planned Organizational Change,** Paul S. Goodman and Max Bazerman, Carnegie-Mellon University and Edward Conlon, Georgia Institute of Technology. **Work Design in the Organizational Context,** Greg R. Oldham, University of Illinois and J. Richard Hackman, Yale University. **Organizational Growth Types: Lessons from Small Institutions,** A. C. Filley and R. J. Aldag, University of Wisconsin. **Interorganizational Processes and Organizational Boundary Activities,** J. Stacy Adams, University of North Carolina.

A 10 percent discount will be granted on all institutional standing orders placed directly with the publisher. Standing orders will be filled automatically upon publication and will continue until cancelled. Please indicate with which volume Standing Order is to begin.

JAI PRESS INC., P.O. Box 1678, 165 West Putnam Avenue,
Greenwich, Connecticut 06830.

Telephone: 203-661-7602   Cable Address: JAIPUBL